T0100206

Get the eBook FREE!

(PDF, ePub, Kindle, and liveBook all included)

We believe that once you buy a book from us, you should be able to read it in any format we have available. To get electronic versions of this book at no additional cost to you, purchase and then register this book at the Manning website.

Go to https://www.manning.com/freebook and follow the instructions to complete your pBook registration.

That's it!
Thanks from Manning!

The Creative Programmer

WOUTER GRONEVELD

FOREWORD BY FELIENNE HERMANS

MANNING

SHELTER ISLAND

Manning Publications Co.
    20 Baldwin Road
    PO Box 761
    Shelter Island, NY 11964

Development editor:	Connor O'Brien
Review editor:	Adriana Sabo
Production editor:	Kathleen Rossland
Copy editor:	Kathy Savadel
Proofreader:	Katie Tennant
Typesetter:	Gordan Salinovic
Cover designer:	Marija Tudor

ISBN 9781633439054
Printed in the United States of America

contents

iii

foreword

When I heard that Wouter was going to write a book for Manning, I was very excited! Wouter is researching the skills programmers need to be productive and creative, and his work so far had gained attention only in academic circles. How wonderful, I thought, that a larger audience will now be able to read about ways in which we can get more creative in our work!

Creativity, though, is a weird thing. We all agree programming is a creative endeavor, but what is creativity, and how can we get better at it? Isn't being creative simply a matter of knowing a lot of things so you can apply the one that is most relevant? Wouter argues that yes, technical knowledge is a necessary condition, though not a sufficient one. He goes on to fill his book with a fantastic mix of engaging historical anecdotes, concrete practical exercises, and extensive references to papers, books, and essays for deeper reading both in and outside of programming.

I very much appreciate Wouter's honest reflections on his own strategies. It is easy to simply encourage the reader to do a certain thing ("always take notes" or "work well as a team by communicating more"). Wouter openly addresses how hard it is to do these things, talks about his own failures at doing so, and always ends with concrete advice that feels both actionable and doable—a rare combination.

I love the fact that the book is filled with exercises and encouragement to try out techniques because if anything is hard to do in theory, it would be creativity! My own edition has now been filled with pages of scribbles and notes on which I could immediately apply Wouter's lessons on organizing and following up, a sign that his exercises are truly engaging and encouraging!

The book is deep in its different aspects of creativity, from note taking and brainstorming to creative teamwork and creative techniques to apply. In addition to the practical tips, the book is grounded in solid scientific work and introduces relevant theoretical constructs related to creativity. I learned about organizing knowledge, common pitfalls in critical thinking, and how to use constraints to boost your creativity.

I don't doubt that *The Creative Programmer* will be useful to any programmer, from high schoolers taking their first steps in Python to seasoned C++ developers with decades of experience. I can't wait to see what creative projects readers will come up with!

—Prof. Dr. Felienne Hermans
Professor of Computer Science Education
Vrije Universiteit Amsterdam

preface

As much as technicality and program architectures bedazzled me in a good way during my 11 years as a software engineer, it was really the mysticism of nontechnical coding skills that kept calling my name. When I got involved in coaching and onboarding, I noticed a few odd things. Why was it that new recruits mostly caught up with our frameworks and best practices but sometimes failed to grasp what really matters: integrating into the team and solving problems? What does it mean to be a truly great programmer, besides the obvious technical mastery?

This question kept me up at night and eventually lured me back to academia. More than four study-intensive years later, and having published multiple scientific papers on the subject, I can finally say I better understand what makes a truly great programmer: a *Creative Programmer*. The problem is that segregated academic publications—besides their excellent legibility—lack context and barely make it beyond university borders. I was also set on giving something back to the programming community. Thanks to the interest and help of Manning, the idea soon evolved into easily digestible chapters and an early-access release, kicking the feedback–rewrite cycle into overdrive.

The result of our collaboration is a blend of theory and practice—a practical approach backed by scientific evidence that should help you with complex programming problems as a coder in the field. I've done my best to make this book as accessible (and as funny) as possible, both for the junior programmer and for the experienced guru. By the end of the book, all the tools you need to become a Creative Programmer should be in your hands. In total, we'll cover seven distinct but intertwined themes: technical knowledge, communication, constraints, critical thinking, curiosity, a creative state of mind, and creative techniques.

I hope the concepts explained in this book will jump-start your creative thinking and continue to be a useful guide for years to come. If there is anything you'd like to discuss or share, please feel free to reach out. I'm always happy to help, and feedback is more than welcome. As you'll see later in the book, there's no such thing as a Creative Programmer without a creative community.

Thanks again for buying the book, and enjoy!

acknowledgments

While the first draft of this book was written in solitude, many ideas that helped shape it were, of course, based on the superb work of others. Of those, I owe a special thanks to Andy Hunt. If not for discovering his book *Pragmatic Thinking & Learning* in 2009, I would probably never have shown any interest in cognition and the psychology of programming.

I thank all the wonderful people I've ever had the pleasure of working with and previous employers who allowed me to put together experimental courses on various aspects linked to the concepts of this book. A big thanks goes to my PhD supervisors, Joost Vennekens and Kris Aerts at KU Leuven, who let me choose my own path instead of forcing me to limit my topic to their research domain. I also thank all the participants in industry and academia who were interviewed as part of my research.

I probably will never want to admit it, but the first draft of the book, while containing a lot of good ideas, was still in pretty rough shape. I owe a great deal to my editor, Connor O'Brien, for critically reviewing the chapters and forcing me to kill my darlings when needed. It has been a rocky ride, and the need for a careful balance between theory and practice may have caused a stir or two, but in the end, Connor always put me on the right track.

Also, I thank associate publisher Michael Stephens for recognizing this book's potential when we first met. A big thanks goes to all the other folks at Manning who helped put this out there.

I thank the people who put in the effort to provide early feedback on the manuscript during various stages of its development: Abdul W. Yousufzai, Alessandro Campeis, Andres Sacco, Chuck Coon, Diego Casella, Đorđe Vukelić, Edin Kapić, Edmund Cape, George Onofrei, Germano Rizzo, Haim Raman, Jaume López, Jedidiah River Clemons-Johnson, Jeremy Chen, Joseph Perenia, Karl van Heijster, Malisa Middlebrooks, Manuel Rubio, Matteo Battista, Max Sadrieh, Muhammad Zohaib, Nghia To, Nouran Mahmoud, Oliver Forral, Or Golan, Orlando Alejo Méndez Morales, Pradeep Chellappan, Prajwal Khanal, Rich Yonts, Samuel Bosch, Sebastian Felling, Swapneelkumar Deshpande, and Vidhya Vinay.

Other people also deserve special acknowledgment:

- Yannick Lemmens, who laid eyes on one of the earliest versions of the manuscript. His enthusiasm certainly helped push this project forward.
- Linus De Meyere, for always supporting my projects, however silly they may seem at first.
- Peter Bridger, as my retro computing liaison and good friend, for sharing stories, happy and sad, and providing distractions when needed.
- Felienne Hermans, for paving the way with her book *The Programmer's Brain*, also published by Manning, showing coders (and publishers) there is a clear need for nontechnical technical books.
- Daniel Graziotin, for helping to point me toward creativity research in the context of software development, even though he ended up pursuing another related topic himself.

Lastly, the person I probably owe the most to: I thank my wife, Kristien Thoelen, for putting up with my grumbling and whining when hitting yet another (writing) roadblock. I have the feeling this won't be my last book; sorry, honey!

about this book

As the title implies, *The Creative Programmer* is primarily a book for programmers of all levels who are keen on improving their problem-solving skills with the help of creativity. By purchasing this book, you've already unlocked the first and most important part of your creative potential: the curiosity to learn something new! I hope the coming chapters contain enough information to keep that curiosity going.

Unlike many Manning books, this one does not require any prior knowledge of certain programming languages or technologies. Instead, we'll venture deep into the world of cognitive psychology to discover what it means to be a Creative Programmer. It does help if you've programmed before, but it's not a strict requirement. The few code examples present are devoid of language-specific syntax and serve as a use case for specific creative concepts: no extensive programming language or design pattern knowledge is required.

Even though these approaches to creativity, conventional and unconventional, will always be translated back into the world of the programmer, they might also appeal to noncoders who are involved in tech. Technical analysts will certainly also benefit from the revealed concepts, while engineering managers will learn how to better support their team creatively. With a bit of effort, most techniques can be translated into other domains. We'll see examples of this as we make our way through the book.

How this book is organized

Since *creativity* can be a confusing term, we first discuss the origin of the word, what it means to be creative, and how to measure it in chapter 1, which also serves as a guide to the creative road ahead.

In each of chapters 2–8, a central theme related to creativity is revealed and explored in depth. These themes can also be found in the core concept graphic on the inside of the front cover. They are technical knowledge, communication, constraints, critical thinking, curiosity, a creative state of mind, and creative techniques. As you'll soon discover, these themes are highly interconnected. While the book was written with the intention of reading the chapters in order, feel free to flip through them and follow your curiosity, cherry-picking topics here and there. Just make sure you don't skip the important context.

Chapter 9 closes with some final thoughts on creativity in the context of coding and offers a few moments of reflection to help you integrate what you've learned into your daily practice as a programmer. In case you're still hungry for more after finishing this book, this chapter also contains a list of recommended readings, grouped by the main themes.

Each section in chapters 2–8 contains an exercise to make you stop and think. Some of these are easily actionable while others may require more thought or a good night of sleep and a reread. I did my best to design these in such a way that they potentially ignite change, but I do expect you, the reader, to give them a fair chance. If you encounter any difficulties or don't know how to apply something in your specific situation, feel free to reach out. I'm always happy to help where I can!

liveBook discussion forum

Purchase of *The Creative Programmer* includes free access to liveBook, Manning's online reading platform. Using liveBook's exclusive discussion features, you can attach comments to the book globally or to specific sections or paragraphs. It's a snap to make notes for yourself, ask and answer technical questions, and receive help from the author and other users. To access the forum, go to https://livebook.manning.com/book/the-creative-programmer/discussion. You can also learn more about Manning's forums and the rules of conduct at https://livebook.manning.com/discussion.

Manning's commitment to our readers is to provide a venue where a meaningful dialogue between individual readers and between readers and the author can take place. It is not a commitment to any specific amount of participation on the part of the author, whose contribution to the forum remains voluntary (and unpaid). We suggest you try asking him some challenging questions lest his interest stray! The forum and the archives of previous discussions will be accessible from the publisher's website as long as the book is in print.

about the author

WOUTER GROENEVELD is a software engineer, computer science education researcher, and professional bread baker. Wouter was an enterprise software engineer for 11 years with a passion for inspiring and teaching others. After a few years of experience, he became involved in teaching, coaching, and onboarding. Witnessing the failure of many software projects led him to ask the following question: What makes a good software engineer? That question ultimately caused him to quit his job in the industry in 2018 and rejoin academia. Since then, Wouter has been conducting research on nontechnical skills in the software engineering world. He has written extensively about the topic. A list of his academic publications can be found at https://brainbaking.com/works/papers/ (all papers are open access). He also runs a blog at https://brainbaking.com/.

about the cover illustration

The figure on the cover of *The Creative Programmer* is "Homme Ostjak à la Chasse d'Hermine," or "Ostyak man hunting ermine," taken from a collection by Jacques Grasset de Saint-Sauveur, published in 1788. Each illustration is finely drawn and colored by hand.

In those days, it was easy to identify where people lived and what their trade or station in life was just by their dress. Manning celebrates the inventiveness and initiative of the computer business with book covers based on the rich diversity of regional culture centuries ago, brought back to life by pictures from collections such as this one.

The creative road ahead

We humans love to create. *Homo faber*—creating to control our fate and environment—is a manifestation of man's innate being in nature, according to philosopher and novelist Umberto Eco.[1] By buying this book, you've made your first step toward your innate being as a creative programmer. Congrats, and welcome!

Chances are that you've decided to read this book to become a better programmer. You've come to the right place. Only, don't expect the unfolding of the latest technical marvels, such as a just-in-time compiler of some virtual machine, or to learn more about programming language *x* or *y*. This is far from your average programming book.

---

[1] Umberto Eco. The open work (Anna Cancogni, trans.). Cambridge: Harvard University Press, 1989.

1

Instead, we'll be working on a different level. You'll learn how highly creative individuals (and groups) approach problems, what their habits and thought processes are like, and how they arrive at both more productive and more creative solutions. Once you're a certified Creative Programmer™, you'll unravel any technical marvel with ease and learn multiple programming languages at once—well, at least according to the theory. Whether you just picked up programming as a new discipline or you're an experienced developer, my hope is that you will acquire at least a few new creative tricks to have up your sleeve.

More experience in a technical trade such as programming does not necessarily equal more creative output. I've been in the software development industry for more than a decade and have witnessed few highs and a lot of lows. Software seems to be doomed to fail. Pragmatic programmer and cocreator of the "Manifesto for Agile Software Development" Andy Hunt started his book *Pragmatic Thinking & Learning* on a similar troubling note:[2]

> *Whether you're a programmer or frustrated user, you may have already suspected that software development must be the most difficult endeavor ever envisioned and practiced by humans. Its complexity strains our best abilities daily, and failures can often be spectacular—and newsworthy.*

Although Andy's approach is to teach you how to think and learn, my approach is to teach you how to approach problems more creatively. After witnessing so many software failures (and [un]consciously helping conceive them), I've become convinced that the deficit may be one of nontechnical skills, not of technical ability. This obsession even led me back to academia, where I have spent the past four years researching creativity in software engineering. The fruit of my hybrid industry–academia work lies in your hands—provided you're an old-school book person. But before we can get cracking, we first need to get a few questions out of the way.

1.1   *What exactly is creativity?*

Psychology scholars have been squabbling over this question for decades. The result is the existence of about 100 different definitions of creativity. When you ask your 10-year-old daughter what creativity is, she might insist on sharing her paintbrush to find out together. Your stingy neighbor, on the other hand, thinks that tax evasion is creative. After carefully inspecting the internals of a computer, you yourself might conclude that they are all wrong: it's the engineers who come up with this that are creative! Who's right?

One possible solution would be to boil down the essence of all different opinions into a single definition. Creativity researchers Kaufman and Sternberg[3] say an idea is creative if it meets these descriptions:

[2] Andy Hunt. Pragmatic thinking & learning: Refactor your Wetware. Pragmatic Bookshelf, 2008.

[3] James C Kaufman and Robert J Sternberg. Creativity. Change: The Magazine of Higher Learning, 2007.

- It is considered novel and original.
- It is of high quality.
- It is relevant to the task at hand.

Throwing a NoSQL database at a problem might be a qualitative solution, as has been proven in the past, but I doubt it is an original idea. If your problem is not data related, then it might not even be relevant. Still, if you or your team has never worked with NoSQL databases before, it might be considered novel.

This essentialists' take on creativity comes with many drawbacks; for example, it completely ignores context. Creativity research is making a gradual shift toward a more *systemic* approach that takes into account contextual parameters. This sounds complicated, and I can almost hear you bracing yourself for yet another dry academic definition. Fortunately, quite the opposite is true.

> **EXERCISE** When do you think something is considered creative? Ponder that question for a few minutes. When was the last time that something you came up with was considered very creative?

Done? Right. I'll lift the curtain for you: something is creative when someone else says it is. There, isn't that easy? Creativity is a *social verdict.*[4] Your peers decide whether or not your programming efforts led to something creative. You cannot possibly declare that yourself. It is a sociocultural phenomenon.

Art experts who proclaim a particular painting to be a stroke of genius dictate our opinion as laypersons (figure 1.1). In response, we dutifully sigh in awe. If that painting was considered plain and uninteresting by critics, we wouldn't bother to look. It would probably never make it to a museum wall. Because we don't have the necessary technical knowledge about painting, we have to rely on the experts in the field.

The same is true for programming—or any other domain. If your teammates pat you on the back saying, "Nice code! A creative way to circumvent the problem!" then you're suddenly promoted to a creative programmer, on the condition that your teammates as experts in programming are not just fooling around. Yet, that very same solution could be considered boring by another team or in another company: been there, done that.

Thinking about creativity in a systematic way also explains the sad prevalence of unsung geniuses. It goes without saying that if none of Vincent van Gogh's paintings had been found, we would not consider him a creative genius. And if none of the art experts in the field had accepted van Gogh's paintings as evocative and groundbreaking, we would not consider him a creative genius. In fact, that is exactly what happened during his lifetime. His paintings were consistently rejected by the Paris Salon curators, who were responsible for the official art exhibition of the Académie des Beaux-Arts between 1748 and 1890. Their conservatism didn't last long. The critical mass grew and dethroned the classicists in favor of Impressionism, as the Impressionists started holding their own independent exhibitions. Time and place are equally

---

[4] Vlad Petre Glăveanu, Michael Hanchett Hanson, John Baer, et al. Advancing creativity theory and research: A socio-cultural manifesto. The Journal of Creative Behavior, 2020.

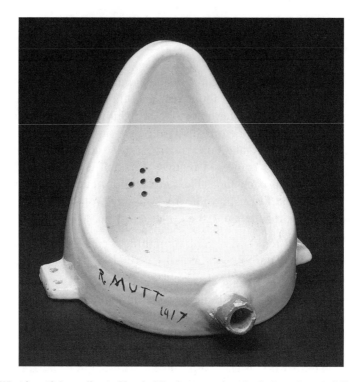

Figure 1.1   What is art? According to Marchel Duchamp, a signed urinal can be art. A New York gallery rejected it. Duchamp's *Fontaine* did manage to shake things up quite a bit in the domain of 20th-century art. It is now considered highly creative. Source: public domain.

important contributors to creativity, as we will see in later chapters. Many of van Gogh's works are now among the most expensive paintings ever sold.

The origins of the creative

The way in which we perceive creativity has changed many times throughout the history of humankind. Nowadays, we immediately think of art when we hear the term. In ancient Greece, art (*technê* in Greek, later adapted to *technology*) involved strict adherence to rules. Painters and sculpturers imitated; they did not create—only poets were allowed "freedom of action." Artists discovered; they did not invent.

In later Christian-dominated Europe, creativity was reserved for God's act of creation from nothing (*creatio ex nihilo*). We humble humans merely made (*facere*) stuff; we couldn't—and weren't allowed to—create.

Only during the Renaissance period did philosophers and artists begin to see themselves as inventors, shaping new objects according to their own ideas, gradually freeing art from craft and moving toward creativity. It would take two more centuries before the term was actually applied—and it was met with heavy Christian resistance.

Creativity would not gain traction in scientific research until the 1950s. It is, just like programming, a relatively new concept!

I might come up with a clever variant of ext4, the most popular journaling file system for Linux. I might perhaps call it *WouterFS*. That does ooze with creativity (and decadence). If I never introduce it to someone else, there's a slim chance it would get picked up after my death. Luckily, I'm a realist. Technology changes too rapidly, and by then, they'll probably be about to roll out ext65, which most likely will make WouterFS redundant. Maybe one day I will find the courage to show my implementation to a few of the ext maintainers. If it is seen as mundane and dismissed—and the chances of that are high—I'll have to accept my defeat. But if my code is seen as creative, they might even patch a few features into ext4. In other words, all I can do is my best, but it is not up to me to declare my work as creative.

1.2   Why creativity?

That does sound rather depressing, doesn't it? Why would you bother reading a book about becoming a creative programmer if it's up to someone else's whims? Because many habits and personality traits explained in the coming chapters greatly increase your *potential* to be a creative programmer.

Still, that does not answer the *why* question. Why bother becoming a creative programmer when you're already a competent programmer? The answer is—again— multidimensional. Let's examine the major reasons to lead a creative developer's life.

The first reason, simply put, is that employers ask for it. For years, nearly every software development job advertisement contains the word "creative."[5] Everyone knows that job ads are bulging with meaningless words made up by the Human Resources department to attract as many candidates as possible. *Soft skills* are all the rage these days. Instead of scanning ads, my colleagues and I conducted our own research by simply asking software development experts: "Which non-technical skills do you think are needed to excel as a developer?"[6] Guess which word popped up? If you want to sell yourself, you'll have to be creative.

> **EXERCISE** When do you consider your own programming work to be creative? When is it anything but creative? When do you consider others' code creative? Is there a difference? You might be reluctant to answer such mundane questions because the answers might yield (un)pleasant surprises.

As for the reason why creativity is such a sought-after skill, the answer lies in problem solving. When conventional methods fail, bringing in a splash of creativity might be the way to go. Knowing how the creative process works is half the solution. For example, if your web application is struggling with handling thousands of requests per second, it might be a good idea to look at message queuing, load balancing, caching, or

---

[5] Judy L. Wynekoop and Diane B Walz. Investigating traits of top performing software developers. Information Technology & People, 2000.

[6] Wouter Groeneveld, Hans Jacobs, Joost Vennekens, and Kris Aerts. Non-cognitive abilities of exceptional software engineers: A Delphi study. Proceedings of the 51st ACM Technical Symposium on Computer Science Education, 2020.

coroutines. If nobody on the team suggests any of these, you'll likely go in circles. A creative programmer breaks those circles.

Sometimes, though, problem solving is not enough. Sometimes, the problem hasn't yet been found—let alone defined. In cases like that, your typical problem-solving skills won't be very effective: you will need to rely on your creative senses to *see* the problem.

When Charles Darwin left Plymouth on the *Beagle* in 1831, a voyage that would last five years, he had no intention of linking natural selection with the origin of species: the problem domain didn't even exist yet. The British Royal Navy researchers were tasked only with charting the coastline of South America. The exotic vegetation and animals Darwin encountered and meticulously kept notes of planted the seeds for his theory that would be conceived only years after the voyage itself.

Darwin wasn't a problem solver; he was a problem *finder*. What can we as programmers learn from Darwin's way of thinking? We're usually swamped with small and well-defined (sub)problems, tasks in a swim lane that somehow have to make it to the "done" column. But perhaps, somewhere along the journey, enough dots are collected and later connected to form an entirely new question. Perhaps we discover a problem our clients didn't even know they had. A creative programmer is both a problem finder and a problem solver. We will revisit Darwin's voyage around the world in chapter 6.

The second reason to care about the creative judgments of others is because the opinion of your peers should matter. In case you haven't noticed yet, software development is a team-based activity. Creativity is meaningless in isolation (more about that in chapter 3) exactly because it is a social construct. The psychological safety that emerges from mutual respect makes everyone feel more at ease, thereby increasing the jelling of the team. This opens up the possibility for you to learn and grow and to help others learn and grow as well.

Creative product vs. process

Note that, when admiring creative work, we almost always admire the *product*: the end result, after the flow of ample blood, sweat, and tears. The end result could be a clever algorithm or a newly invented design pattern. Those would attract admiration primarily from software developers. The end result could also be the whole application, which, ideally, your end users also would call creative.

Instead of the end product, the *process* that leads up to the work can also be creative. However, the process is mostly invisible and hence impossibly difficult to evaluate. Creative processes might yield creative products. The emphasis is on *might* here: the result could also be a train wreck. The opposite also is true: a creative product can be the result of a conventional process.

Inviting experts to judge the creativity of a product is called the *Consensual Assessment Technique*, a popular term coined by Teresa Amabile in 1988. Next time you're watching *America's Got Talent*, remember that it's adhering to sound academic methods!

A third reason to be creative is because creativity equals *fun*. Many experts we interviewed mentioned the sole reason for being a programmer is the possibility of being creative. Creative programmers deeply enjoy their work. They love taking a deep dive, getting out of their comfort zone, connecting unusual ideas, discussing different approaches with others, and being in the flow. In short, creative programmers give in to their *creative urge*. They become Umberto Eco's *homo faber*.

Many creators hope to achieve immortality through their creative work that might outlive their feeble body. The lucky few who realize their dream of leaving a permanent mark on the world are hailed as true geniuses. We, as programmers, working with highly volatile technology, might be better off taming our immortal aspirations. I bet by the time this book is published, dozens of existing technical books on programming can be safely moved to the "vintage" bookshelf. And we all know what that means.

1.3 Different levels of creativity

You might have noticed I've casually used the word *genius* in the context of creativity. Of course, it doesn't take a genius to be creative. Researchers tried to classify different levels of creativity and came up with the following taxonomy:[7]

- *little-c, or everyday creativity*—This is personal creativity: doing something original you haven't done before, for instance, cross-compiling your C++11 game of life implementation to the Game Boy Advance.
- *Big-C, or eminent creativity*—Doing something original nobody has done before, for instance, porting Ruby 3 to run on your 486 machine under DOS 6.22. Hey, there's an idea . . .

Linus Torvalds is a Big-C creator. He completely changed the domain of operating systems (and version control). According to some scholars, "geniuses" are responsible for important creative products that alter the whole domain. On the other hand, coming up with a creative solution for your web app's request throughput problem won't likely shake things up.

Of course, as with all things in this world, the taxonomy had to be criticized. little-c is sometimes portrayed as too mundane and bland. The greatness of Big-C might have creators succumb to the pressure. Creativity researcher Mark Runco completely dismisses the distinction between little and big, proclaiming that reality is not categorical.[8] Others develop their own version in response: there are *H-creativity* (historic: does the invention affect the history books?) and *P-creativity* (personal creativity), and there are more hidden layers between little-c and Big-C called *mini-c* and *Pro-c*. Some researchers, such as Mihaly Csikszentmihalyi, interview creative geniuses to extract practices for everyday creators, whereas others claim this gives a distorted picture. In short, academic creativity research is a bit of a mess. Still, thinking about creativity in terms of different "levels," as clarified in figure 1.2, can be helpful.

---

[7] Peter Merrotsy. A note on big-C creativity and little-C creativity. Creativity Research Journal, 2013.

[8] Mark A Runco. "Big C, little c" creativity as a false dichotomy: Reality is not categorical. Creativity Research Journal, 2014.

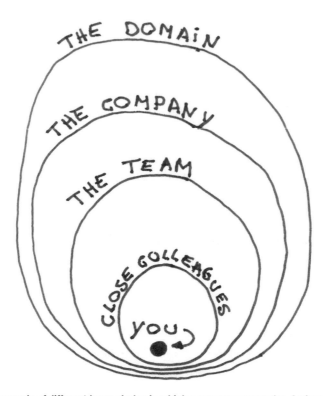

Figure 1.2   An example of different inner circles in which a programmer works. A piece of code deemed creative by close colleagues might bubble up and be lauded as creative by the team. However, another team might have done the same: at the company level, your fame comes to an abrupt end. Because creativity is socioculturally dependent, switching teams also changes the interpretation of creativity. Being mindful of these inner circles can be very useful. Helping the team and company be creative means spreading the word, but starting with yourself.

1.4   *A road map to becoming more creative*

This book is not about how to become a genius, which has little to do with "creative genes": you will soon discover, there is no such thing. Instead, it is about the process of problem-solving. By applying different creative methods and insights into creativity, neatly wrapped in seven distinct but heavily intertwined themes, it is my hope that you will be able to become a better programmer. In case you are not a programmer, don't worry: you will see that many of these methods can be easily transferred to other domains.

Andy Hunt's *Pragmatic Thinking & Learning* starts with a beautiful hand-drawn mind map that doubles as a road map. Because his book also leans to the softer side of programming, I've let myself be inspired by his drawing and used it to brighten up a research[9]—which was considered very creative and promptly accepted. The mind map, as visible in figure 1.3 and at the beginning of this book, also serves as a guide

---

[9] Wouter Groeneveld, Laurens Luyten, Joost Vennekens, and Kris Aerts. Exploring the role of creativity in software engineering. 2021 IEEE/ACM 43rd International Conference on Software Engineering: Software Engineering in Society.

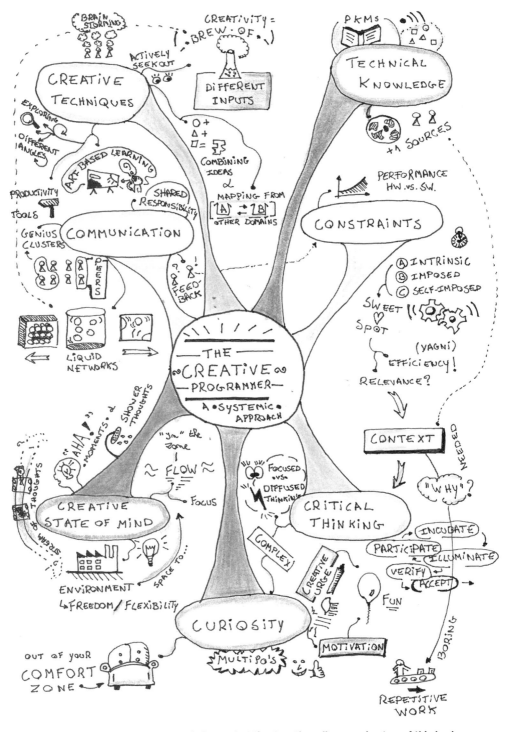

Figure 1.3   *The Creative Programmer* mind map that ties together all seven chapters of this book.

for this book. Each "tentacle" in the map represents a chapter with a distinct theme related to creativity.

> **NOTE**   All illustrated figures in this book are hand drawn by me to better fit the creativity theme.

1.4.1   *The seven Creative Programmer themes*

The following adventures await us.

TECHNICAL KNOWLEDGE

Anyone who produces something creative must have a firm grasp of the state of affairs in their domain. This might sound so obvious that it almost seems excessive to waste a whole chapter on. A programmer can't be a creative programmer if they are not a programmer in the first place. Even though learning before doing is quite self-evident, pausing and thinking about various ways to consume information, continuously learn, be aware of cognitive biases, and manage knowledge still pay off.

Creative programmers understand how to convert a steady stream of knowledge into new ideas.

COLLABORATION/COMMUNICATION

Creativity never happens in isolation: refinement of ideas is a social process. Without any kind of feedback, it will be impossible to upgrade your slightly original idea into an excellent one. Your peers can act as catalysts for change. In chapter 3, we'll explore the concept of genius clusters, how to build dream teams, and techniques to enhance the creativity of teams. In a paper my colleagues and I published,[10] this theme is called *communication*, so we stuck with that term, but in hindsight, *collaboration* might be a more fitting name.

Creative programmers are always aware of the subtle interplay between ideas, individuals, and teams.

CONSTRAINTS

Tackling any kind of problem involves taking constraints into account, whether they are self-imposed or external. Contrary to popular belief, constraints actually spark creativity instead of diminishing it. We will explore multiple cases of creative outbursts that are the result of converting what might look like annoying limitations into sudden advantages.

Creative programmers know how to take advantage of imposed constraints instead of only complaining about them in retrospect.

CRITICAL THINKING

Coming up with a lot of ideas is only half the work: the other half, which is arguably more difficult, involves vigorous scrapping until the best idea is left standing. Then

---

[10] Wouter Groeneveld, Hans Jacobs, Joost Vennekens, and Kris Aerts. Non-cognitive abilities of exceptional software engineers: A Delphi study. Proceedings of the 51st ACM Technical Symposium on Computer Science Education, 2020.

and only then, it might be time for action. In chapter 5, we'll try to engage in a symbiotic relationship between critical thinking and our everlasting fountain of crazy ideas. We'll discover that creativity is not only about generating ideas but also about decision making and execution.

Creative programmers are able to fluently switch between sprawling ideation and critical evaluation.

CURIOSITY

Why did you pick up this book? Were you curious about its contents? Are you eager to learn? Are you determined to read this book cover to cover? If the answer is yes, we're off to a great start here! According to creativity researcher Mihaly Csikszentmihalyi, curiosity and perseverance are the two most defining personality traits for creativity.[11] We'll regularly revisit Csikszentmihalyi's excellent work on this subject in the coming chapters.

Curiosity leads to an implicit motivation to learn new things (technical knowledge). Curiosity leads to asking "why" questions (critical thinking). We'll discuss why having a sense of wonder is advantageous, not only for the absent-minded professor but also for the creative programmer.

CREATIVE STATE OF MIND

We all know that frequent interruptions are detrimental to the programming flow. Getting into the right state of mind will greatly improve your creative work. We'll inspect how flow and insight work, what insight priming can bring to the table, and how to increase those ever-so-important but fickle "aha" moments.

Working on your individual state of mind is one thing. Enhancing the collective state of mind of your team or company is another—and both are equally important to a creative programmer.

CREATIVE TECHNIQUES

Last, we will discuss several practical, creative techniques that can positively affect the concepts explained in all of the preceding chapters. Just like creativity's systemic definition, these techniques are intertwined with all dimensions of creative problem solving. They do not necessarily fit neatly into one distinct theme. We'll take a critical look at classic brainstorming sessions and more unconventional techniques, such as giving your ideas some legs.

1.4.2   The Creative Programming Problem Solving Test

What if you wanted to follow along in this book and gauge your growing creative programming potential related to a specific assignment or project? A lot of creativity assessment tools exist that measure specific bits and pieces, as we'll soon discover in the coming chapters. Some determine your divergent thinking skills, and others are mostly focused on evaluating the end product. Unfortunately, none of the existing tools are composed from within the computing domain and apply a systems view.

---

[11] Mihaly Csikszentmihalyi. Creativity: Flow and the psychology of discovery and invention. Harper Perennial, reprint edition, 2013.

To do exactly that, my colleagues and I have designed a self-assessment survey for creative problem-solving based on the seven themes discussed in this book.[12] The survey has been validated for first- and last-year software engineering students and was verified by several industry experts. It is by no means a catchall solution to measure creativity, but it's the closest thing we have nowadays for programmers to identify the level of engagement for each of the seven themes.

The questions will make more sense as soon as you've finished reading each particular chapter. Some questions will leave you wondering whether or not they neatly fit into a single theme. Don't worry; many don't: as we'll soon discover, creativity doesn't easily let itself be pushed into a single category.

Perhaps it's a good idea to fill in the questionnaire now, before moving on to the first chapter, to get a general idea of your current state as a creative programmer. Remember, it's a self-assessment test, so try to be honest—lying will only trick you into thinking there's little room for improvement! When filling in the test, try to relate the questions to a recent specific assignment. The answers will likely vary from project to project.

Each question should yield a number: 1 (completely disagree), 2 (disagree), 3 (neither agree nor disagree), 4 (agree), or 5 (completely agree). Feel free to take out a pencil and insert "X"s in the rubric where appropriate.

Table 1.1   The full set of 56 questions from the Creative Programming Problem Solving Test rubric

1. Technical knowledge	1	2	3	4	5
I have gained a lot of knowledge during the project.					
I learned and applied new practical programming techniques.					
I have gained insight into the problem domain.					
The technical aspect of programming appealed to me.					
I thought about my learning process and how to improve it.					
I felt comfortable with this project because many aspects were unknown.					
I tried to relate the new knowledge to something I know.					
Thanks to the project I also gained knowledge of other things outside of coding.					
2. Communication	1	2	3	4	5
I regularly asked for feedback from my fellow colleagues.					
I visualized the problem on a whiteboard or on paper.					
I regularly asked feedback from my clients and/or end users.					
I helped my teammates with their own tasks.					
My own tasks were completed on time so that teammates did not run into deadline troubles.					

[12] Wouter Groeneveld, Lynn Van den Broeck, Joost Vennekens, and Kris Aerts. Self-assessing creative problem solving for aspiring software developers: A pilot study. Proceedings of the 2022 ACM Conference on Innovations and Technology in Computer Science Education, 2022.

Table 1.1   The full set of 56 questions from the Creative Programming Problem Solving Test rubric *(continued)*

	1	2	3	4	5
I supported the ideas and efforts of my teammates.					
I was so proud of our result that I showed it to everyone.					
I thoroughly thought through suggestions made by others.					
3. Constraints	1	2	3	4	5
I regularly thought about the correctness of my solution.					
I did not perform less well due to time pressure.					
I tried to make my code as elegant as possible.					
I tried to identify the constraints of the assignment.					
I had the program tested by friends and/or family (if possible).					
I could make good decisions even though there was a lot of creative freedom.					
Coding on short notice accelerated my learning process.					
I regularly tested the program myself and paid attention to its ease of use.					
4. Critical thinking	1	2	3	4	5
In discussions about problems, I often suggested alternatives.					
I regularly carefully weighed up the various options we had.					
I dared to completely rewrite my code when it didn't go well.					
I used multiple sources to find out information myself.					
I think it was important to ask teammates how they implemented something.					
I always check the credibility of the source when I look something up.					
It was important that I 100% understood why something works the way it did.					
Looking at other projects made me reflect on my own.					
5. Curiosity	1	2	3	4	5
During the project, I got very much out of my comfort zone.					
Many parts of the project piqued my curiosity.					
I enjoyed getting involved in many aspects of the project.					
I enjoyed really immersing myself in some aspects.					
I was stimulated by the complexity of the project.					
I felt the urge to implement extras.					
I had a lot of fun while developing the project.					
I didn't have to commit and push myself to finish the project.					
6. Creative state of mind	1	2	3	4	5
I remained focused for a long time on one part of the project.					
I used productivity tools to focus more on the essence of the problem.					
I found the experience to be very rewarding.					

Table 1.1   The full set of 56 questions from the Creative Programming Problem Solving Test rubric *(continued)*

Time seemed to fly while working.					
I found that I knew enough to meet the high demands of the project.					
Programming went almost automatically.					
I knew exactly what I wanted to achieve.					
I was not concerned with what outsiders thought of my code.					
7. Creative techniques	1	2	3	4	5
I used many different methods to solve a single problem.					
I employed knowledge from another domain to solve something.					
I combined different ideas to tackle a problem.					
I deliberately took occasional breaks to let things sink in.					
I brainstormed with others to come up with new ideas.					
I took a step back now and then to see things as a whole.					
In case of problems I let myself be inspired by other projects.					
I never felt completely stuck.					

If you calculate an average for each theme, you can sketch out the results in the form of a spider diagram, such as the one in figure 1.4. In contrast with other assessment tools we'll encounter in later chapters, it is impossible to further reduce the outcome

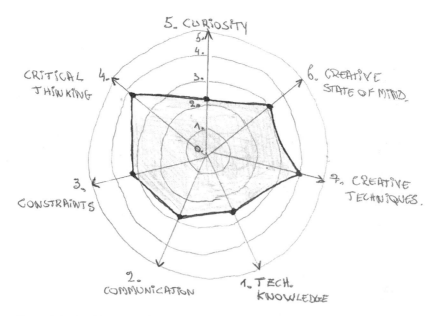

Figure 1.4   A spider graph of a possible Creative Programming Problem Solving Test (CPPST) result. If you're too lazy to draw something like this, try out the online survey at https://brainbaking.com/cppst/.

to a single digit. That would completely negate contextual links of creative problem solving that we have so carefully tried to preserve.

Filling in the questionnaire can yield interesting and different results depending on the project you're working on: it's purposely very much context bound. Perhaps you're bored with one project, resulting in a low curiosity score. Or you're going all out at a technical level with another project, resulting in a high technical knowledge score. Again, don't worry too much about that score—the CPPST tool primarily serves as a way to gain some insight in your current personal creative process. As you work your way through the book, consider going back to the questions now and then to see whether you're improving in practice.

1.5   The structure of the following chapters

Each chapter after this one starts with a background story to set the scene and provide examples of creative thinking inside and outside the world of technology. You might also notice my tendency to use video game references as contextual assistants, next to conventional examples. This isn't just because I happen to like games. Dozens of studies—including those of my colleagues and I—have proven that visual examples better capture interest, and game use triggers playful learning. Because this is a book about creative programming, it would be a shame not to dig up stories about game development. After all, aren't they also considered pieces of art?

Chapters are also generously sprinkled with exercises marked with a distinct border. This isn't a technical programming book, so the exercises aren't as hands-on as you might be used to. However, they are still valuable as thinking exercises and can serve well as subjects of retrospectives. Of course, I can't force you to suddenly be creative—all I can do is point in the right direction. Converting those pointers into action is up to you.

Sometimes, as an aside, I'll digress from the topic to provide additional amusing and insightful background stories. You will recognize these off-topic sections as gray blocks in between the regular text. If you're in a hurry, they can be skipped, although you'll likely miss out on creative triggers if you decide to do so.

Each chapter ends with a checklist that summarizes the new concepts covered in that particular chapter. These can serve as a reminder, but please take their context into account: just scanning the summaries isn't going to get you closer to creative coding mastery; neither do they serve as a complete overview of best practices.

You are now ready for your creative adventure. Let's dive in.

Technical knowledge

This chapter covers

- How to gather, internalize, and act on knowledge
- The Zettelkasten knowledge management technique
- A workflow for keeping smart notes

A lonely crow disturbs the otherwise peaceful silence of an ancient Corsican night. A Spanish-born Roman citizen passes the evening with his two best friends: pen and ink. After being exiled from Rome by the dictator Claudius, Seneca the Younger spent eight highly productive years on the island of Corsica, publishing various consolations on anger and death. Writing, as Seneca proclaimed, is how one should exercise oneself. Not a single night would pass without him writing in his journal. As he explained to a friend, "I scan the whole of my day and retrace all my deeds and words. I conceal nothing from myself, I omit nothing. For why should I shrink from any of my mistakes, when I may commune thus with myself?" The sleep that would follow his self-examination felt particularly satisfying.

Seneca's daily note-taking habits gained traction during his extended stay in Alexandria. His struggle with tuberculosis forced him to take an extended leave from Rome. For almost 10 years, in convalescence, he did what any Stoic philosopher would do: study and write, building both mental and physical strength. Seneca

16

looked into combining Stoicism with Pythagoreanism. He read and debated the works of Epicurus, who ended up being the most cited writer in Seneca's works. Seneca said we should read like spies in the enemy's camp, always looking to learn from our intellectual and philosophical opponents. Sadly, all works from Seneca's Alexandrian period are lost. According to recent estimations, about half of his tragedies and philosophical essays are gone.

Seneca's journaling served three main purposes: (1) self-examination, (2) gaining and connecting knowledge, and (3) retaining knowledge. He would argue that to lead by example, you first have to analyze your own actions—and those of others. Unlike other journalers of that time, Seneca wrote with the intention to publish. He wanted his writings to be discovered and read, to influence others and conserve ideas.

Nineteen centuries later, a German academic rummages through paperwork in a set of small drawers of a heavy apothecary cabinet. He holds a small piece of paper in his hand, speedily scanning the contents of certain drawers, until a mumbled "aha!" announces his arrival at the right drawer. The paper disappears into the cabinet, and the academic sinks back into his office chair, returning his attention to that huge stack of papers in dire need of grading (figure 2.1).

Figure 2.1 Niklas Luhmann in his home office, consulting his notes. Photo © Michael Wiegert-Wegener / University Archives Bielefeld.

That person is Niklas Luhmann, one of the most productive and renowned social scientists of the 20th century. During his academic career, he published 50 books and more than 600 articles. When asked how he managed such a feat, his answer was humble: he said his productivity stems from a "conversation" with his notes. His famous systems theory—an integrated take on communication, societal, and evolution theory—was the product of conversations with his *Zettelkasten* ("slip box").

Thanks to his ingenious knowledge storage and generation system, Luhmann managed to connect seemingly unrelated domains and produce novel insights. These new insights would in turn be stored in the *Zettelkasten*, steadily growing his external body of knowledge. Although Luhmann wasn't the first to use an interlinked index card system to organize intellectual work—16th-century polymath Conrad Gessner had already mentioned writing down ideas on slips of paper to arrange into larger clusters—his (now fully digitized) *Zettelkasten* archive provided more insight into the prolific brilliance of it, inspiring many contemporary note takers and digital note-taking apps.

Another century passed. In 2010, Russian software engineer Andrey Breslav and the JetBrains R&D team discussed development and production problems in large-scale back-end codebases. Whiteboard sketches would later become the groundwork for a new programming language known as *Kotlin*; however, Breslav and his language design team had little intention of creating yet another shiny new toy for fashion-conscious developers to play around with. Kotlin was designed to be "pragmatic, concise, safe, and interoperable," according to the Kotlin website.

Those four cornerstones caused the team to thoroughly inspect existing programming languages and steal ideas that work but, more importantly, leave out the fancy fluff. As Breslav said in his GeekOUT 2018 talk "Languages Kotlin Learned From,"[1] being wary of using existing ideas is counterproductive. Instead, they turned toward Java (classes, autoboxing, runtime safety guarantees, etc.), Scala (primary constructors, the `val` keyword, etc.), C# (some ideas of `get`/`set` properties and extensions, internal visibility, easy string interpolation, etc.), and Groovy (the `it` shorthand, passing lambdas without parentheses, etc.), and implemented what worked. "Thanks a lot, authors of Groovy; it's been a pleasure borrowing features from you," concluded Breslav.

Their design philosophy clearly paid off. Next to Java, Kotlin is now the most popular language on the Java Virtual Machine (18%, according to Snyk's 2020 JVM Ecosystem report[2]), and yearly Stack Overflow Insights[3] report a steady increase in overall popularity, surpassing Ruby and closely following Go.

2.1   *No input, no creative output*

What is the greatest common divisor of Seneca's knowledgeable and still-popular Stoic writings, Niklas Luhmann's *Zettelkasten* apothecary cabinet that is fed index cards, and the birth of the Kotlin programming language? All three examples showcase that creativity begets creativity. Every intention is based on a previous one. Seneca closely followed rival schools and internalized that knowledge to produce something new. Luhmann conversed with his notes, which told him to connect information he otherwise would have forgotten. Breslav first turned to other programming languages, inspecting what worked there, to avoid creating something original but ultimately unsuitable.

All creative work starts with input. If there is no input, there can be no output. In an effort to better understand the role of creativity in software engineering, my colleagues and I asked many developers to identify the requirements for creativity.[4] Technical

---

[1] See https://youtu.be/Ljr66Bg–1M.

[2] See https://snyk.io/blog/jvm-ecosystem-report-2020/.

[3] See https://insights.stackoverflow.com/survey/ for the years 2020 and 2021.

[4] Wouter Groeneveld, Laurens Luyten, Joost Vennekens, and Kris Aerts. Exploring the role of creativity in software engineering. 2021 IEEE/ACM 43rd International Conference on Software Engineering: Software Engineering in Society (ICSE-SEIS).

knowledge was consistently mentioned first. I'm sure this won't come as a big surprise—that's the reason this is the first major Creative Programmer theme.

Creativity can be approached from different perspectives, such as *inspirationalist* (free association, playfulness, lateral thinking, etc.), *situationalist* (depending on social context, embedded in the community), and *structuralist* (studying and analyzing techniques and methods). Let's get the structuralist approach to creativity out of the way before moving on to the situationalist approach in chapter 3 and the inspirationalist in chapters 4, 5, and 6.

A musician with little knowledge of instruments, existing play styles, and perhaps various vocal techniques cannot be expected to deliver a truly creative record. A painter can't produce creative work without extensive knowledge of drawing techniques. Although we might get fooled by the simplicity contemporary art pieces seem to embody, art usually requires technical knowledge and years of experience to deconstruct colors and compositions to their essence. Of course, there are always exceptions to the rule.

The same is true for us programmers: we can't be creative with Java code without extensive knowledge of the Java Virtual Machine (JVM) and its ecosystem. In his Geek-OUT talk, Breslav admitted to having overlooked Swift as a potential influence. At that time, it was also very new, and nobody on the team knew about it. Without Groovy's influence, the keywords `with` and `it` would not exist in the Kotlin world.[5]

But what exactly is *extensive* knowledge? What is the best way to gain, retain, and create new knowledge? And when it comes to creativity, are we really only talking about *technical* knowledge here? Welcome to the wonderful world of cognitive psychology.

Many forward-thinking technology firms take continuous learning seriously. They offer learning days, hackathons, innumerable books and courses to plow through, and even Google-inspired "20% time," where one day a week you can toy with a pet project that ideally grows into Gmail-like greatness. (Google gradually dialed back on this creative free time. We'll get back to this in chapter 8.) Whether it's called *continuous learning*, *lifelong learning*, or *self-improvement*, the premise remains the same: we're here to learn.

One of our interviewees managed to beautifully set the scene for this chapter by stating the following:

> *The bottom line is that creativity is the brew of different inputs—and usually, I actively look up those inputs . . . , or something forms in my mind by structuring those inputs, or when I ask for feedback to take into account; that's something I often do.*

But where does that input come from? Some developers might answer with their preferred tech news site (e.g., <u>dzone.com</u>, <u>slashdot.org</u>, <u>lobste.rs</u>) or the blog of their favorite coding idol. These would all be valid yet very narrow-minded sources of information. Let us start by considering the big picture.

---

[5] The "it" and "me" keywords are in fact much older than Groovy. Breslav's team probably zoomed in on those via Groovy because that language also sits on top of the JVM.

2.2   *Gathering knowledge*

Curiosity will inevitably lead to the accumulation of new knowledge—we'll learn more about that in chapter 6. Before continuing, I'd like you to think about the way you typically gather information.

> **EXERCISE** What are your regular sources of new input? When was the last time you actively pondered the contents of those sources instead of zipping through them? When was the last time you took notes? Finally, when was the last time you effectively used something you've picked up from those sources?

I hope you didn't struggle to remember the last time you applied something from those sources. If so, it might be worth reconsidering what goes in. As they say, garbage in, garbage out. I wouldn't put it that bluntly, but if you stick to scrolling through Facebook—which *can* be a valuable source of input—you won't make much progress in helping to solve that programming problem your team is having difficulties with.

The knowledge-gathering problem is much more severe today than it was in the nineties. The days of a simple bookmark in Netscape Navigator, the only door to the internet, are long gone. How should we keep track of the stuff we're interested in?

2.2.1   *Diversify what goes in*

Diversifying means two things. First, don't put all your eggs in one basket. As a Java developer, read about threading models on the JVM as well as on Goroutines in Go and concurrent actors implemented in Ruby. Having an idea of how concurrency works in other languages will allow you to better reflect on what works and what doesn't in the language you're currently working with. If you love the ease of use of Goroutines but you're stuck with the JVM, you might come up with a few cleverly written wrappers to take away the rough edges.

As a developer, read books on compilers and programming languages as well as on philosophy and psychology. It is only natural to go deep into the technical side of things: after all, that is probably one of the reasons why you're a programmer in the first place. However, do not neglect other domains! I felt the need to add an exclamation mark here because investing in a variety of technical topics seems to be universally accepted, while the nontechnical topics are left Alone in the Dark. Creative programmers excel at making connections *across* domains, not merely within their comfy programming domain. Learning about psychology will help you better understand the various moral implications of technology. Learning about history is a great way to situate and help evaluate the rapidly evolving technologies. Many workplaces increasingly expect programmers to be experts in one or two topics. That view is very narrow minded and anything but creative. We'll delve into the specialist versus generalist debate in detail in chapter 6.

Second, diversify in the medium. Pick up a book or two. (I'll admit that writing "Read more books!" in a book is not the best way to convey the message. If this all sounds a bit too obvious, it's probably because it is.) Attend a conference or a class. Subscribe to a newsletter. Become a regular blog reader—or, even better, a writer. Talk to others about the things that puzzle you. Ask for feedback. Join a reading group. And so forth.

> ## Domain general vs. domain specific
>
> Is creativity domain general or domain specific? This is another question that academics like to answer with knives out.[a] On the one hand, you'll need to invest a good amount of time and effort to get to know Ruby before being able to express yourself fluently in that language: perhaps the magical 10,000 hours, as suggested by famous Canadian journalist and author Malcolm Gladwell in his book *Outliers*? The Dreyfus model of skill acquisition also claims that you'll likely need 10 years of deliberate practice to fully master something. According to the model, to change a domain, one must first fully master it. The question is whether the domain is Ruby programming or programming in general.
>
> On the other hand, many creative techniques explained in this book can be seen as domain general. A curious attitude, smart management of knowledge, the incubation of ideas: they can all be transferred from the programming world to the garden landscaping world. Furthermore, some domain-specific knowledge from one domain is even advantageous in another, given that cross-pollination is what really gets creativity going. The Dreyfus model seems to omit this. The conclusion? It does not matter. Creativity is domain specific *and* domain general!

[a]Jonathan A. Plucker and Ronald A. Beghetto. Why creativity is domain general, why it looks domain specific, and why the distinction does not matter. American Psychological Association, 2004.

2.2.2 *Moderate what goes in*

My wife loves reading books but regularly panics after yet another buying spree. She'll state something like, "So many books to read, yet so little time!" And she's right. In a good year, my Goodreads account tells me I manage to squeeze in 24 books. At the time of this writing, I'm at 36. Let's say I can keep up this trend until, at age 80, my eyes are about to pop. That's still 44 great years and thus 1,056 books ahead of me. The average bookstore probably sells about five times that many books every year. As a writer, it almost seems futile to publish yet another book that takes up one of those precious slots.

Moderating your knowledge calorie intake like a dieter counting food calories is the only solution. You will have to decide for yourself—or let others guide you on— what is worth reading and what can be safely ignored. This analogy extends to the web, where we probably spend way too much time poking around. Instead of wasting your time and eyesight on ads, redundant news items, and predictions of possible pregnancies of the royal family, it might be a better idea to rely on something as simple as an RSS reader, which gives you full control over the information stream.

Although feed aggregators like RSS readers can be combined with read-it-later bookmark systems, the danger of information overload reemerges when carelessly subscribing to and saving everything you come across. Treating these systems like yet another inbox to Get Things Done,[6] as time management guru David Allen taught us,

---

[6] David Allen. Getting things done: The art of stress-free productivity. Penguin, 2001.

might do the trick. Just remember that sorting through items to decide what is still relevant and what is not will come at the cost of extra cognitive load—or, in programmer's terms, extra RAM and CPU usage.

Does too much knowledge impede creativity?

An omniscient programmer is not necessarily a creative programmer. Sometimes, what we do know blinds us and effectively *reduces* our openness to potentially creative ideas. We're quick to reject silly proposals because we "simply know" it's not possible: "Trust me, I'm an expert on this; this ain't gonna work." Perhaps if we naively tried anyway, it would work out.

Researchers call this *knowledge priming*. A brainstorming experiment showed that participants primed with knowledge produced more ideas but, compared with an unprimed control group, the ideas were less original.[a]

In chapter 4, we'll explore the effect of naivety on constraints, while chapter 5 introduces critical thinking as a tool to evaluate what we (don't) know.

[a] Eric F Rietzschel, Bernard A Nijstad, and Wolfgang Stroebe. Relative accessibility of domain knowledge and creativity: The effects of knowledge activation on the quantity and originality of generated ideas. Journal of Experimental Social Psychology, 2007.

2.3 *Internalizing knowledge*

Great, so you've inhaled a bunch of new and exciting things. Now what? The next step is to *internalize* that knowledge by translating it to your own personal context.

Do you remember painstakingly hand-writing summaries of physics and math during high school? You might have hated it then, but it is one of the more effective ways to internalize knowledge. First, writing information by hand increases the chance that it will be stored in long-term memory. Pam Mueller and Daniel Oppenheimer published a study with the catchy slogan *The pen is mightier than the keyboard*, in which they suggested that laptop note-taking is less effective than longhand note-taking for learning.[7] Second, the same study suggested that reframing information might be key:

> We show that whereas taking more notes can be beneficial, laptop note takers' tendency to transcribe lectures verbatim rather than processing information and reframing it in their own words is detrimental to learning.

Medieval monks copied manuscripts with pen and ink. Did they learn better because of it? Perhaps: some studies have indicated that copying notes and texts with a pen might enhance learning because the slower pace of hand-writing compared with typing on a keyboard increases focus; also, the tactile feedback involved in any form of hand-writing activates multiple areas of the brain simultaneously, notably, the same areas as working memory.[8]

---

[7] Pam A Mueller and Daniel M Oppenheimer. The pen is mightier than the keyboard: Advantages of longhand over laptop note taking. Psychological Science, 2014.

[8] Richard Tindle and Mitchell G Longstaff. Working memory and handwriting and share a common resource: An investigation of shared attention. Current Psychology, 2021.

Still, the most important part of internalizing knowledge is reframing information so you can transfer it from the source context to your own, which can of course also be achieved by typing on a laptop. Mueller and Oppenheimer's subjects were students in academia: during lectures, it is often faster to literally copy what is being said. Internalizing (one hopes) happens afterward, when rummaging through the notes.

I've had colleagues who use a wiki system—a web-based, interlinked set of pages that acts as their knowledge base—for this. Some have published wikis on the internet for other team members to access or even modify. Snippets of intricate regular expressions, Bash scripts, command-line-based search commands to quickly go through the production log, code patterns used in previous projects, you name it: it was all there. At one point, my colleagues and I banded together and created a shared team-based wiki knowledge base.

Shared knowledge bases have become rather common in software engineering. However, I'm sad to see a decline in what could be considered a knowledge *base*. Slack and Discord are excellent in facilitating fleeting communication, not in building a permanent shared knowledge base. These tools do not replace forums or wikis, where information is permanent and searchable!

Your team does have a way to share knowledge, right? No, email does not suffice. If not, stop reading, remove all Post-Its™ from the scrum board, and put "sharing knowledge" on it as a call to arms!

Rather technical code snippets or tutorials on how to create a new service inside the existing system arguably don't need a lot of reframing. Some wiki maintainers don't stop there and add personal notes on books they've read, mechanics of noncoding hobbies, recipes and cooking techniques, and so on.

Wikis are far from the only way to gather and internalize knowledge. The following is a subset of the digital possibilities:

- Some kind of simple fat-file structure to keep track of notes
- A plethora of note-taking apps, such as Microsoft OneNote, DEVONthink, and Evernote, that include features like OCR searching, scanning documents, and cloud saves
- Note-taking apps such as Obsidian and Zettlr that emphasize hyperlinking
- Mind map software or sketching systems
- Static site generators powered by Markdown files

Avoiding vendor lock-in

As you choose a digital tool to support your note-taking habits, be mindful of the data format it uses. Your external knowledge base will always outlive the software used to create it, so export capabilities into human-readable formats are important.

Be prepared to write custom scripts to convert your database if needed—which was what I had to do when switching from Evernote to DEVONthink, because Evernote unfortunately uses a proprietary XML-like format instead of simple text-based files.

> **(continued)**
> Similarly, think about where you want your notes to be stored. For example, Evernote uses a cloud-based solution on top of the Google Cloud Platform. That means it's easy to sync between your laptop and smartphone, but it also means your notes are not your notes. I know several former Evernote users who effectively lost crucial notes because of "server inconsistencies." Whoops.

2.3.1   *Knowledge management*

Leadership expert and public speaker John C. Maxwell was right when he wrote in his million-copy-selling book *Developing the Leader Within You*, "You gotta have a system."[9] This system is not just to develop the leader within you but also to keep track of knowledge and generate new ideas: a consistent system to collect and process information in, also known as (personal) *knowledge management*.

The idea of knowledge management is far from new, as are the tools used to do so. Cicero wrote letters to his friends on all things politics and philosophy to both organize his own thoughts and humor others. Leonardo da Vinci meticulously categorized his thoughts and ideas in multiple volumes of notebooks, accompanied by equally detailed sketches. He used mirror writing to keep out prying eyes—or simply to avoid making ink stains because he was left-handed. Marcus Aurelius kept notes. Charles Darwin kept notes. Michel de Montaigne kept notes. Arthur Conan Doyle kept notes. Computer pioneer Alan Turing kept notes. Eric Evans, the software expert who coined the term *Domain-Driven Design*, has notebooks full of scribbles.[10] Can you spot the pattern?

Somehow, in the past few millennia, journaling lost its appeal. Of course, until the invention of typewriters and computers, taking notes with pen and paper was the only possible way of storing knowledge. Still, the great minority of people I know keep track of their own thoughts—whether on paper or digitally. Yet, when creativity researcher Mihaly Csikszentmihalyi interviewed creative geniuses, all indicated that analog note-taking acted as the catalyst for their creative success.[11]

In 1685, English philosopher John Locke wrote an essay on how to make what he called *commonplace books*: works that contain quotes, ideas, and parts of speeches to ponder on. The idea was to keep a scrapbook of sayings, idioms, maxims, poems, letters, and recipes that, from time to time, one could flip through, reread, and gain new insights. After copying a quote from another author, personal remarks were added: the knowledge was internalized. During the 16th and 17th centuries, commonplace books were the most popular way to record knowledge (figure 2.2).

Locke's idea was far from new. During Aristotle's rhetoric lessons in his Lyceum, *commonplace* was used to refer to wise sayings of well-known historians, poets, philosophers,

---

[9] John C Maxwell. Developing the leader within you. Harper Collins Leadership, 2019.

[10] Evans lets people take a peek within during a 2017 Domain-Driven Design conference; see https://youtu.be/Zm95cYAtAa8.

[11] Mihaly Csikszentmihalyi. Creativity: Flow and the psychology of discovery and invention. HarperPerennial, reprint edition, 2013.

and politicians. Later, Seneca hinted at collecting commonplace quotes to learn from and "turn the words into your own."

Nowadays, keeping a journal—or even using a pen—is regarded as excessively old-fashioned, especially among us technology geeks. Whether it's an analog journal or a digital wiki, *you gotta have a system.* For me, analog writing tops digital keypads any day. I can easily add drawings, use different pens and colors, stick a newspaper clipping or a photo in there, draw arrows, write upside down, squish blueberries and dry tea leaves in there (works wonders!), and so on.

Figure 2.2   The commonplace book of British voyager and entrepreneur Henry Tiffin (1760). These pages were used to contemplate sailing methods. If you, like me, love peeking into both ancient and modern notebooks, *Great Diaries: The World's Most Remarkable Diaries, Journals, Notebooks, and Letters,* **published by DK, makes for a beautiful addition to the bookshelf. Photo courtesy of the Phillips Library, Peabody Essex Museum.**

Most of my ideas come to me at unexpected moments—moments when I'm not usually in front of my computer screen. I'm not great at handling an Android keyboard, and the battery of my smartphone is likely to be dead anyway. The simplest solution is to keep a notebook (figure 2.3) or a stack of Post-Its™ in the car and on the bedside table.

The biggest drawback of digital note-taking is exactly the fact that it's digital: you'll have to stick to ASCII or use awkward drawing software that doesn't have the proper export capabilities. I've seen others use their iPad to great success. Do whatever works for you, but remember: *you gotta have a system.* Try not to get hung up on the setup of the system itself: use the *Pragmatic Programmer*'s KISS—Keep It Simple, Stupid—solution here!

EXERCISE   Next time you enter the office, take a look around. Which desk contains a notepad with scribblings? (Doodles do not count, sorry.) Next time you're in a meeting, who whips out a notebook? Try to find out if these people are copying items verbatim or internalizing what is being discussed. Can you guess whether the notebooks are strictly used during working hours? These questions might be a good conversation starter!

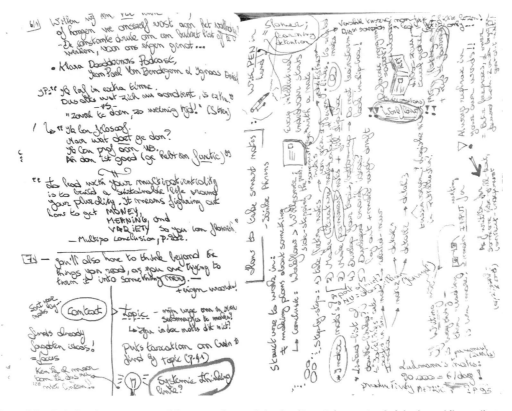

Figure 2.3   A gloriously messy excerpt from one of my notebooks. It contains quotes I picked up while reading or listening to podcasts (left), and my own synthesis of Sönke Ahrens' *How To Take Smart Notes*, intertwined with links to other pages and concepts I'm working on.

Diaries vs. journals vs. notebooks

What's the difference between a journal and a notebook? And where should you write "Dear diary, today I've read *The Creative Programmer*, and it sucks?"

Ancient intellectuals did not make that distinction, so why should you? I keep just one notebook with me at all times to simply record anything that comes to mind, including private tales of dreaded family dinners. It has served me exceptionally well so far—a strict separation of concerns would not have enabled the making of novel connections across domains.

The point here is to let go of the idea that programming thoughts should be written in a programming notebook and that cooking experiments belong in a booklet reserved for kitchen adventures. Diaries that are merely used to record mundane day-to-day activities might not spark many ideas. The opposite is also true. Notebooks that are merely used to summarize how lexical parsing during compiling works might never touch on lexical parsing of natural languages.

2.4 *Acting on knowledge*

After deciding how to consume new information and buying a notebook, or experimenting with a digital note-taking system to put that information into context, you are ready for the third and most important part: actually doing something with that ever-growing pile of knowledge. The sole purpose of collecting and translating information is to produce both novel and actionable insights. Novelty is the product of the unusual combination of knowledge, whereas action transforms that into a tangible outcome, such as piece of code or a publication. Don't fall for what avid note takers call *The Collector's Fallacy*: hoarding loads of seemingly interesting pieces without ever looking at them again. Especially in our line of work as programmers, technical knowledge becomes obsolete pretty fast. Better do something useful with it, then!

Creative Programmers combine previous knowledge and experiences in new ways to solve the current problem they're facing. Therefore, they'll need a way to keep track of what worked and what didn't. Don't be fooled into thinking your memory will suffice, because it won't. Do you remember the contents of most of the books you've read in the past year? Do you remember why some sections appealed to you back then? That context is likely to be completely gone, unless you've taken notes, although even that won't suffice: I sometimes forget where I noted what. That's an indication that your system is not working properly! My solution was to make notes searchable by digitizing them.

Countless studies on knowledge retention all end on the same note (pun intended): if you don't want to forget, jot stuff down. Discovering links between supposedly unrelated bits and pieces is the real reason why the overhead of gathering and internalizing is worth it. Edward O. Wilson invented the concept of sociobiology. When he was interviewed about his creative process, his response was simple: his ideas come from synthesizing extensive notes from both social and biological sciences.

Niklas Luhmann attributed his productivity to conversations with his notes. Without extensive note-taking and acting on those notes, this book would have taken form as a vague—and, above all, fleeting—idea.

You may be wondering what this has to do with programming. Not everyone is looking to invent a new scientific field or publish hundreds of articles. Interviews with developers, and my own experience, indicate that there is little difference between publishing text and publishing code. Both require knowledge, fluency, and a good idea. Both dictate thinking, contemplation, and rumination. Both will be read by others.

2.4.1   *From notebook to memex to genex*

Preserving knowledge has been done since ancient times with the help of codexes, manuscripts, or commonplace books. Vannevar Bush's thought experiment of a "memory expander" took the concept of a codex one step further. In 1945, he explained in his article "As We May Think" how he sees the future:[12]

> *A memex is a device in which an individual stores all his books, records, and communications, and which is mechanized so that it may be consulted with exceeding speed and flexibility. It is an enlarged intimate supplement to his memory.*

This memory expansion pack—I wonder whether it's DDR (otherwise, I'll need to upgrade my now-old motherboard)—would be used not only to store knowledge but also to facilitate idea generation, by semiautomatically bringing related ideas together to promote insights and, thus, creativity. Data could be stored in the form of associative links, not unlike hyperlinks on the web, which was heavily inspired by Bush's experiment.

"As We May Think" might not have turned into reality just yet, but we're getting quite close. Personal interconnected thought databases took on the form of blogging in the early 2000s, perfectly mimicking what the memex machine was supposed to do. Self-improver John Naughton even called his blog *Memex 1.1*,[13] and blogger and author Cory Doctorow named his *Outboard Brain*.[14] Articles published on these weblogs are all littered with links to related internal and external blog posts.

Hyperlinking in blogging is still a task reserved for the writer. Technology can help us in discovering these links. Digital tools such as Obsidian and Zettlr make it easy to create a personal memex. A repository of notes, called a *vault*, contains Markdown files that can link to other files using the special `[[link]]` syntax. Obsidian also detects unlinked but related notes by scanning the content for words that might appear as an explicit link somewhere else. These are the most interesting links because they are probably the ones you didn't think of.

Another novel feature of Obsidian is its use of backlinks: instead of reading a note and seeing where it links to, Obsidian gathers links from other notes pointing to the current one. For instance, I might consult a note named "creativity," as shown in figure 2.4. The "linked mentions" pane shows I've also written about creativity in notes "diffuse thinking" and "Big Five personalities." Exploring backlinks might lead me to new insights.

> **NOTE** In case you prefer wikis or blogs, countless plugins exist for displaying backlinks on your HTML-powered memex.

---

[12] Vannevar Bush et al. As we may think. The Atlantic Monthly, 1945.
[13] See https://memex.naughtons.org/.
[14] See https://pluralistic.net/.

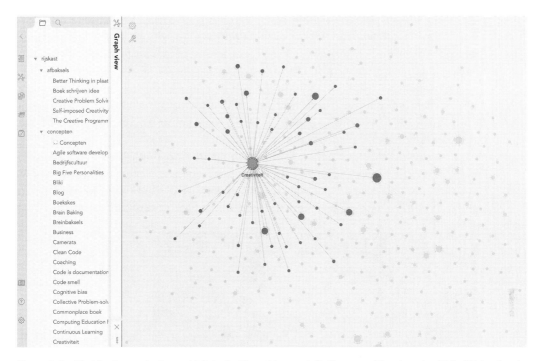

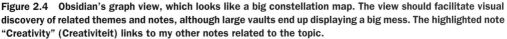

Figure 2.4 Obsidian's graph view, which looks like a big constellation map. The view should facilitate visual discovery of related themes and notes, although large vaults end up displaying a big mess. The highlighted note "Creativity" (Creativiteit) links to my other notes related to the topic.

Ben Shneiderman took the memex concept another step further by introducing the term *genex*, generators of excellence:[15]

> *A genex would be an integrated family of direct manipulation tools that supports users in creating innovations in art, science, engineering, etc. A genex would help users initiate hopes, fabricate plans, and implement dreams in a highly social framework. It would facilitate dialog with peers and mentors, and then dissemination to potential beneficiaries.*

Shneiderman envisioned memexes as going beyond a digital interconnected library: they should become tools to support creativity. Genex is memex 2.0.

2.4.2 From note to action

Note-taking is one thing; actually doing something with notes is another. Ideally, your workflow incorporates moments of reflection where you go through all the relevant notes again. Just stowing notes in a system is useless if you don't reread and rework them. Even if you merely use notes to manage `TODO` items, not a lot of boxes will get ticked without regularly going over them.

---

[15] Ben Shneiderman. Codex, memex, genex: The pursuit of transformational technologies. International Journal of Human-Computer Interaction, 1998. Published online 2010: https://www.tandfonline.com/doi/abs/10.1207/s15327590ijhc1002_1.

David Allen's popular *Getting Things Done* system works like that. He wrote about wearing two hats: *thinking* (taking notes) and *doing* (box-ticking).[16] Programmers will feel right at home because we're used to switching back and forth from *refactoring* to *writing* hats.

I particularly like Allen's "Mind Like Water" attitude, inspired by Buddhist sayings. While *doing*, your mind should not be troubled with other chores that need to be done. Instead, take note and forget. Of course, failing to revisit notes still causes chores to pile up.

Let's investigate how Niklas Luhmann managed to publish so many books on a wide variety of topics. According to him, the biggest indicator of his success was a peculiar note-taking system he called a *Zettelkasten*, or a "slip box" in English. A *Zettel* is an index card or a note that Luhmann stored in a big drawer—the *Kasten* (figure 2.5).

Figure 2.5   A portion of Niklas Luhmann's note-taking system: a big filing cabinet filled to the brim with handwritten index cards. Photo courtesy of Bielefeld University.

To quickly find related notes, Luhmann came up with a simple but effective method to connect them. By adding a number, optionally followed by a letter on the top left, the cards supported both a linear continuation of previous notes and the possibility of branching out (figure 2.6). For example, a note with number 32 could be continued with 33, even if its contents weren't related. At the same time, additional information could be added to Note 32 by creating Note 32a. Weird IDs such as 45/7a/21b were not uncommon.

A set of keyword index cards that point to bigger themes further optimized the navigation of Luhmann's cabinets. After a certain note was pulled out, re-creating a certain idea was only a matter of following the trail to related notes.

Digital note-taking systems such as Obsidian and Zettlr are heavily inspired by Luhmann's *Zettelkasten* method. We no longer need a big office space to accommodate clunky filing cabinets. Notes no longer need to carry a numbered ID: a unique file name to reference suffices. The powerful fuzzy search engine that autocompletes your half-baked attempt to retrieve an existing note does the rest.

---

[16] David Allen. Getting things done: The art of stress-free productivity. Penguin, 2015.

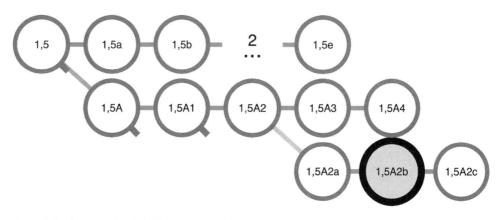

Figure 2.6 An example of the linking capabilities of Luhmann's method. Zettel 1,5A2b, as seen in https://niklas-luhmann-archiv.de/bestand/zettelkasten/zettel/ZK_1_NB_1-5A2b_V.

Luhmann's *Zettels* were groundbreaking in many ways. Each card only contained one idea or thought. Think of it as the software design principle separation of concerns applied to note-taking. While consuming new information, you might be tempted to create a note called *The Creative Programmer* and jam everything that sparks your attention in there. These notes might be related, but to get the most out of your system, they should be treated as separate entities.

Another interesting fact is the style of the notes, as visible in figure 2.7: they're scribbled in full sentences. Luhmann wrote *Zettels* in his own words—thereby translating them into his personal context. He never copied passages, as commonplace writers used to do. Even the backs of the notes were sometimes decorated. Because he

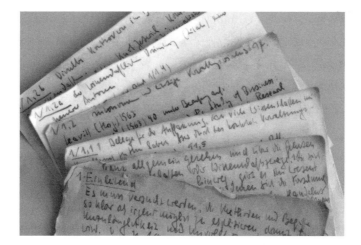

Figure 2.7 A few numbered *Zettels* from Niklas Luhmann's note-taking system. In case you'd like to test your German, all notes have been digitized as part of the Niklas Luhmann Archive project and are available at https://niklas-luhmann-archiv.de/ bestand/zettelkasten/suche/. Photo courtesy of Bielefeld University.

went through a lot of paper, he was always reaching for something to write on; some notes were written on the back of his children's drawings.

Obviously, setting up a *Zettelkasten* system and injecting daily notes requires a hefty time investment. Luhmann famously said that the *Zettelkasten* method costs more time than actually writing a book. As the notes grow in size and more links are made, it becomes easier to extract and publish something worthwhile. *Zettelkasten* was Luhmann's *genex*—his personal generator of excellence.

Writer and educational researcher Sönke Ahrens[17] described in great detail how Luhmann's system works and why it can be a powerful tool, rightfully calling it "smart note-taking." In his book *How to Take Smart Notes*, Ahrens elaborated on how learning by writing works:

> *We learn something not only when we connect it to prior knowledge and try to understand its broader implications (elaboration), but also when we try to retrieve it at different times (spacing) in different contexts (variation), ideally with the help of chance (contextual interference) and with a deliberate effort (retrieval) . . . . Manipulations such as variation, spacing, introducing contextual interference, and using tests, rather than presentations, as learning events, all share the property that they appear during the learning process to impede learning, but they then often enhance learning as measured by post-training tests of retention and transfer.*

During the course of the coming chapters, we will revisit and expand on these learning themes (*elaboration, spacing, variation,* etc.). If you are interested in setting up a similar system, I recommend you check out Ahrens' book or visit https://zettelkasten.de/ to get a sense of how to get started.

2.4.3   *A note on note maintenance*

Some note takers lovingly call their system a *digital garden*. Just like Steve Freeman and Nat Pryce—early adopters of eXtreme Programming, and Test Driven Development advocates—called programming *growing* software, note-taking can be called *growing ideas.*[18]

The analogy doesn't stop there. When growing software, one needs to tend to the garden now and then. Instead of reaching for the garden shears, we'll start restructuring code without modifying its functionality: refactoring. When note-taking, the same rules apply: some notes can be rehashed by appending and linking new notes to them, and others might have withered and can be safely pruned.

Don't be afraid to throw away or completely rework notes. Remember to place everything in its context—context that is bound to change depending on your technical knowledge and the environment you're in, two factors that will likely change over time. Although he was not the first to say it, novelist William Faulkner put it more bluntly: "Kill your darlings." To write is to delete, both in code and in notes.

Pruning dead branches is one thing; completely eradicating all notes is another. I know of analog note takers who love to tear up paper as soon as either the task is done

---

[17] Sönke Ahrens. How to take smart notes: One simple technique to boost writing, learning and thinking–for students, academics and nonfiction book writers. Sönke Ahrens, 2017.

[18] Steve Freeman and Nat Pryce. Growing object-oriented software, guided by tests. Pearson Education, 2009.

or everything is digitized. As much as I recognize that destroying analog notes as soon as they are processed can be a real space saver, I just can't bring myself to do it. My notebooks are more than just notes: they are embedded within a certain stage of life and period. Physically flipping through them not only reminds me of past ideas: it also brings me joy. I'll admit, I'm a sucker for nostalgia.

Digital gardening—or note-taking, for that matter—is a skill and therefore subject to the Dreyfus model, as shown in figure 2.8. At first, you'll need clear rules on how to structure and refactor your notes. As your skill level increases from novice all the way to expert, you'll rely less on rules and more on context and that important gut feeling.

Think of it this way. My wife hates cooking and doesn't bother learning it because I'm the chef at home. When she makes spaghetti, she strictly follows the guidelines as printed on the packaging: cooking for 12 minutes means setting a timer and cooking exactly 12 minutes. The problem is, most of the guidelines are wrong. Sometimes the spaghetti is overcooked. Sometimes it's undercooked. As you cook more and more, you'll develop a knack for getting the spaghetti out of the boiling water at the right time—without having to set a timer.

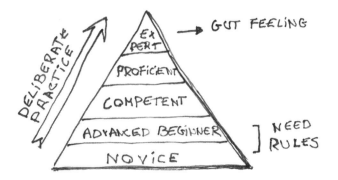

Figure 2.8   The Dreyfus model of skill acquisition—from complete novice in dire need of strict rules as guidance to experts who transcend reliance on those rules

Public vs. private gardens

Public gardens are meticulously maintained. People generally don't like nettles blocking pathways; they like neatly trimmed hedges perfectly shielding a bed of luscious roses. Private gardens are more likely to be an ever-evolving work in progress, for your eyes only. The same is true for digital gardens. Your thoughts are exactly that: your thoughts.

Yet, some note takers prefer to keep their notebook open to the public. It forces them to write their notes in a particular way, providing more context for visitors to understand their premises. Writing for an audience can help convert incoherent thoughts into a chain of concrete ideas. If your team maintains a wiki to store development information on, you'll have to make sure your teammates easily understand information posted on the site. Misunderstanding can easily lead to yet another software bug.

2.4.4   *From interruption to action*

Sometimes, a note can serve as a simple but powerful cue to jump-start action. In that case, it doesn't necessarily need to be interconnected and contextualized: it functions only to get you back on track after a brief period of interruption. In 2010, behavioral computing scientists Chris Parnin and Robert DeLine inquired into developers' strategies for resuming interrupted tasks. They discovered that the vast majority of the interviewees heavily relied on note-taking across several types of media.[19]

These kinds of notes are not *permanent* notes: they are disposable, one-shot scribbles that serve no function after the work has been picked up. Most programmers reading this—or, more generally, most knowledge workers who are frequently interrupted and blocked in their tasks—will probably be familiar with these kinds of TODO notes. We will cover interruptions and recovering from them in chapter 7. The scribbling works only in the short run, as a participant from the above study observed:

> *I take notes on random scraps of paper. Sometimes I refer to them again, but often they migrate to odd corners of my office where they are never looked at again, except right before I throw them away the next time we change offices . . . . When I don't throw the notes away I invariably leave them at home and then I don't have them at the office the next day.*

Luhmann's *Zettelkasten* is overflowing with notes that helped him learn—not that helped him get back or stay on track. To get something out of note-taking, your note skills should evolve from *temporary* notes on random scraps of paper, like the participant quoted here, to *permanent* notes that help you learn, like Luhmann.

Both note types have their merits, and both note types ultimately lead to action. Just be sure not to underestimate the differences.

EXERCISE   What do you do with your notes once they're jotted down? Are all TODO items consistently revisited and checked off? What about more permanent notes—can you find a way to link these to previously made notes to generate original insights?

2.5   *A workflow example*

Personal knowledge-management guru Harold Jarche summarized his workflow as *Seek > Sense > Share*,[20] three essential ingredients of a personal knowledge-management framework with an emphasis on knowledge representation by continuously sharing knowledge. This is the framework, in a nutshell:

---

[19] Chris Parnin and Robert DeLine. Evaluating cues for resuming interrupted programming tasks. In Proceedings of the SIGCHI conference on human factors in computing systems, 2010.

[20] Harold Jarche. The seek-sense-share framework, 2014. http://jarche.com/pkm/.

- *Seeking*—Finding things and keeping ourselves up to date by building a network of colleagues, allowing us not only to pull information from classical sources but also to have it pushed to us by trusted sources (e.g., through RSS). Jarche called good curators, who filter data for you, valued members of knowledge networks.
- *Sensing*—How we personalize and internalize information. This includes reflection and putting things in perspective, next to previously gained knowledge, and can involve experimentation.
- *Sharing*—Exchanging resources, ideas, and experiences with others. Suddenly, you've become the curator for someone else's *sensing* input!

Jarche's emphasis on knowledge sharing does not only benefit others: it forces us to rethink how we understood something, just like Luhmann's notes written in his own words. As physicist Richard Feynman said, the best way to learn is to teach (and thus share).

Something that really surprised me while rummaging through Jarche's extensive notes was the following excerpt:

> Today, content capture and creation tools let people tell their own stories and weave these together to share in their networks. It's called narrating your work and has been done by coders and programmers for decades as they learn out loud. What started as forums and wikis quickly evolved into more robust networks and communities. Programmers who share their work process and solutions in public are building a resource for other programmers looking to do the same type of work. This makes the whole programming environment smarter. Organizations can do the same.

Let's contemplate that for a moment. When it comes to knowledge sharing, we tech nerds are recognized as pioneers! Don't sit on your laurels for too long, though. Pretty much every coder I know consumes public knowledge, but only a small percentage actively contribute to it. We're all *lurkers*. It's time to level up and become a contributor— as long as you remember not to feed the trolls.

A simplified version of my own workflow is outlined in figure 2.9, which might or might not work for you. It is just one of the hundreds of possibilities to implement a system to gather, internalize, and act on knowledge. Feel free to swap out parts or build your own from scratch.

As your programming brain might have already told you: yes, this is an incremental process! I regularly threw out things that didn't work until I had a stable workflow that was right for me.

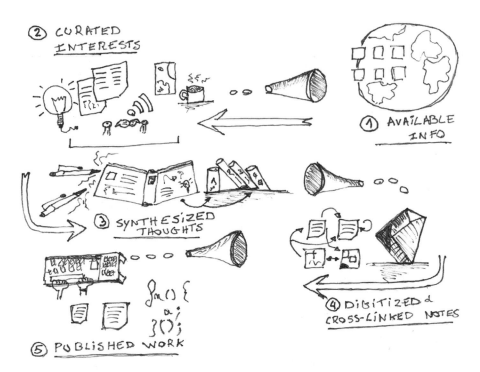

Figure 2.9   A simplified version of my information-processing workflow with filters in between each step, from available info to published work.

2.5.1   *A five-step workflow*

1. AVAILABLE INFORMATION

Available information comprises the collective works of everything and everyone: a big pile of knowledge, impossible to tame without the use of a system.

2. CURATED INTERESTS

Curated interests are a selection of things that spark my interest, served via RSS, email, browsing Wikipedia, conversations, museum or library visits, magazines, and so forth. Some things are pulled as I reach out for specific information for my research, and others are pushed by peers I trust and subscribe to, like Jarche's *seeking* element.

3. SYNTHESIZED THOUGHTS

Synthesized thoughts are the curated interests, contextualized and solidified in note-books with pen and ink: *sensing*. In practice, this step also acts as a filter: not every bit of knowledge and information consumed turns out to be valuable for the things I'm working on.

Remember to use a loose hand here. Make a mess. Draw diagrams, symbols, arrows. Cross out parts. Spatial cueing and emphasis on relationships strengthen insights. Mind map or note-taking software might be clean and hyperlinked, but at this stage they are rarely useful in facilitating learning. Andy Hunt explained the details of how this works in his book *Pragmatic Thinking and Learning.*

4. Digitized and cross-linked notes

Once a month or so, I digitize my notes by scanning and tagging them. Then they end up as linked notes in Obsidian. This sounds tedious (and it is), but I've found it to be a necessary evil to comfortably cross-reference notebooks of previous years. This also makes it much easier to quickly locate anything I've ever written down—unless I make a mistake with tagging, of course. Unfortunately, OCR technology is still very unreliable.

I do scan everything since it's easy to do with mobile apps like Genius Scan, but I do not tag every single page. Diary-like stories do not need to be cross-linked. Some digital-only systems combine steps 3 and 4 into a single step. I urge you not to do this, as you'll lose the learning benefits gained by capturing thoughts with a pen; it will also blur the lines between different filters and complicate your decisions about what to keep and what to throw out. In short, you're violating separations of concerns.

5. Published work

Finally, by pulling up all linked notes in a digital repository, all I have to do is arrange them in a certain order and start summarizing. At step 5, most of the writing and thinking work should have been done. Like Luhmann said, this makes publishing trivial. Watch out with that false sense of productivity, though: most of the work is off-loaded in previous steps. The work still needs to be done. Most of the notes never make it into publication, and that's okay. Some notes take multiple years to bubble up, and that's okay, too. Creative writer, photographer, and avid journaler Susannah Conway calls this *composting*.[21] I've heard software development managers calling it *Nemawashi*, referring to the lean Toyota production system whereby the groundwork is laid to build the foundations for major future changes by gathering and sharing information. Like aged wine or cheese, good ideas need to ripen.

As a professional baker myself, I like to resort to the process of *fermentation* when explaining how ideas make it into production. Decent bread can be pulled out of the oven after 4 hours of starting from scratch. Excellent bread takes 36 hours and requires planning ahead—although most of the time, you just let the dough do its thing: develop flavor.

Sometimes, the sourdough starter overreacts and ferments too quickly, taking the baker by surprise, like the jar depicted in figure 2.10. Working out ideas too soon without taking the time to mull them over achieves the same result: blandness.

Sometimes, the acidity from a (too) long fermentation ruins the bread. Stale ideas usually do not make it to step 5.

Of course, to let an idea ferment, you first have to "catch" it, which is, in essence, what step 3 does. American journalist and author Elizabeth Gilbert lamented the possibility of losing an idea to someone else in her creative self-help book *Big Magic*.[22] According to her, if you fail to capture a thought in time, it will fly away to another open mind better capable of catching it. Big ideas "bounce" from entrepreneur to

---

[21] See https://www.susannahconway.com/.
[22] Elizabeth Gilbert. Big Magic: Creative Living Beyond Fear. Penguin Publishing Group, reprint edition, 2016.

Figure 2.10 A sourdough starter, perhaps too happily fermenting away. Next to flour, water, and salt, time is the most important ingredient for a great loaf of bread.

entrepreneur until someone is willing to take big action. Although it is hard to digest that fairy tale, the message here is clear: get your net out and be ready to catch fleeting ideas.

2.5.2   *The workflow in practice: Coding*

A couple of years ago, through my filter of curated interests, I read about other programmers' experiences on writing end-to-end tests for their web applications and their struggles with it. At work, my colleagues and I were getting frustrated with our own approach, because these automated tests proved to be unstable at best and involved a lot of maintenance, to the point that we considered dropping them all together.

A blog post I read triggered a discussion of our current approach in which we laid out a first rough revision to better tackle the myriad asynchronous client-side requests. My personal knowledge-management system contained more cross-linked notes about end-to-end testing from previous projects that could also be factored in, including the reasoning behind the choices made.

Without (re)reading any prior stored (self-)knowledge on how to write end-to-end tests, our test strategy would have been altered for the worse. I can't count the number of times my system has saved me from reinventing the wheel or implementing the inferior solution. Other examples include reaching for that complex search routine you once put together, a drawing of sort algorithms to pick from, saved URLs of longer articles on the internals of the Linux kernel that might come in handy, rereading what went wrong last time you tried integrating OAuth in a legacy codebase, and so on.

This isn't limited to coding or software architecture: I also like "stealing" other's search bars; web accessibility style guides; various UI considerations, such as button and label placements; and so forth. I provide more information about stealing ideas from others in chapter 8.

2.5.3   *The workflow in practice: Learning new programming languages*

This year, I've learned to program in Go. I was keen to convert a Node-based project from JS to Go. Several little and big problems were successfully tackled along the way, thanks to my notes. Not sure how to structure REST requests without resorting to reflection or copying and pasting, I consulted my database. It told me I had watched a couple of GopherCon videos just over a month ago where best practices on Go web services were presented—videos I again completely forgot about.

If, instead, I had resorted to good ol' Google or Stack Overflow, I would have missed the context of my notes on these videos, which linked to related practices I've accumulated over the years. Sometimes, that's good enough. It makes no sense to cram an entire API documentation into your note system.

2.5.4   *The workflow in practice: Writing*

It goes without saying that the workflow is also perfectly applicable to writing—in fact, without it, this book wouldn't exist. But you're a programmer, not a writer, so why should you care? Because programmers have to communicate ideas, not only through clean code but also through requirement documents, project proposals, API documentation, performance reviews, remote chat messages, technical demonstrations, blog posts, and more.

Many software engineering leaders are also prolific technical writers. Writing is becoming so important that companies like Amazon start their engineering manager screening process with a writing exercise.[23] As Sönke Ahrens mentioned, learning is done through writing—even if it's just for yourself.

Writing is a whole lot easier if you have something to fall back on: your system, containing outlined notes and ideas. Then, you can start puzzling. Create a new note, give it an appropriate name, and start linking concepts from previously collected insights. These will turn out to be the building blocks for your text.

The system tells us we should reread notes we've written years ago and completely forgotten about. It suggests possible connections between refactoring, domain-driven design, and creative problem solving. In short, it helps us become a better coder *and* writer.

> **EXERCISE**   Note-taking can be daunting to newcomers. The best way to start is to just start. For the next two weeks, try to simply gather the things you've learned on (digital) paper on a daily basis. Be as quick or as thorough as you want—don't be encumbered by the process. Visual thinking expert and creative director Dan Roam illustrated that this can even be an ugly sketch on "The Back of the Napkin."[24]

After 14 days, reread your notes. Does anything stand out? Is there a connection between seemingly disparate records? Cross-link if you feel like it. Can you do something with that new knowledge in the near future?

If you did not enjoy the exercise, simply retry with a different approach. Eventually, you'll end up with your own version of figure 2.9—a workflow that filters available

---

[23] See https://blog.pragmaticengineer.com/becoming-a-better-writer-in-tech/.
[24] Dan Roam, The back of the napkin: Solving problems and selling ideas with pictures. Portfolio, 2008.

info, curated interests, synthesized and digitized thoughts, into something that is worth publishing.

Summary

- No Python knowledge equals no Python creativity. Without any input and a baseline of technical knowledge, creative problem solving will prove to be next to impossible.
- Creativity begets creativity. Every intention to create is based on a previous one. Thus, it's important to keep your knowledge base up to date.
- Gather new knowledge and refactor your existing knowledge. Think about your regular sources of information. Is it perhaps time to diversify or moderate your intake?
- Gathering knowledge is one thing; internalizing that knowledge is another. Do not just summarize what you've read: rewrite it in your own words to add your own context.
- What's the purpose of internalizing all that information if you never intend to do anything with it? Remember that the point is to produce both novel and actionable insights.
- A well-oiled personal knowledge management system greatly simplifies the gather-internalize-act loop. Try to develop a system that works for you based on the examples that are provided in this chapter. This system, if used correctly, can act as your "external memory."
- The most interesting novel insights arise from the connection or combination of information that at first sight seems unrelated. This is yet another reason why the personal knowledge management system—where everything is centralized—is important.
- Notes do not have to be static; they can be revisited, reworked, scrapped, and more. Note maintenance is just as important as note creation. New ideas will certainly arise from regularly rereading previous notes.

Communication 3

Mysterious voices echo from a colonnade just outside of Athen's city wall. The Peripatetics—scholars and disciples interested in Aristotle's teachings—are gathered in a series of open buildings called the *Lyceum*. The predominant voice that bounces off the *peripatoi,* or walkways, belongs to Aristotle himself, who is giving a lecture on how the squid reproduces. Among the regular listeners are Demetrius of Phalerum, one of the first Peripatetics; Alexander the Great, who would later build one of the largest empires in history; and Theophrastus, who initially studied in Plato's Academy but would later succeed Aristotle as the head of the Lyceum.

Aristotle was first and foremost interested in the *why*. Starting from facts, his scientific approach to philosophy ultimately formed the baseline of inductive and deductive reasoning. Reasoning wasn't a one-way street: ample discussions between fellow Peripatetics were held on matters of politics, metaphysics, ethics, and logic—

preferably while walking around. The Lyceum wasn't a private affair like Plato's Academy: many lectures and discussions were held free of charge. Its open approach would ultimately improve Aristotle's works, which are nowadays seen as the foundation of modern science.

Centuries later, at the end of the 16th century, similar patterns emerged in Florence. A group of humanists, musicians, poets, politicians, and philosophers gathered under the roof of Count Giovanni de' Bardi—yet another wealthy Italian with perhaps too much time on his hands—to discuss, and successfully change, the trends in arts, music, and drama (figure 3.1). The gathering was known for its famous Florentine guests and would later be known as *The Florentine Camerata*.[1]

The premise of The Camerata was simple. Music had become boring and corrupt, according to the members. They intended the art form to be restored to the way the ancient Greeks had styled it. An open view of the composition and the flow of music was the greatest legacy of The Camerata. Although only indirect influence was attributed to them, without the Florentine Camerata, Bach and Mozart would probably never have composed world-class musical pieces that tell a story.

Figure 3.1 Anton Domenico Gabbiani's "The Musicians of Prince Ferdinando de' Medici." The painting was linked to de' Bardi's Camerata at work, although that has been disputed recently. The Camerata's efforts played a major role in the forming of later symphonies and operas, proving that collective creativity trumps individual ideas. Source: public domain.

---

[1] Ruth Katz. Collective problem-solving in the history of music: The case of the Camerata. Journal of the History of Ideas, 1984.

Again centuries later, we turn our attention to Paris and its bustling cafés, at the very end of the 19th century. Tired of the persistent clinging to classicism, a small group of sculptors, art dealers, and painters decided to challenge the Paris Salon art curators by giving birth to an endless slew of new art *-isms*: impressionism, pointillism, cubism, modernism, Dadaism. Lively discussions about art and its future were consistently held in cafés, dutifully accompanied by a selection of wine as well as cigar smoke.

The Parisian avant-garde art movement attracted young talent from within France (Paul Cézanne, Georges Braque, Claude Monet, Edgar Degas) and far beyond it (Pablo Picasso, Vincent van Gogh, Piet Mondrian, Wassily Kandinsky). Foreigners like the Dutchman Mondrian and the Russian Kandinsky would eventually bring back ideas to their homeland to unleash artistic revolutions there, establishing *De Stijl* and *Bauhaus*.

Fast forward another century, to the early to mid-2000s. This time, we are in London, specifically, inside its plethora of business hubs. These centers took turns hosting The Extreme Tuesday Club.[2] The Club acted as a platform for software developers at the early beginnings of the agile and extreme programming movements, where ideas were proposed and critically evaluated on a weekly basis. Several well-respected software developers would make a guest entry in The Club: Jez Humble, Dan North, Chris Read, and Chris Matts. It even proved to be an effective way to recruit competent programmers into ThoughtWorks—another well-known consulting firm.

The Extreme Tuesday Club was a unique and fertile test bed that managed to successfully breed Continuous Integration, Continuous Delivery, DevOps, Kanban, and Technical Debt concepts, microservices, mocking techniques—the list is, again, endless. Other like-minded people mirrored The Club elsewhere, resulting in The Silicon Valley Patterns Group, The Portland Patterns Group, The Salt Lake City Round Table, and so forth. The spirit of The Club lives on in innumerable software craftsmanship and testing meetups around the globe.

3.1 Collaborative teamwork

What is the greatest common divisor between The Peripatetics, The Camerata, The Extreme Tuesday Club, and countless other examples the history books can show us? These gatherings somehow managed to completely change the field they worked in, which, according to Csikszentmihalyi, qualifies as genuine creativity. I'd like to take this a step further and call it *collective creativity*: without a collective, the creativity of each genius partaking in these meetings would never have reached that far.

Teamwork is a word that, in our 21st century, is all too eagerly used. Teamwork is required to bring big and dangerous software projects to a happy end. Teamwork is required to motivate each other to keep on trucking, day in, day out. Teamwork is required to learn as an individual, as a team, and across teams. Teamwork can be found in job ads, books on how to succeed, books on how not to succeed, in videotelephony

---

[2] See Chris Matts's report on his blog at https://theitriskmanager.com/2019/05/25/the-london-agile-software-camerata/.

software, in company announcements, in remote-work guidelines, in curriculum outcomes, in conference slides, on the back of a menu card in restaurants, in popular hashtags on social media, in TV ads, in every sport, during joyful team building days—teamwork, teamwork, teamwork!

Research indicates that teamwork is the most commonly taught nontechnical skill, appearing in the learning outcomes of 34% of European university computing courses. Written/oral communication and presentation skills are similar academic all-stars. The term *creativity*, on the other hand, is encountered in less than 5% of university course descriptions![3]

Was an ancient gathering in the Lyceum one of the very first team-based efforts to advance the field of philosophy? Is there any difference between de' Bardi's Camerata and our contemporary programming teams? Let's dig a little deeper to see what exactly caused those collectives to be successful—besides the obvious use of communicative skills.

3.1.1   *What makes a Camerata tick*

Thanks to Jessica Kerr's 2018 blog post, which manages to connect the Renaissance's music collective and Gregory Bateson's cybernetics ideas with programming,[4] the term *Camerata* has become quite popular among programmers. According to Kerr, we should learn from The Camerata's methods to successfully launch software engineering into the future.

First, what were the members of The Camerata trying to do? They were fed up with classic Renaissance music and partially wanted to return to the greatness of ancient Greece; that is, there was a problem to solve: a *shared* problem. Every member of The Camerata was equally invested in the problem at hand. Nobody was forced to join. In fact, you weren't particularly welcome if you weren't intrinsically motivated to join the common cause.

Second, not only the problem was shared, but also the knowledge of every single individual. They taught each other. The Camerata resembles a kind of invisible college, which is the key to creativity in science, according to Kerr: this "invisible college" is an association of people who share ideas, who build a new reality together, then spread it to advance the wider culture.

This sounds mundane but is key to the success of a group. A stream of knowledge acting as a one-way street will not get you far. Furthermore, The Camerata consisted of people with vastly different backgrounds, which facilitated the cross-pollination of ideas.

Third, The Camerata system was a *living system*. Remember our premise that creativity is systemic, as explained in the introduction? The same is true for a creative collective such as The Camerata: each part is interconnected, to both each other and the

---

[3] Wouter Groeneveld, Brett A Becker, and Joost Vennekens. Soft skills: what do computing program syllabi reveal about non-technical expectations of undergraduate students? Proceedings of the 2020 ACM Conference on Innovation and Technology in Computer Science Education.

[4] See https://jessitron.com/2018/04/15/the-origins-of-opera-and-the-future-of-programming/.

environment. Since a living system is a *learning system*, it constantly evolves. The environment changes, and so do we as we adapt to it. We learn from our comrades; they learn from us. The system gets shuffled around a bit; new links appear, and old ones disappear. Think of it as a never-ending feedback loop:

```
func changeSelf() {
 changeEnvironment()
}
func changeEnvironment() {
 changeSelf()
}
```

Cybernetics pioneer Gregory Bateson was a systems thinker. Instead of looking at the individual parts, or a few relationships in between those parts, he liked to think in terms of the *whole*. He once said that evolution is in the context—not in the subject, or, as our modern self loves to think, the individual. Nora Bateson, his daughter, further refined her father's ideas. She thought it was peculiar that we don't have a word for mutual learning in living contexts. Her introduction of the term *symmathesy* fixed this problem.[5] Nora combined the Greek prefix *sym* ("together") with *mathesi* ("to learn"). Her working definition of the concept is as follows:

> *Symmathesy (noun): an entity composed of contextual mutual learning through interaction. This process of interaction and mutual learning takes place in living entities at larger or smaller scales of symmathesy.*

> *Symmathesy (verb): to interact within multiple variables to produce a mutual learning context.*

The Camerata was a symmathesy: a living, learning system (figure 3.2).

Fourth, the collective not only provided feedback; they provided *critical* feedback. This prevented the gatherings from becoming an echo chamber where no idea truly managed to break free. I discuss critical thinking and its role in creative programming further in chapter 5.

Limiting the exposure to diverse perspectives and a formation of groups of like-minded people framing and enforcing a shared narrative is called *the echo chamber effect* in sociology.[6] Such a segregation is prevalent not only on social media platforms but also in a lot of discussion groups, where the living system is more or less on life support.

EXERCISE When was the last time you attended a coding-related meetup where ideas were openly discussed instead of simply presented and accepted? Can you remember how prevalent the echo chamber effect was? Perhaps next time it might be good to start the discussion with that.

---

[5] Nora Bateson. Small arcs of larger circle: Framing through other patterns. Triarchy Press, 2016.
[6] Matteo Cinelli, Gianmarco De Francisci Morales, Alessandro Galeazzi, Walter Quattrociocchi, and Michele Starnini. The echo chamber effect on social media. Proceedings of the National Academy of Sciences, 2021.

During the creativity research of my colleagues and I, the developers we interviewed also emphasized the importance of context, just like Bateson's focus on contextual learning:

> *We assumed a bit that, eventually, we work in teams, so if you put someone, perhaps less creative, in the right context and surround that person with the right people, you'll still arrive at a creative solution, within its limitations.*

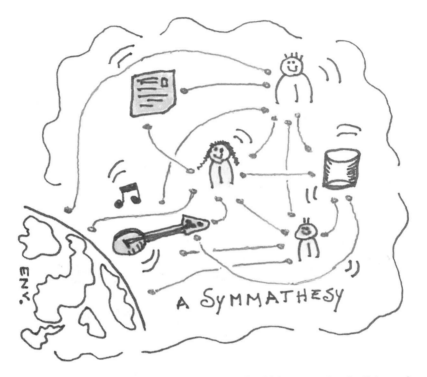

Figure 3.2   A symmathesy: a living, interconnected system in which every part mutually learns from each other, including the environment it's in. Actually drawing such a system betrays what it stands for, since it is now frozen in time. The environment pictured encompasses anything that interacts with the group: your clients, other teams, the company, and so on.

Great teams make great people

Serious software development is the practice of symmathesy. According to Jessica Kerr, great teams make great people, not the other way around. Sure, you can't simply hire a bunch of great developers, usher them into a room, and call it a day—don't forget to throw in a couple of bananas. But does this mean you can't engineer great teams?

My own view of this is more nuanced. I've had the privilege to be "dropped" into a great team (thank you, consultancy work), which undoubtedly made me a better programmer. For a couple of years, I, too, tugged the symmathesy ropes and was part of the system.

> But I've also cocreated teams with other competent developers where the team was yet to be formed: the symbiotic relationship was still very unstable. As we got to know the problem domain (and each other), some teams flourished. Other teams withered pretty quickly. The chicken or the egg? A little bit of both, thank you.

Cameratas, living or coevolving systems, symmathesies, systemic teams, symbioses—whatever the term, its methods always consist of four principles: having a shared problem, learning from each other, being interconnected, and providing critical feedback.

Ben Shneiderman's genex system, which we explored in chapter 2, can take you only so far. He concluded that refinement of the genex system is a social process. Only your peers' constructive feedback can take your creative work to the next level.

3.1.2   Dream teams

A heterogeneous group of well-communicating individuals has a better chance of solving problems creatively than fiddling on your own. I'm sure you've experienced this yourself at some point when working in well-oiled teams, compared to trying to crack a tough problem by yourself.

Collectives such as The Camerata not only identify and solve bigger problems faster, they also increase emotional engagement. This effect is clearly visible in interviews with creators who fondly reflect on their time "back in the day," often referring to their past collective as a "dream team." The team is a dream, not only when you get along well with your peers, but also when it consistently churns out highly creative products.

Take LucasArts, for example. During the early nineties, the Games Division of Lucasfilm was rebranded as LucasArts thanks to a few successes in the games industry, most notably *Maniac Mansion* and its SCUMM (Script Creation Utility for *Maniac Mansion*) engine, which came with it. Since then, LucasArts consistently released one hit after the another: *Monkey Island 1* and *2*, *Loom*, *Indiana Jones and the Fate of Atlantis*, *Day of the Tentacle*, *Sam & Max: Hit the Road*, *Full Throttle*, *The Dig*.

Some sources claim that after George Lucas lost interest in games; after the rebranding, the company gradually went downhill; although, judging from the results, the software development division was still successful for at least five consecutive years.

Retro Gamer interviewed a part of the original crew to rediscover the legacy Lucas-Arts left behind.[7] The former members mused about the "correct alignment of the stars" and admitted they never quite reached the same height ever again (figure 3.3). When asked why not, the interviewees provided two reasons: the perfect composition of the team, which sadly broke down and scattered after the release of *Monkey Island 2* for various reasons, and it wasn't the right time for that kind of adventure game.

The productive combination of different skill sets, where everyone influences each other, clearly surfaces when reading the interview. Dave Grossman, codesigner and

---

[7] The legacy of Monkey Island. Retro Gamer, no. 212, p. 18.

writer, relished the daily brainstorm meetings led by director Ron Gilbert, where artist Steve Purcell would often draw funny illustrations. Dave Grossman recalls:

> *I wrote a poem once about ideas being like lint and dust—they're just kind of floating around everywhere and the trick is to make something interesting out of them.*

Tim Schafer chimes in, commemorating Ron's effort to lead the team and fondly remembering his time at LucasArts:[8]

> *Those were really special times, especially working at the Lucas Ranch in this incredible environment that was set up just to make creative people relaxed and comfortable. It was a fun environment and all these people were so fun to work with. Getting that job right out of college was a lucky break for me, and I'm glad I was ready for exactly that job description.*

Ron Gilbert and his crew's latest point-and-click game, *Thimbleweed Park*, was highly inspired by Monkey Island's early success, not only because they wanted to recreate a pixelated 2D adventure but also because they tried to emulate what made those nineties adventure games so special. Ron replays *Monkey Island 1* and *2* every time he starts a new game, to recapture the atmosphere. He admitted he never really figured it out. The original crew has since set sail. *Retro Gamer* concludes that the secret of *The Secret of Monkey Island* might very well be group dynamism.

Figure 3.3   Members of the LucasArts crew pose for "Ron Gilbert Day," one of the many gags that kept them entertained. Everyone is wearing Ron's style of clothing (a striped top). Photo courtesy of The International House of Mojo.

An ample number of other veterans within the software development industry provide more evidence for the significance of group dynamism. Adam Barr (Microsoft), David Heinemeier Hansson (Ruby on Rails, Basecamp), Gergely Orosz (Uber, Skype): in any success story interview, former core members implicitly or explicitly call their team a dream team.

Nostalgia goggles aside, I think it is safe to assume there is some truth behind this— backed up by yet another pile of academic publications on team jelling, methods,

---

[8] The Retro Gamer guide to Tim Schafer & Double Fine. Retro Gamer, no. 216, p. 46.

composition, affects, and so forth. *Dream work makes the team work.* Or is it the other way around?

> **EXERCISE** Does your current development team resemble a symmathesy? If not, what do you think needs to be changed to become one? For example, how is critical feedback handled between team members, what is the atmosphere like, is everyone open to mutual learning, is there a constant flow of shared ideas that moves the team forward, are the actions by the team supported by the company? What could be the first small and achievable step toward such a dream team?

3.2 Collective geography

In his book on the psychology of flow and creativity, Mihaly Csikszentmihalyi takes off with a rather sobering message: the creative power of the individual is negligible. And yet, our ideal image of the lone creative genius who single-handedly manages to change an entire domain of expertise somehow stubbornly persists.

Einstein might have submitted a paper on the theory of relativity that indeed completely altered how we think about physics, but even Einstein had his group of friends, called the *Akademie Olympia*, who discussed philosophy and physics. The first few but important seeds of his theory were likely planted during those discussions. As Csikszentmihalyi said: creativity is systemic.

What, then, can we as individuals do to increase our chances of creative success? The previous discussion on dream teams reveals that being part of or creating a great team might be the answer. Surround ourselves with high achievers who can improve our own performance. Seek out experts. But where to look for like-minded people? Indeed, *where*—the physical location of Cameratas has proven to be significant in history.

3.2.1 Liquid networks

Has your attempt to sell an idea to your family or friends only managed to evoke a lukewarm reception? Perhaps you're approaching the wrong target audience. Did your presentation of the idea get lost in the enormous sea of ever-evolving—and possibly better—ideas from others? Perhaps that environment was literally too volatile.

Innovation expert and science communicator Steven Johnson managed to capture this phenomenon in a neat symbolic representation in his story "Where Good Ideas Come From."[9] He explains that the birth, success, and death of ideas can be summarized in a *liquid network*.

In chemistry, matter is in a state of either solid, liquid, or gas, as shown in figure 3.4. Molecules are less mobile in blocks of ice than in their liquid form: water. Heating water results in another state change during evaporation, in which molecules are extremely mobile. For brevity, we omit plasma, which is even more unstable than gas.

Johnson compares early hunters and gatherers to gas matter: highly mobile, nomads traveled from place to place, never really exchanging ideas with other small

---

[9] Steven Johnson. Where good ideas come from: The natural history of innovation. Penguin Publishing Group, 2011.

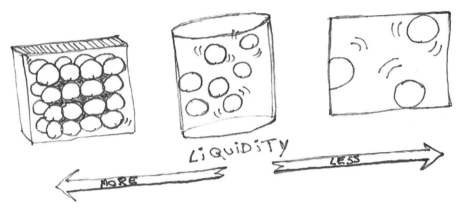

Figure 3.4 **Left: solid matter, ideas set in stone due to the definite shape and volume. Middle: liquid matter, allowing the creation of new connections. Right: gas matter, too volatile to make ideas really stick.**

groups of humans until they started settling and forming cities. Condensation forms, and more liquid-like networks of people emerge. It was then that many inventions were conceived that boosted early civilizations. Settling down made it possible for ideas to "spill over" from human to human, as Johnson likes to call it.

However, for ideas to spread, the network has to stay liquid and not solidify, as otherwise, innovation stagnates and, in the worst case, evolution becomes devolution. Johnson also argues that this is the reason why innovation is sometimes geographically clustered in big and boisterous cities.

Embracing foreign ideas—but not too much—increases the likelihood of creative achievements. Psychology and history researcher Dean Simonton concluded the same[10] when studying the effects of cultural influx on one of the world's most closed societies: medieval Japan. For many fields, such as medicine, philosophy, writing, poetry, and especially the arts, achievement was positively associated with national openness to alien influences.

We can use the concept of liquid networks to describe how, both within the mind of a single human and within clusters of humans, the process of making novel connections is amplified. Business venture specialist Seth Godin chimes in by emphasizing happy accidents of ideas: "Ideas occur when dissimilar worlds collide."[11]

Think back to your personal knowledge system from chapter 2. If most notes just rehash the same ideas again and again, your knowledge stream might have solidified. On the other hand, if only a few but highly original ideas are noted, they do not get the chance to bounce into others to evolve into a vastly superior idea. Your knowledge system ideally floats in between those two extremes: it's a liquid network.

---

[10] Dean Keith Simonton. Foreign influence and national achievement: the impact of open milieus on Japanese civilization. *Journal of* Personality and Social Psychology, 1997.

[11] Seth Godin. Linchpin: are you indispensable? How to drive your career and create a remarkable future. Piatkus Books, Hachette UK, 2010.

The same is true for group dynamics. Too many wild ideas blurted out with nobody taking the time to sit down and summarize or combine them will likely end in diffusion. On the other hand, not enough ideas, or too many of the same ones, won't exactly end in creativity either. The group composition of collective creators floats in between those two extremes: they're a liquid network.

According to Steven Johnson, the places people visit, work, and live in are also solid or liquid networks; that is, geography becomes a determinant of creative success. If you grew up in a rural area, your chances of creative success were slim unless you moved to one of these places where "it is happening."

Of course, in our age of globalism, a fiber network and Zoom radically altered that, although not entirely. Eminent companies and research universities still attract many young and promising people across the globe, convincing them to move thousands of miles, lured by the promise of working with the best of the best, hoping it will spark that much-needed creativity. And it probably will.

EXERCISE Initiatives such as Meetup, Skillshare, Eventbrite, and Airbnb Experiences are a great way to get a taste of other cultures' ideas. For this exercise, take part in one of the many unique virtual communities. Try to push your boundaries beyond all things coding. For instance, engage in a philosophical discussion, draw together with hundreds of other like-minded people, or learn the basics of bookbinding. Have a look at the various possibilities; then pick one and click Register. Numerous experts across the globe are willing to share their knowledge. They are waiting for you to join them!

3.2.2 *Creativity is contagious*

Johnson's clever analogy borrowed from the chemistry world also teaches us that, as chemical components bump into each other, they influence each other's state. In other words, as Albert Einstein said, creativity is contagious. Studies confirm that we are more creative when surrounded by creative coworkers.[12] Just by having them in the vicinity, our own urge to be creative rises. We've seen the same effect when organizing interdisciplinary hackathons across universities. Student pairs operating in the same large room reported that their inspiration rose precisely because they were surrounded by other groups—even if they interpreted the assignment completely differently. By walking around and engaging with other groups, students gathered others' ideas to bend and apply to their own solution.

This may not be so surprising. We are social animals, and our brains are prewired to copy behavior—any behavior. If we surround ourselves with creative programmers, our chances of becoming "one of them" increase. This sounds a lot like the *broken window* theory, brought into the world of programming by the pragmatic programmers Andy Hunt and Dave Thomas.[13] Leave a lot of junk behind, and people will throw

---

[12] Randall G Holcombe. Cultivating creativity: market creation of agglomeration economies. Handbook of creative cities. Edward Elgar Publishing, 2011.

[13] Andy Hunt and Dave Thomas. The Pragmatic Programmer: from journeyman to master. Addison-Wesley Professional, 1999.

more onto the pile. Be consistent in tidying up the code, and coworkers will automatically behave a bit more like responsible coding citizens.

3.2.3   *Moving to stimulating environments*

In 1952, when he was 27, Swiss sculptor Jean Tinguely moved to France with his wife to pursue a career in art. He grew up in Basel, which, with its almost 180,000 inhabitants, is far from a small city. Basel has been a commercially and culturally important hub since the Renaissance. And yet Tinguely hated it there, feeling asphyxiated, almost creatively burned out. The moment he arrived in Paris, he felt rejuvenated: "Switzerland is not a stimulating environment. Paris is. I felt like a fish in water."

In Paris, as part of the New Realist avant-garde, he found his liquid network, which in Basel was too solid for his taste. The fruits of his move are showcased in museums all over the world—at least, a part of it. Tinguely's most famous works are self-destructing machines he liked to let detonate in front of a gasping audience. No worries, the Las Vegas desert didn't feel anything.

During my own training as a professional baker, I was on the lookout for a bakery with internship possibilities. Since I was mainly interested in sourdough bread and wanted to learn from the very best, I ended up at De Superette in Ghent. Why? Because the then-head baker was Sarah Lemke, an American expert who had learned the craft together with Chad Robertson from Richard Bourdon.

For the uninitiated in all things sourdough, Chad's Tartine Bakery in San Francisco is one of the most well-respected and famous bakeries in the world. Chad is one of my many bread-related idols. Of course, as a famous baker, Chad also published a slew of bread-baking books, one of which, *Tartine Bread* (Chronicle Books, 2010), has become a timeless classic. Feel free to switch books if baking bread gets you more excited than typing a bunch of brackets and semicolons.

Since I live in Belgium, working at De Superette proved to be the next best thing—wild ideas like this require a stamp of approval by my significant other. In hindsight, dropping everything to head to San Francisco and face the heat of an oven at 5:30 a.m. might have pushed things a bit too far.

If you're from Belgium and are genuinely committed to baking great bread, sooner or later you'll end up at De Superette. During my internship, I've encountered several like-minded people, visiting the bakery to chat with Sarah to share ideas and be inspired by her methodology and usage of very wet dough. De Superette is also a restaurant, where distinguished chefs from all over Europe work together to produce original and tasty dishes.

Of course, there are ample bakeries closer to home, and I'm sure I would have scored an internship in my own neighborhood. But I wanted to work in the midst of the baking idea highway interchange. I was looking for a liquid network. I can't say it ever became a Camerata, because my time there was very short, and as an intern, my responsibilities were limited to shutting up and doing as I'm told—which worked out quite well, to be honest.

The appeal of a stimulating environment is what makes developers flock to high-tech campuses such as Google's and Yahoo's, where they "push the boundaries of the workplace," according to a Google spokesman in an interview with the *New York Times*.[14] Carefully engineered casual collisions between employees drive both creativity and production.

3.2.4 *Genius clusters*

Why did Western philosophy originate in and around Greece, where so many other culturally important concepts come from? Why was Florence the center of innovation during the Renaissance, influencing the future not only of music but also that of art, architecture, economy, and politics? Why did so many artistic talents gather in Paris in the 19th century? A century later, the epicenter of art was somehow moved from Europe to New York. Why is working in Silicon Valley a dream for so many technologists nowadays?

Foreign correspondent and reporter Eric Weiner traveled around the world to explore these questions in his work, *The Geography of Genius*.[15] Weiner is fascinated by creativity and wanted to find some answers that might help him better raise his daughter. "It's already too late for me, so I'll content myself with writing about creativity instead," he concludes.

This might disappoint, but most of the time there is no single answer to the big geographical creativity question. These clusters of inventiveness, which Weiner calls *genius clusters*, appear and dissolve as power is concentrated and lost in certain geographic areas.

For example, Alexander the Great's unquenchable thirst for conquest eventually helped distribute Greek literature well into ancient Persia. Alexandria was founded during his brief stay in Egypt, which would evolve into one of the most influential cities of the world with the help of Ptolemy and his successors.

Alexander, who always carried a copy of Homer's *Iliad*, was fascinated by Greek literature. Ptolemy, a then-faithful companion of Alexander, recognized this and started seizing and copying every single piece of written papyrus paper that arrived in Alexandria. It wouldn't take long before the Great Library of Alexandria was bursting with books—of which a great deal sadly got lost in flames thanks to Roman carelessness and the later Muslim invasion.

The Great Library attracted a lot of intellectuals. In a way, Alexandria became one of the first international academic research centers. It is said that Archimedes invented his Archimedes' Screw while studying at the Library. Irene Vallejo, an academic history researcher fascinated by all things classical antiquity, shares her excitement for the ancient library in her exposition on the history of books:[16]

The electrifying atmosphere around those fully written rolls and their accumulation had to be something like the current eruption of creativity brought about by [the] internet and Silicon Valley.

---

[14] James B. Stewart. Looking for a lesson in Google's perks. New York Times, March 15, 2013. https://www.nytimes.com/2013/03/16/business/at-google-a-place-to-work-and-play.html.

[15] Eric Weiner. The geography of genius: a search for the world's most creative places from ancient Athens to Silicon Valley. Simon & Schuster, 2016.

[16] Irene Vallejo. *Papyrus: een geschiedenis van de wereld in boeken*. Meulenhoff, 2021.

Knowledge wasn't the only reason to fear or respect Alexandria. The papyrus plant thrived across the Nile Delta, making it an ideal export product, next to grain. Ancient Egypt acted as the granary of the Mediterranean world: when the grain flow stopped, famine and war erupted across the region. Grain was then what oil is now: an ideal way to apply pressure.

Other genius clusters also originated organically—and gradually. Weiner notes that in Florence, the Church's invention of purgatory and the subsequent selling of "indulgences" to cleanse the sinful spirit introduced a big flood of money that would be spent to commission the impressive monuments we still admire today. The gold rush naturally attracted the geniuses of that era. Weiner concludes that, not the individual, but the organization and city that commissions (creative) work is the real genius.

Most creators Weiner studied did not become geniuses in their place of birth: they flourished only when becoming immigrants. Geniuses are not born; they are made. If the conditions are right, geniuses are attracted to certain places, like Jean Tinguely was to Paris.

What, exactly, those conditions are remains unclear, although it hasn't stopped us from trying to replicate genius clusters in fancy business parks—or *campuses,* as the trends dictate, like the one in figure 3.5—that should spark creativity. While these commendable efforts undoubtedly increase cross-business conversations and perhaps partnerships, synthetically creating true genius clusters might prove to be impossible.

Figure 3.5   The Corda campus close to my home in Hasselt, Belgium, is an example of a modern technology site that focuses on what business conglomerates and owners call "business communities": where people and companies, both large and small, come together to grow ideas. In short, it is one of the many business parks engineered as a genius cluster skeleton. Photo © Karel Hemerijckx.

Game designer Tim Shafer did mention the Lucas Ranch, which presumably was designed to accelerate creative flow, as a special place to work. We'll cover the physical work environment as a creative stimulant or blocker in chapter 7.

Urban planners and architects love to cite the following quote from urban studies theorist Richard Florida's book *The Rise of the Creative Class*,[17] which is echoed by Weiner's conclusion, mentioned earlier: "It is not companies but places that provide a pool of talent." And yet we continue to put the companies instead of the places on a pedestal. If that quote is in the vicinity of terms like *entrepreneurship, policy review*, and *strategic*, it might be time to play a round of buzzword bingo.

Cluster sizes and creativity

Should teams/Cameratas/genius clusters be big and bold or modest in size to facilitate creative outcome? That's a tough question to answer that, again, depends on many variables.

Creativity researchers You-Na Lee and colleagues discovered that, on the one hand, team size has an inverted-U relation with novelty but, on the other hand, a continually increasing relation with effect.[a] Thus, in general, teams that are too tiny or too large equal not much creative work, but large teams equal more reach. There are, as always, exceptions.

Note that Lee et al.'s investigation took place in scientific teams in academia, not software developers in industry. Other papers hint at an increased amount of conflict within groups that are too large, leading to a lot of squabbling and little productive outcome.

What is the ideal team size? Scrum rules dictate around seven, but scrum never mentions creativity—it's just a way to get the job done. In general, smaller means more agility, and bigger means more communication overhead. Take the worrying trend of nearshoring or offshoring in technology companies, for example. I expect anyone who has had the (dis)pleasure of working in and syncing with multiple (remote) teams to nod while reading this.

---

[a] You-Na Lee, John P. Walsh, and Jian Wang. Creativity in scientific teams: Unpacking novelty and impact. Research Policy, 44(3), 2015.

EXERCISE Does your current work environment resemble a liquid network where you, like Tinguely said, feel like a fish in water, or does it feel like a solid network, where hardly anything is stimulating and too few ideas flow? If so, what action could be taken to facilitate the happy collision of dissimilar worlds?

3.3 Creative work in time

Time is, next to geography, another major factor that facilitates or impedes creativity. Remember that your creation is accepted as a creative outburst only when experts conceive it as such. Sometimes, the world simply isn't ready yet for your invention.

---

[17] Richard Florida. The rise of the creative class, volume 9. Basic Books, 2002.

Municipal workers might shake their heads in disbelief as you pave the streets with marshmallows, while the effort certainly would be approved by Roald Dahl's Willy Wonka. Sometimes, an idea as sticky as that one is considered a bit too progressive.

Sociologist and creativity researcher Pieter J. van Strien acknowledges the importance of creating at the right moment. In his book *Het Creatieve Genie* (The Creative Genius),[18] he laments the many misguided geniuses that never made it into the history books. If only they had waited a few more years to show their work.

The world is full of technological inventions that appeared ahead of their time. Take the 1999 video game *Outcast*, for example. Despite critical acclaim, the game sold poorly, which ultimately forced the developer, Appeal, to cancel its sequel and file for bankruptcy. In 2006, seven years after its release—which is a very long time in the highly volatile environment of gaming—several journalists praised *Outcast* as revolutionary thanks to its free-to-explore 3D open world, which was unheard of at the time. In 2001, *Grand Theft Auto III* took that concept and ran with it. Why? In 1999, the world wasn't ready yet.

Do you think cloud-powered services like Microsoft 365 or Xbox Cloud Gaming are novel inventions? As early as 1994, the Sega Channel service took a first stab at bringing an online content delivery system to the market, through a coaxial cable television interface. It was praised for being innovative, but its launch was poorly timed, making the product disappear into obscurity almost as fast as it appeared. Or how about the mid-1990s set-top box WebTV systems that marked the first television-based use of the internet? Or what about Apple's 1987 HyperCard software, which uses hypermedia to link a stack of virtual "cards"? Again, the web (and the wiki and JavaScript) took those concepts and ran with it.

Multiple former LucasArts members mused about "the right time" to create *The Secret of Monkey Island*. They were competing with Sierra On-Line's *King Quest* series, which was outselling *Maniac Mansion*, possibly because of the medieval setting. With their SCUMM engine in place, more time could be spent on the story, puzzles, and graphics. History proved that it was high time for a pirate game.

If the first *Monkey Island* appeared a year or so later, Sierra On-Line might have churned out something that would have dwarfed it. If the idea popped into Ron Gilbert's mind a few years earlier, *Monkey Island* might have been *Monkey Village* because of hardware limitations. The window of opportunity is always small.

In the introduction to this book, we encountered Vincent van Gogh's bad luck while trying to make a living as a painter. This is typical for art: first, new techniques or ideas are seen as ridiculous and promptly rejected. Georges Braque and Pablo Picasso iterated on cubism for many years before it became a proper art movement. It usually takes at least a decade of persistence to convince the critics—unfortunately, a decade too late for van Gogh.

Sometimes, though, it takes more than a century. Gustave Courbet's *L'Origine du monde* (*The Origin of the World*), a close-up view of the genitals of a naked woman,

---

[18] Pieter J van Strien. Het creatieve genie: het geheim van de geniale mens. Amsterdam University Press, 2016.

painted in 1866, needed 122 years before a forward-thinking curator deemed it ready for the general public, in 1988 in New York. And even then it shocked everybody. It is said that the person who commissioned the painting bought another one of the same size depicting a conventional landscape to place in front of *L'Origine* when receiving guests. Better to hide it than to cause a big outrage. I didn't have the guts to include a photo of the artwork; I'm sure you'll know where to look.

Italian contemporary artist Lucio Fontana managed to baffle me while visiting the City Museum of Amsterdam. Instead of gazing at paint strokes neatly brought together on a canvas, I found myself looking at a hole. Fontana called it *Concetto Spaziale*: a white canvas with a curving cut made by a sharp knife. It renounces the idea that a painting is a flat surface that can create the illusion of depth by painting on it.

I tried imagining the artist, standing in front of a stretched canvas. Concentrating, taking a deep breath. Perhaps standing there for an hour. Then, suddenly, whipping out a knife and taking a jab at the canvas, revealing a portion of the darkness behind it. I gave up. I wasn't ready for that artwork yet.

3.3.1   *The adoption curve*

New ideas, products, and practices take time to diffuse. This idea was made popular by agricultural researchers Ryan and Gross, who published a classic study on the diffusion of hybrid corn as early as 1943.[19] The authors plotted a curve that categorizes farmers willing or unwilling to adopt the new corn species (figure 3.6). The study revealed two things:

- The adoption process began with a small percentage of farmers who were willing to try out something new. From there, the innovation cascaded to other farmers.

- The most influential factors were the neighboring farmers. When they saw and talked to farmers who had adopted hybrid corn, they adopted it, too.

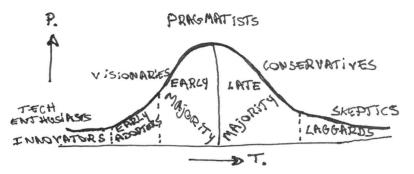

Figure 3.6   An innovation curve, still widely used in business and marketing to explain how new products are gradually adopted. In theory, the innovators and early adopters should help you win the early and late majority market. In theory.

---

[19] Bryce Ryan and Neal C Gross. The diffusion of hybrid seed corn in two Iowa communities. Rural Sociology, 8(1): 15, 1943.

Other researchers began taking interest and drew their own innovation curve, describing different stages of the process: awareness, information, evaluation, trail, adoption. Programmers following ThoughtWorks' well-known Technology Radar[20] will certainly recognize these terms.

In essence, trying to conquer the whole market from left to right takes time. Sometimes, it's a good idea to try to influence the innovators who will carry on to spread the word on your behalf. Sometimes, it's not, as the group is too small. Over the past 70 years, Ryan and Gross's adoption curve has been met with a fair amount of criticism. Innovation spread through word of mouth is never homogeneous, and farmers never neatly stay in one category.

Despite its flaws, the adoption curve remains popular and insightful when trying to break into a new market. The nineties video game *Outcast* never made it past the tech enthusiasts. Van Gogh's paintings did, but it took too long. Who knows where this book will land on the curve.

> **EXERCISE**   Does your team take the adoption curve into account when deciding which new technology to use on a certain project? Did your team, as an early adopter or a laggard, ever regret that choice afterward? How about positioning your clients on the curve—do they always upgrade to your latest software, or are they more skeptical?

3.4   *When creative flow is impeded*

So far, we know that it's important to lean on others to fuel our own imagination—to stand on the shoulders of giants. We also know that these giants like to cluster together in certain places. Last, we need to meet the giants at the right moment. Too soon, and they won't be there to embrace our ideas. Too late, and someone else will have stolen our plans.

During our interviews to investigate the role of creativity in software engineering, many programmers recognized the need to communicate, remembering several disastrous projects where the number one thing that went wrong was . . . the coordination within the team (or between teams).

3.4.1   *Social debt*

Behavioral software engineering researcher Damian Tamburri has a special word for communication gone awry in software development teams: *social debt*. The first thing that must have sprung to mind while reading this was probably *technical debt*. At least, that was my first thought when I read about social debt in an academic article titled "The Architect's Role in Community Shepherding."[21]

We as software developers are more than aware of technical debt when working with outdated or legacy code and the many code problems that come with it. When in

---

[20] See https://www.thoughtworks.com/radar.

[21] Damian A Tamburri, Rick Kazman, and Hamed Fahimi. The architect's role in community shepherding. IEEE Software, 2016.

luck, a small portion of the smells eventually get translated into technical user stories and picked up in a sprint. When less lucky, these smells breed more smells, and before you know it, things will have grown completely out of control.

We software developers talk about code smells all the time. We organize working groups and ensemble programming sessions to identify and get rid of them, we read books such as the aforementioned *Refactoring* and Robert Martin's *Clean Code*,[22] and we might even complain to our partner at home about yet another shortcut that had to be made today because of time constraints, introducing a smell instead of cleaning one up. But the software development problems do not end there—technical debt is only the most obvious problem.

Code smells and technical debt

Just to be clear, let us rehash a few definitions. What, exactly, is technical debt? It is the cost that comes with doing things "the easy way," when a better technical approach should have been taken instead. If it is not fixed in time, it accumulates "interest," meaning certain improvements will become harder over time.

An example is a few design patterns that are repeatedly abused but tolerated until it is too late to refactor the code without breaking a bunch of things. Abusing static variables is also a well-known characteristic in code indicating a bigger underlying problem, also called a *code smell*, a term coined by Kent Beck but really popularized by Martin Fowler's *Refactoring* book.[a] Of course, some technical debt, just like regular debt, can be justified: it is not always a lazy choice.

---

[a]Martin Fowler. Refactoring: Improving the design of existing code, 2nd ed. Addison-Wesley, 2019.

3.4.2 *From technical to social debt*

Technical debt might be annotated with `@TechnicalDebt` in code—I've seen it inserted and then happily ignored—but what about social problems in development teams? We all know it severely affects team performance—perhaps orders of magnitude more than a few "simple" code smells you have to work around (or, ideally, fix). We also all implicitly know a couple of community smells: just like code smells, they're anti-patterns that emerge time and time again in (development) communities and negatively affect the creative efforts of the team.

I really like the terms *social debt* and *community smells*, because they perfectly accompany their better known counterparts *technical debt* and *code smells*. I encountered these terms in Damian Tamburri's papers, in which he talks about the "shepherding" role of the software architect (or team/DevLead, for that matter), who is a negotiator who should try to minimize the effects of both kinds of smells.

---

[22] Robert C. Martin. Clean code: A handbook of agile software craftsmanship. Pearson, 2008.

3.4.3   *Community smells*

The following is a selection of community smells identified by Damian Tamburri's team, from interviewing many practitioners:

- *Time Warp*—An organizational change that leads team members to wrongly assume that communication will take less time and that coordination isn't needed, leading to unresolved problems, code smells, and thus low software quality
- *Cognitive Distance*—Perceived distance between peers on physical/technical/social levels that causes distrust, misinterpretations, and wasted time
- *Newbie Free-Riding*—Newcomers being left to themselves, which causes irritation and high work pressure
- *Power Distance*—The distance that team members with less responsibility perceive, accept, or expect with power holders that impedes knowledge sharing
- *Disengagement*—Thinking the product is mature enough to ship when it's not, due to unchecked assumptions and a lack of engagement
- *Priggish Members*—Extremely demanding and pointlessly precise people who cause unneeded delays and frustrations within the team
- *Cookbook Development*—Programmers who are stuck in their ways and refuse to adapt to new technology and new ideas
- *Institutional Isomorphism*—Imposed sameness of processes and frameworks between different teams that reduce flexibility, morale, and collaboration
- *Hyper-Community*—A too-volatile thinking environment where everything constantly changes, which results in buggy software
- *DevOps Clash*—A strict separation of development and operations teams, perhaps even geographically, that causes culture clashes and a lack of trust
- *Informality Excess*—Excessive informality due to a total lack of protocol, causing low accountability
- *Unlearning*—New technologies that become unfeasible to adapt because older employees refuse to do so, causing a loss of new knowledge and practices
- *Lone Wolf*—"That guy" who commits without taking others' opinions into consideration
- *Black Cloud*—Information overload without a clear way to manage it within teams and between teams, resulting in a loss of potentially great ideas

I love these analogies because it suddenly makes it much easier to actually talk about the problem. It is important to note that the names of the smells emerged simply from analyzing and grouping together what programmers said during interviews. Some might resonate very much with you, and others not so much. You can easily come up with variations or completely new smells to take your team's unique context into account.

You might be wondering what this has to do with creativity. Well, *everything*! Easy access to information and resources is crucial to expressing creativity. Got a Black Cloud or stuck with Unlearning problems? Tough luck. The dangerous combination of Cognitive Distance and Time Warp with a DevOps Clash thrown in for good measure can have devastating consequences for the team morale.

Psychology academics devoted a whole research subdomain to *team* creativity, next to *individual* and *organizational* creativity,[23] where team processes, composition, dynamics, and methods are investigated in relation to creative output. Their conclusion? An excess of conflicts is bad. Who would have thought?

Jumping from code smell to community smell isn't a big stretch, and everyone knows communities don't build themselves. As mentioned in section 3.1, Jessica Kerr went as far as saying great development teams are symmathesized.

My own personal experience isn't far off: work with people, not technology. That means, when programming in teams, the community smells just listed should receive more attention than "mere" code smells. Thorough readers will have noticed that many community smells are responsible for code smells.

Nowadays, most software-centered conferences include a social problems track. There certainly is some attention for social and psychological aspects of software engineering, but not nearly enough. That is the most important reason why I chose to rejoin academia and ultimately write this book.

Damian asserts that it is primarily the role of the architect to act as a shepherd to take care of the flock: "We've always claimed that architects are much more than just a 'technical lead,' but now they must also be an active community shepherd." While I think it is dangerous to explicitly give that responsibility to a single person on a team, I do agree that making implicit problems explicit is the beginning of a solution. However, the jelling of the team isn't the work of one architect. Rather, it's the accumulated effort of every single person who interacts with the system, and the system that interacts with every single person, which is all the more reason for everyone on the team—including nontechnical people—to familiarize themselves with the concepts of social debt and community smells.

The work of Damian's academic colleague, Gemma Catalino, builds on Damian's. In 2021, she published a paper on her team's understanding of the variability of community smells.[24] The paper isn't as powerful as the introduction of the concept itself, although it contained one sentence that really resonated with me: "Communication is the key factor to reduce social debt."

Let us bring the concepts of social debt and community smells outside of the academic software engineering circles and inside the development teams in industry, where it belongs and is critically needed. Or perhaps simply scribble @SocialDebt on a sticky note and smack it on the back of one of your peers to call it a day.

---

[23] Ming-Huei Chen. Understanding the benefits and detriments of conflict on team creativity process. Creativity and Innovation Management, 2006.

[24] Gemma Catalino, Fabio Palomba, Damian Andrew Tamburri, and Alexander Serebrenik. Understanding community smells variability: A statistical approach. IEEE/ACM 43rd International Conference on Software Engineering: Software Engineering in Society, 2021.

3.4.4   *Getting out of social debt*

There are countless books, articles, best practices, methods, models, insights, experiments, and theories out there to help identify and minimize team-based problems. It would not make much sense to attempt to summarize every work here.

A few things stand out, though. The programmers my colleagues and I interviewed mentioned accountability, for example—not simply holding others responsible for actions gone wrong, but instead sharing responsibility as a group. Behavioral expert and former management consultant Christopher Avery expanded this idea into a *Responsibility Process*[25] specifically focused on teamwork. Avery teaches us to stop reveling in deny, justify, or blame states we can't seem to get out of and instead take (shared) responsibility to face the problem and do something about it.

A shared responsibility should minimize Cognitive Distance, DevOps Clashes, and Disengagement community smells. I've read questionable practices that require developers to even check in their cellphone number together with code changes in case things break. Companies that enforce such dubious methods seem to have forgotten the essence of responsibility—that it is shared.

Another way to mitigate social debt is the effective use of pair programming. Pair programming effectively negates Lone Wolf, Unlearning, Cookbook Development, and Newbie Free-Riding smells—that is, as long as the team takes the shared responsibility to regularly switch pairs.

Pair programming not only helps in battling social debt; its long-term effects include facilitating insight (the "aha!" moment—more about that in chapter 7) through collective learning, higher quality code thanks to two pairs of watchful eyes, and even more happiness and confidence in the work—both for experienced coders in industry and software engineering students.[26]

If pair programming leads to happy programmers, what, then, is the result of that increased happiness? More creativity. There is plenty of evidence for that in both academic and popular literature. Companies are starting to become well aware of the fact that happy employees are better-performing employees. HR managers are suddenly promoted to "Chief Happiness Officer," to dedicate their efforts to increasing well-being at work.

Don't be fooled, though: the only reason employers are interested in your well-being is your work performance—including your creative skills to solve their complex problems. The happiness–creativity relationship functions as a reinforced feedback loop: more creativity also leads to more happiness. Mihaly Csikszentmihalyi summarizes it as follows[27]:

> *For many people, happiness comes from creating new things and making discoveries.*
> *Enhancing one's creativity may therefore also enhance well-being.*

[25] Christopher M Avery, Meri A Walker, and Erin O Murphy. Teamwork is an individual skill: getting your work done when sharing responsibility. Berrett-Koehler, 2001.

[26] Max O Smith, Andrew Giugliano, and Andrew DeOrio. Long term effects of pair programming. IEEE Transactions on Education, 2017.

[27] Mihaly Csikszentmihalyi. Happiness and creativity. The Futurist, 1997.

EXERCISE Which of the above community smells cause alarm bells to ring in context of your current development team? If none do, congrats, you're part of a dream team! Or perhaps the hidden social debt present in your team doesn't neatly match any of the above. If that is the case, feel free to make up your own smells.

Summary

- A collective creativity significantly improves our individual creative efforts. Engage in a community with like-minded but diverse people to discuss and improve your and others' work.

- That same collective has the tendency to organically cluster in creative regions, or genius clusters. Synthetically engineering genius clusters has proven to be quite difficult.

- Time is, next to geography, another major factor that potentially facilitates or impedes creativity. The innovation curve teaches us that ideas take time to diffuse.

- Engaging in mutual learning is, as the word implies, beneficial for both the trainee and the trainer. Mutual learning is much more effective than either transmitting or receiving knowledge.

- Seek to cross-pollinate ideas across multiple domains and groups. Do not limit your interest to the things you know. Seek out experts. Broaden your horizon.

- Creativity is systemic: it is a complex (living) system that is more than the sum of its pieces and wholes.

- Provide—and welcome—genuine critical feedback instead of mirroring others' opinions, to avoid the echo chamber effect.

- Be mindful of the kind of network you find yourself in when working or attending gatherings. Are ideas stagnating (solid), following each other at a dazzling pace (gas), or effectively spreading (liquid)?

- The creative flow of software development teams can be easily impeded by social debt. Communication is the key factor to reduce social debt. Identifying and naming community smells might be a good place to start.

Constraints

4

The whispering whizz of mowing scythes startled sleepy birds nesting near the ancient Nile Delta. Workers harvested the papyrus plant quickly and efficiently, before the unbearable heat of the Egyptian sun turned the labor into an even bigger nightmare. The fibers of these plants were to be converted into a valuable writing material similar to paper by expert papyrus makers.

In the 2nd century BC, King Ptolemy V promptly ordered craftsmen to stop exporting one of their treasured national products. The reason was as simple and mundane as jealousy. A rival library in Pergamon, in Mysia (now western Turkey), had gained enough traction to greatly annoy the king, who wanted to protect the fame and power of his Great Library of Alexandria at all costs.

The sudden papyrus shortages did not stop the Hellenistic King Eumenes II from expanding the library in Pergamon. His hunger for literature was much,

much bigger than the literary ambition of his predecessors. The papyrus plant does not grow well outside of the Nile delta, and resorting to clay tablets greatly decreases the capacity of a single book. Instead of accepting defeat, Eumenes's experts perfected the Eastern art of writing on animal skin, a method that until then was only used locally and not highly regarded.

Ptolemy's masterstroke turned out to be a painful mistake. It was called *parchment*—*pergameno* in Latin—as a memory to the city where this technique was perfected, and it was parchment that made sure Ptolemy's already crumbling Alexandria lost even more political power: texts could suddenly be relatively cheaply copied without the need of papyrus.

Twenty-one centuries later, the rhythmic scratches of swift and wet brushstrokes rubbing against a canvas entranced a lone painter in a big mansion near Aix-en-Provence in the south of France. Paul Cézanne's daily exercise of drawing a basket of apples, again and again, gradually shifted his ideas of painting a subject from a single viewpoint to a combination of multiple angles.

Cézanne attempted the impossible: to paint different compositions using only one canvas. Yet, the end result achieved in 1893 was a surprisingly balanced but disjointed perspective, precisely because of the unbalanced parts, which were all drawn using a slightly different vantage point.

Cézanne's *Le Panier de Pommes* challenged the idea of linear perspective. Painters had been using a single vantage point for centuries to create the illusion of space and depth. Everyone just assumed it was impossible without resorting to another canvas. This achievement earned Cézanne the title "The Father of Modern Art," because his paintings paved the way for Fauvism and especially Pablo Picasso's and Georges Braque's art movement, Cubism.

At the end of the next century, the busy sound of mechanical keystrokes filled The Black Cube, an office space in Mesquite, Texas. A small team of designers, programmers, and artists were working on their next video game that would take the world by storm: John Romero, Tom Hall, Sandy Petersen, John Carmack, Dave Taylor, Adrian Carmack, and Kevin Cloud—the team of developers at id Software—were developing *DOOM* in 1992.

The keystrokes did not come from classic, beige-looking keyboards attached to 80386 IBM PCs. They came from sleek black keyboards connected to NeXTstation computers running the NeXTSTEP operating system, the UNIX-based precursor to macOS. Carmack and his team found that cross-compiling on NeXT hardware dramatically increased their productivity. The workstations shipped with 17-inch monitors that could handle more colors and larger resolutions,[1] helping *DOOM*'s map designers get the job done much faster.

---

[1] $1,120 \times 832$ pixels with a density of 92 DPI, compared with standard 14-in. monitors delivering a resolution of 640×480 pixels, which already was considered high end on PCs. Read more about this awesome technology and how id Software used it in Fabien Sanglard's Game Engine Black Book. https://fabiensanglard.net, 2018.

Carmack admitted to spending more than $100,000 on NeXT computers during the entire course of the development of *DOOM* and *Quake*.[2] For many developers and designers, even the "cheaper" NeXTstations were well beyond their budgets. Still, their high price tag turned out to work well for id Software. By rejecting conventional IBM PCs as workstations, they were able to churn out the bloody space marine shooter in just over a year, making millions within the first year of release.

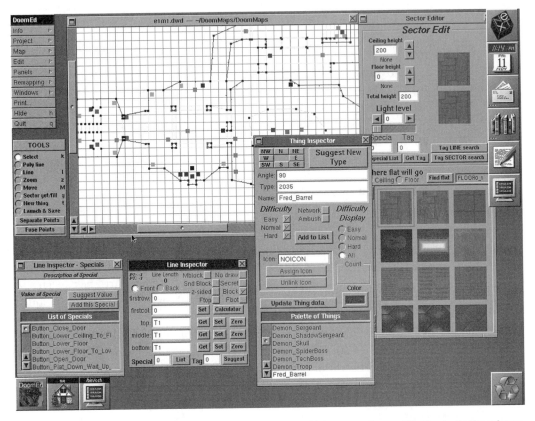

Figure 4.1   The DoomEd map editor running on the NeXT OS, which was made possible thanks to the release of the *DOOM* source code in 2015. Without the raw power of the NeXT machines, simply creating the DoomEd software (which also took 20,000 lines of code) would have taken at least twice as long. Screenshot courtesy of Fabien Sanglard.

4.1   *Constraint-based thinking*

What is the greatest common divisor between Eumenes' reaction to being cut off from Ptolemy's papyrus supplies, Paul Cézanne's stubbornness in clinging onto a single canvas to paint multiple viewpoints, and id Software's decision to move a majority of the development process onto NeXT computers? All three examples showcase a challenge to overcome, and all three resulted in radical, forward-thinking inventions.

---

[2] Fabien Sanglard. Game Engine Black Book: *DOOM* v1.1. https://fabiensanglard.net, 2018.

These challenges can be seen as *constraints*. Pergamon suddenly lost access to papyrus. How could he supply paper to scholars to keep on feeding the library and expand cultural and political influence? Cézanne stubbornly insisted on painting two vantage points on one canvas. How could he fill one blank space to represent two similar but dissimilar views? Carmack and his team refused to work with lower-resolution and slower hardware. How could they exploit technology to (partially) diminish hardware limitations?

Constraints prove to be of paramount importance when it comes to creativity. These can be self-imposed, such as in the case of Cézanne, who stubbornly kept painting on a single canvas. Later artists do this often: adhere to a muted color palette, draw only rectangles, don't use paint at all, and so forth. Musicians and photographers often use the same self-imposed constraint technique to create truly unique pieces of art. On the other hand, constraints can be forced on you: in that case, you'll have to either work with what is given to you or find a way around it.

The end result of a process influenced by constraints can be very progressive. No constraints, no creativity. Just like collective creativity from chapter 3, it is one of the many important factors to take into account when trying to solve problems creatively. As 19th-century novelist and scientist Johann Wolfgang von Goethe keenly observed: "He who'd do great things must display restraint; The master shows himself first in confinement, And law alone can grant us liberation." Remember that the next time you're forced to work with legacy code and a cruddy existing database system.

4.1.1   Greenfield or brownfield?

Constraints drastically improve creativity. This might come across as counterintuitive because constraints are widely regarded as bad. Too little time or money. Too much pressure, too limited hardware to realize that ambitious software project. Too old software architectures to build a new layer on, too outdated Java Development Kits to comfortably program in. Too many requests in one second to handle flawlessly, too unstable network connections, or too little bandwidth. Too much whining about constraints in the team.

Working on what is called a *greenfield* project certainly can be a lot of fun—and creative: you get to choose a fancy new technology, there are virtually no limits when it comes to development and deployment pipelines, and most important, there's no annoying, existing, decaying but still-important piece of software you have to build around. Great!

On the other hand, a *brownfield* project, where you cannot simply start with a clean slate, is likely to trigger more creative behavior, precisely because of the limitations you're forced to deal with. I'm not claiming it's a lot of fun; I'm simply trying to convince you that constraints *can* be a good thing. Guess which of the two types of software projects you'll encounter most often in the wild?

This also shines through in our developer interviews. A few participants stated that working on a problem without any form of constraints ultimately results in boredom. There's no frustrating but exciting deadline to meet or manager to convince, no annoying but valuable feedback from clients to take into account. You can do whatever you want, whenever you want. Sounds fun, right? It is—for the first few weeks—until the boredom sets in.

Learning software development: Greenfield or brownfield?

In higher education, software engineering students are usually served neatly preprocessed and carefully defined programming problems to solve—in other words, small greenfield projects. If the aim is to train the syntax, this works.

However, if the aim is to learn how to apply design patterns in the real world, how to cope with large software projects, and above all, how to cleverly work with existing constraints to arrive at a creative solution, this doesn't work. Adam Barr, a Microsoft veteran who analyzed 50 years of software engineering history, advocates for the use of real-world open source projects in academia precisely because of that. And yet computing education research turns a blind eye and keeps on dutifully studying and applying greenfield approaches. I admit I'm guilty of this, too: greenfield lab exercises are easier to come up with, maintain, and grade.

This story can serve as an interesting thought experiment. How do you train your junior programmers or interns? Are they handed a separate, nicely self-contained playground where nothing can go wrong, and when it comes to constraints, little will be learned? Or can they code along with a more experienced colleague to learn how to properly and creatively deal with constraints?

If constraints are universally bad, then why do so many innovators and artists willingly choose to adopt them? They use constraints to break through, to "think outside the box"—you knew that was coming. Let's investigate a few archetypes of constraints to better understand the relationship with creativity.

4.1.2   *A taxonomy of constraints*

The structure of the following sections has been adapted from Norwegian social and political theorist Jon Elster, who specializes in rationality and constraints. His beneficial taxonomy of constraints, as shown in figure 4.2, allows creativity scholars—and us—to gain more insight into which constraints are of paramount importance when it comes to radical decision making.

Not all constraints are beneficial to the task at hand, but for the purpose of creative problem solving in software development, we're interested only in those that are. Elster calls constraints that evoke some kind of benefit to the constraint agent—but are not chosen by him—*incidental*. On the other hand, constraints that are self-imposed for the sake of some creative benefit are called *essential*. A third typology is the distinction between *hard* (material, technical, financial) and *soft* (conventions) constraints. The

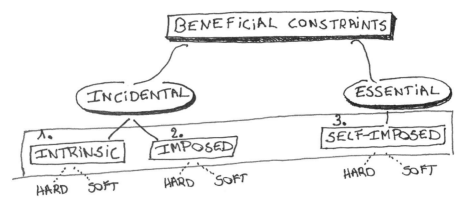

Figure 4.2   A taxonomy of beneficial constraints adapted from Elster's work *Ulysses Unbound*[3]

most important personal freedom is found in self-imposed constraints. But first, let us take a closer look at the two categories of incidental constraints.

> **EXERCISE**   As a software developer, do you consistently identify every constraint of the current task? Do you approach incidental constraints with a different creative mindset compared to essential constraints? If so, why do you think that is the case?

4.2   Intrinsic constraints

Perhaps the most obvious ones, intrinsic constraints are inherent to the properties of the problem to which the specific task belongs. If you're an artist and produce paintings on canvas, the physical material of the canvas and the paint (whatever the type) are intrinsic constraints. If you're a programmer, you'll have to work with code—whether it's JavaScript or an Assembly dialect, the principle stays the same. Squirting acrylic tubes onto a canvas won't help you deliver that software to clients, unless you come up with a paint code image recognizer, converting your contemporary art back into code. Intrinsic constraints are considered incidental: they're simply there, and we have to work with them (or around them).

4.2.1   Intrinsic hardware constraints

By investing in expensive NeXT hardware, the *DOOM* team rejected intrinsic constraints bound to typical IBM PC hardware at the time. Of course, they were still bound to some form of intrinsic constraints: a quad core CPU wasn't invented yet, and NeXT motherboards didn't exactly come slotted with gigabytes of DDR RAM. In the wonderful world of computing, these constraints constantly evolve, but they hardly ever completely disappear.

---

[3] Jon Elster. Ulysses Unbound: Studies in rationality, precommitment, and constraints. Cambridge University Press, 2000.

Other game studios chose to embrace the shortcomings of the current generation hardware. LucasArts'[4] *Monkey Island,* for example, first encountered in chapter 3, has a distinct, pixelated art style. This isn't because the team decided to work with a muted color palette, but rather because of hardware limitations.

In 1984, the Enhanced Graphics Adapter (EGA) superseded the then-standardized CGA graphics display system present in IBM PCs. The 8-bit ISA EGA cards had usually up to 64 KB of working memory. Take that, gigabytes! Even though daughter boards could expand the RAM, allowing for higher resolutions (640×350), EGA produced a display of only 16 colors, of which the palette was fixed.

Sixteen colors. Sixteen. I'll let that sink in for a while. Yet, *The Secret of Monkey Island* is an extremely charismatic game precisely because of its artful and dark background renderings. Mark Ferrari, one of then-LucasArts' artists, found a way around the intrinsic EGA constraints by using the *dithering* technique: drawing pixels of alternating colors in checkerboard patterns to create the illusion of a broader color range that is more appealing to the eye. The clunky early-nineties monitors further magnified the dithering effect thanks to CRT's natural tendency to blend pixels.

Loom was the first game to receive the full dithering treatment, allowing Mark to further perfect the technique while taking on *Monkey Island*'s scenery. The team found a way to compress the dithering graphics, allowing for even bigger scenes and character art. At the time of release in October 1990, VGA graphics would have superseded EGA, although the new hardware was still very expensive. Many people playing the adventure game on their old EGA-powered IBM PC thought their computer had somehow been upgraded overnight. It looked like VGA thanks to creative use of hardware despite its limitations, thereby overcoming constraints. A VGA version of *Monkey Island* would eventually be released that implemented 256-color support, allowing for even more advanced background and character art (see figure 4.3).

Mark calls *Monkey Island* his "PhD thesis in dithered EGA artwork,"[5] thanking constraints for the team's creative results:

> *All those extreme limitations made it an extremely creative environment to work in, because you had to take any idea you had as far as you could figure out how to take it, to get anywhere.*

Painstakingly drawing these impressive scenes pixel by pixel in DPaint not only shows dedication but also proves that sudden outbursts of creativity are propagated by intrinsic constraints. Mark's mastery over the DPaint tool sprouted even more creative tricks present in *Monkey Island,* such as smart color cycling to animate burning campfires and let the reflected firelight dance on the nearby rocks in the background.

---

[4] During the development of Monkey Island, LucasArts was still Lucasfilm Games.
[5] See The legacy of Monkey Island. Retro Gamer, no. 212, p. 24.

Figure 4.3 One of the first scenes in *The Secret of Monkey Island*, pictured in EGA (top) and VGA (bottom). If you look closely around the curb, on the house behind Guybrush, and in the sky, you should notice slight differences and the checkerboard pattern. The abundant night scenes helped further reduce the need for a larger color palette since EGA's blue tints were the most flexible to work with. Its successor, *Monkey Island 2: LeChuck's Revenge*, fully embracing VGA's 256 colors, is much brighter.

Crashing the color cycle with Mark Ferrari

If you're inclined to learn more about EGA, DPaint, or Mark's professional career—which he summarizes as "falling backward into things"—be sure to watch the Retro Tea Break interview at https://youtu.be/e-aJ8YNSYGs (also available as a chapter in the *Selected Interviews Vol. 1* by Neil Thomas). The interview also touches on serendipitous creativity and chapter 3's genius cluster concept.

4.2.2   *Intrinsic software constraints*

When working with a certain medium to express yourself, intrinsic constraints help to shape the artistic outcome, whether you want them to or not. For instance, different types of paint have not only their own distinct look but also their own painting practices, longevity based on moisture level and lightfastness, consistency, and so on. Acrylic paint dries quickly and is opaque, meaning you can paint from dark to light colors, while in watercolor, it's the other way around.

The same principle applies to software. If you want to write software, you'll have to work within the intrinsic bounds of a software development ecosystem: inputting symbols using a peripheral such as a keyboard, issuing commands for compiling (or interpreting), etc. You can't paint code on a canvas and expect it to magically compile and run.

To tell a computer how to work, you need a set of instructions: this is intrinsic to software development. The programming language choice may be up to you (a self-imposed constraint) or not (an imposed constraint), but on a higher level, it needs to adhere to the nature of software development. Let's first see what happens when someone else tells you to use a certain programming language.

> **EXERCISE**   In your daily practice as a programmer, which constraints are just there, intrinsically connected to the job? Instead of fighting these, can you figure out a way to creatively work around them? For example, in some embedded operating systems, there's no native threading support. Coroutine-like *green threads* (e.g., in Go, Lua, PHP, Perl) that run in user space instead of kernel space emulate threads and "fix" this shortcoming—just like Mark Ferrari "fixed" EGA's limited color palette.

4.3   *Imposed constraints*

While intrinsic constraints are inherent to the material you choose to work with, imposed constraints are limitations that emerge from the stakeholders. In essence, these constraints are the same, except this time you don't get to choose the material: someone else does. Your client wants the problem solved before next Tuesday, and it should be done in PHP since their maintenance team has to take over afterward. Most classic, project-based constraints you have been struggling with fall within this category: budget, time, efficiency, relevance, and so forth.

The difference between intrinsic and imposed constraints sounds marginal: either way, they're still imposed and not chosen freely. However, the psychological consequences have a big effect on the team. For one, with intrinsic constraints, (almost) nobody complains. If you were an eighties PC developer, you worked with very limited hardware capabilities, such as a few hundred kilobytes of RAM and EGA. There was nothing else out there. If you're a skilled programmer and are keen to do things the 2022 way, you might be looking into modern programming languages, CQRS, domain-driven design, and so forth. Being forced to extend an existing, horizontally sliced PHP system and having to work your way around a decaying SQL database suddenly doesn't sound very creative or motivating.

That doesn't mean it's impossible to bring modern best practices to older projects. For example, in one project, I found myself plodding through incomprehensible domain logic tightly locked into an endless set of Oracle SQL stored procedures. The C++ layer, "the program," was in fact an empty box that endlessly transformed data until it was pushed to the "domain layer": the stored procedures. Completely discouraged and unable to apply my beating stick, test-driven development, I tried to tag along, feeling more and more depressed, until I discovered SQL Developer's capabilities to unit test PL/SQL statements. The command-line `ututil` tool even made it possible to integrate it into the build system!

My joy didn't last long. I was the only one on the team who saw the benefit of relying on unit tests, and my feeble attempts to convince others didn't work out. Six months later, frustrated with any lack of advancement on their part, I moved on. Creativity requires willingness from everyone involved.

In another project, we were gradually migrating customers from a fat client software system built using Visual Basic 6 to a modern web browser–based solution powered by C#. Since both software systems had to be well maintained, we were occasionally required to make changes in the legacy system to adhere to various new laws, as the software was a complicated payroll engine. There were only a few employees left who knew what was going on in the VB6 codebase. It felt like a game of Jenga: pull out the wrong piece and the whole thing falls apart.

SimplyVBUnit to the rescue! After a bit of fiddling, we managed to come up with a working system that, although it never got fully integrated, increased our confidence up to a point that we dared to check the code changes into Visual SourceSafe (figure 4.4). The unit test code is quite readable, too, thanks to NUnit's influence:

```
Public Sub MyTestMethod_WithSomeArg_ShouldReturn45
 Dim isType As Boolean
 isType = MyTestMethod(arg1)

 Assert.That isType, Iz.EqualTo(45)
End Sub
```

A few years ago, an ex-colleague told me he was fed up with those typical DTO (Data Transfer Object) practices and managing their life cycle. "It felt like all we did is converting from one layer into the next," he said. The last stop before persisting to disk is probably yet another data layer portrayed by yet another acronym: ORM (Object-Relational Mapping). He continued:

> We were fed up with Hibernate's whining and the endless lazy-loaded one-to-many annotations gone wrong. Why do we always mindlessly import these dependencies? So we decided, let's just persist the first layer straight into the database. And that's exactly what we did. Simple serialization. And that worked surprisingly well!

When you can't work with a NoSQL system, just pretend the SQL instance is a document store. Don't forget to take data migration problems into account. Instead of adopting a negative view toward imposed constraints—resources are limited, ideas

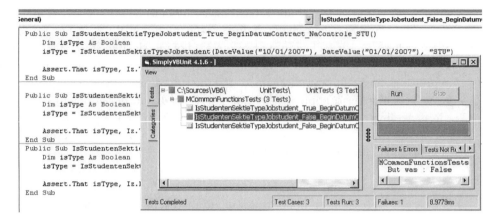

Figure 4.4   A portion of our VB6 unit tests running in SimplyVBUnit. See http://simplyvbunit.sourceforge.net.

easily rejected, and thus creativity is stifled—try to adopt a more positive viewpoint. Limited resources can still be worked with, ideas require perhaps more thought, and thus creativity is pushed past the obvious. A constraint isn't necessarily a restraint!

> **EXERCISE**   Which imposed constraints do you have to work with currently? Why do you think these are imposed rather than intrinsic? Do some constraints make you want to tear your hair out? How do you and your team cope with these?

4.4   *Self-imposed constraints*

However useful constraint-based thinking is to spark creativity, intrinsic and imposed constraints are still viewed by creativity and design researchers as *incidental*.[6] Self-imposed constraints, on the other hand, can be seen as *essential*, according to Michael Mose Biskjaer, a researcher who specializes in constraints of creative processes and who picked up where Jon Elster's beneficial constraint taxonomy left off. These types of constraints are deliberately and voluntarily imposed for the sake of some expected benefit: to boost creativity and invent original works. In his dissertation on self-imposed creativity constraints, Michael clarifies the idea:[7]

> *By abandoning the notion of divine inspiration and genius, a number of classic and current avant-garde movements from around the 1920s and onwards have conceptualised, devised and applied several highly innovative and efficient creative intervention techniques all based on self-imposed constraints. By intentionally setting up obstructions, "tripwires," imperatives, random input stimuli etc. for themselves, many of these artists have soon come to discover that such strategies help ignite and stimulate their creative processes considerably.*

---

[6] Michael Mose Biskjaer and Kim Halskov. Decisive constraints as a creative resource in interaction design. Digital Creativity, 2014.

[7] Michael Mose Biskjaer. Self-imposed creativity constraints. PhD thesis, Department of Aesthetics and Communication, Faculty of Arts, Aarhus University, 2013.

Who would want to voluntarily impose a time or budget constraint on a project? We universally resent the dangerous predicament we're in when managers say it had to be done yesterday with half the money that's already been spent. There's a big difference between a tight but reasonable constraint and an impossibly ridiculous one. The "trip-wires" Michael is talking about are in the former category.

According to Biskjaer, acts of self-binding fall into one of two main categories: (1) boosting productivity and (2) affecting and transforming the creative process itself as a means to open up new opportunities for creative action, ultimately (one would hope) resulting in a more original outcome. Strict daily routines to block distractions and promote productivity when it comes to coding fall into the first category. Productivity tools, such as banning internet access or reducing your workspace to a clean white screen, intentionally block out distractions, allowing you to get stuff done. Software like Serene for macOS is designed to block distracting apps and social media, thereby increasing your focus.

The dangers of always-on messaging

The Serene promo video at https://sereneapp.com/ classifies Slack and Skype as distracting applications, and rightly so. The always-on mentality is extremely destructive to creativity, as indicated in countless publications. Yet we somehow choose to ignore what the research says and carry on messaging away.

It's funny to see both Serene and Slack appear in many "Top 10 best productivity apps" lists on various tech websites. Be very mindful when your employer asks for your presence in various enterprise-like communication apps. Your productivity and creativity are also in their best interest.

The second category, transforming the creative process, should open the possibility of arriving at more original outcomes. Artists are much more aware of the benefits of self-imposed creativity than we programmers are. Famous Russian composer Igor Stravinsky talked about imposing limits to free oneself: "Human activity must impose limits upon itself. The more art is controlled, limited, worked over, the more it is free."[8]

But how can more limits equal more freedom? Because creative freedom and creative self-binding by means of self-imposed constraints are intimately entwined. Such a constraint is both limiting *and* freeing. As we'll see in the later examples, limiting yourself to writing code of only 64 KB to produce a visualization means you'll have to be much more inventive and, thus, creative.

The evolution of imposing self-binding is clearly visible when comparing early and late works from famous painters exploring modernism, such as Pablo Picasso, Piet Mondrian, and Wassily Kandinsky. Some even went as far as removing everything there was to remove. In 1960, Jan Schoonhoven cofounded the Dutch *Nul-beweging*

---

[8] Igor Stravinsky. Poetics of music in the form of six lessons (The Charles Eliot Norton Lectures). Rev. ed. Harvard University Press, 1970.

(Zero-movement), creating art while banning everything that smells and looks "painterly." Paint and emotion were replaced by cardboard and geometrical repetition.

Laugh all you want: Schoonhoven's unusual works are now part of prominent art centers such as the Dutch Kröller-Müller Museum and the French Centre Pompidou. A few years ago, one of his white-textured reliefs fetched £780,450 at Sotheby's in London. Schoonhoven was a postman and did all this in his spare time. Thank you, self-imposed constraints. The following sections demonstrate how deliberately transforming the creative software development process using self-imposed constraints can remove the shackles of the mundane.

4.4.1   *Passionate pixel artists*

Many self-imposed constraints originated as imposed constraints. Let's take a look at Mark Ferrari's 2017 swan song, *Thimbleweed Park*, cocreated by point-and-click veterans Ron Gilbert and Gary Winnick. Released 27 years after *The Secret of Monkey Island*, *Thimbleweed Park* was designed to look like an unopened 1987 classic Lucasfilm adventure game, patiently accumulating dust until someone rediscovers the big box. Only, the world has moved on since the 8-bit era of EGA, DOS, and DPaint, which is fortunate, because nobody on the team *really* wanted to go back to using crude tools of the eighties. Mark calls *Thimbleweed*'s art "8-bitish": all the background art is created in Photoshop with a reduced resolution, harsh interpolation, and anti-aliasing turned off. Some new features, like transparency layers and parallax scrolling, managed to sneak into the game without breaking the nostalgic atmosphere.

Ron, Gary, and Mark deliberately made *Thimbleweed Park* look like an 8-bit game, not only because they were craving big pixels, but also because their audience was 15,623 Kickstarter backers who had raised $626,250, almost twice the initial goal.

According to Mark, pixel art has evolved from a crappy technique inherent to the hardware to a full-blown art movement that surpasses the gaming medium:

> *These days, you have pixel artists who are passionate about pixel art because of the pixels. Back then, it looked horrible and was a huge step down from drawing with colored pencils. But now, it has become an art movement that perhaps even transcends gaming itself.*

The recent resurgence of retro-inspired games proves that *Thimbleweed Park* wasn't a one-off. Some game designers choose to fully embrace old technologies on new systems, such as *Ion Fury*, a 2019 first-person shooter made in *Duke Nukem 3D*'s Build engine, initially released in 1995. Ion Fury runs on a highly optimized revision of the open source EDuke32, but still. Others (*DUSK*, inspired by *Quake*; *Project Warlock*, inspired by *Wolfenstein 3D*) opt to mimic the style and atmosphere of their ancestors but prefer the comfort and flexibility of the modern Unity engine.

Vblank Entertainment's Brian Provinciano belongs to a small and perhaps crazy subset of programmers wanting to downgrade their PlayStation 4 software until it runs comfortably on the 40-year-old MS-DOS platform. *Retro City Rampage*, first released in 2012 on modern platforms, was later ported to much more limited environments, as "a programming exercise."

Figure 4.5 The opening scene in *Thimbleweed Park*, where again extensive use of dithering techniques was applied. This time though, it was a deliberate artistic choice, not a way to work around hardware limitations. Can you again spot Mark Ferrari's signature checkerboard pattern in the sky?

The game was originally created as an 8-bit homebrew homage to *Grand Theft Auto* on the Nintendo Entertainment System. Provinciano somehow even managed to build his own NES development kit to help overcome the limitations of the old console. This guy clearly knows how to work with constraints. Provinciano managed to squeeze his game onto a single 1.44-MB floppy disk, running smoothly on my 486DX2-66 retro PC. A Game Boy Advance port is on the way—another challenging passion project. Curious programmers wanting to learn more about bit shifting and floating-point optimizations can watch Provinciano's GDC 2016 talk at https://youtu.be/kSKeWH4TY9Y.

Does this mean that creativity is reserved for game art?

Of course not. While this chapter indeed contains ample examples from the video gaming world, there's a specific reason for doing so. Game development showcases many interdisciplinary factors that each has to overcome very clear intrinsic, imposed, and self-imposed constraints, making these examples the perfect fit to explain the concepts behind creative software constrainedness.

> *(continued)*
> I don't want you to think that creativity is exclusively reserved for pixel artists like Mark Ferrari just because there are colors involved or the term "art" happens to be used. As I hope you're aware of by now, *any* programmer can be a creative programmer: creativity isn't limited to the arts. We'll delve more into the psychological mindset of creativity and its creative experts in chapter 7.

4.4.2   *Let limitations guide you to creative solutions*

The software-as-a-service company Basecamp is well aware of the beneficial effects of constraints, so much so that it actively imposes what seems to be an impossible six-week budget for most major product work. Instead of writing more and outperforming their competitors, the team at Basecamp decided to write less software and add fewer features and settings. Its self-imposed budget and business constraints paid off well: although its market share isn't big by any means, Basecamp is now a high-revenue company and is famous for its unconventional approaches to software development that should perhaps become the convention.

Build half a product. Underperform your competitors. Say no to meetings. Go to sleep. Grow slowly or not at all. Basecamp's collective business philosophy was written down in *Getting Real: The Smarter, Faster, Easier Way to Build a Web Application*,[9] and has constraint-based thinking placed front and center:

> *Constraints also force you to get your idea out in the wild sooner rather than later—another good thing. A month or two out of the gates you should have a pretty good idea of whether you're onto something or not. If you are, you'll be self-sustainable shortly and won't need external cash. If your idea's a lemon, it's time to go back to the drawing board. At least you know now as opposed to months (or years) down the road. And at least you can back out easily. Exit plans get a lot trickier once investors are involved.*

Basecamp proved that being mindful of the beneficial effects of constraints can put your product out there much sooner, even with a limited budget and a relatively small development team. It calls this strategy "shipping software on a budget" rather than "on a deadline." "Constraints will occasionally hurt—that's when you know it's working," says David Heinemeier Hansson, cofounder of Basecamp.

4.4.3   *Game Boying into constraints*

The Game Boy, first released in 1989, was one of the last dedicated 8-bit gaming devices and undoubtedly the weakest performing of its generation. This was far from a design flaw. The decision to use cheap and well-established technology in new ways fit right into Nintendo's philosophy. Gunpei Yokoi—the creator of the *Game & Watch* devices, the Game Boy, the D-pad, and the *Metroid* series—called it "Lateral Thinking With Withered Technology": fun and gameplay before cutting-edge technology, something that still stands when looking at Nintendo's later consoles such as the Wii and the recent Switch.

---

[9] The book is available for free at https://basecamp.com/gettingreal/.

Relying on "withered" technology came with more advantages besides reduced production costs: robustness and a huge battery life span, lasting up to 30 hours. That proved to be too tough to beat, although SEGA did try to put up a fight.

The as-advertised "more powerful" SEGA Game Gear was just as weak in reality, but it wasn't a case of lateral thinking: SEGA's rushed effort to quickly counterattack the Game Boy led to the recycling of older Master System hardware. As a result, the Game Gear, released one year after the Game Boy, also housed a variant of the Zilog Z80 8-bit CPU clocked at a meager 3.5 MHz. Strangely enough, it also has 8 KB work RAM, and even the screen has the same resolution as the Game Boy. The thing swallowed six AA batteries—two more than the Game Boy— that didn't even last five hours.

Nintendo's self-imposed design constraints may have led to many frustrating inherent constraints for game developers. There wasn't much to work with, the unlit screen struggled with ghosting problems, and "coding" was a matter of bit-shifting registers in Assembly.

Figure 4.6 The "living" proof of the Gray Brick's robustness: the GB of U.S. police officer Stephan Scoggins, destroyed during a bombing in Operation Desert Storm, still plays Tetris! Photo courtesy of Evan Amos.

NOTE Inventive hardware accessory companies made clever use of the GB's crappy screen to create the GB Light, the GB Magnifier, the "all in one accessory" Joyplus Handy Boy that came with two heavily amplified external speakers and an illuminated magnifier, the GBA Worm Light, the Hyperboy, the BoosterBoy, and more.

Super Mario Land, a 1989 launch game, clearly suffers from the multitude of limitations inherent to the GB. Barely any sprites are displayed on screen, everything has almost the same 8 × 8 sprite size, there are only four short worlds, and there's no way to save the game. For being an iconic Mario game, *Super Mario Land* is technically pretty unremarkable and hard to go back to these days.

Its successors, *Super Mario Land 2: Six Golden Coins* (1992), *Wario Land: Super Mario Land 3* (1994), and *Wario Land II* (1998) pulled out all the stops, as if the programmers were using other hardware. This effect is typical for a console: as it ages, developers get more familiar and creative with its limitations.

Wario Land games are filled to the brim with such creative tricks: coins that aren't sprites but part of the background to circumvent the arbitrary maximum number of

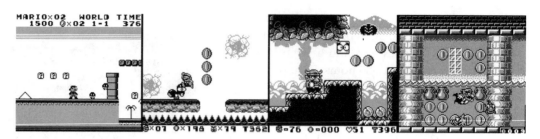

Figure 4.7   Nine years of *Super Mario/Wario Land* evolution, all released on the same platform

sprites the GB can handle; huge multi-sprite bosses to sidestep sprite dimension limits; multi-sprite coins that allow coins to be drawn with four colors instead of the usual three because of the transparency system; smart palette swapping to create variations of enemies or when Wario is hit to avoid cluttering VRAM with yet another sprite; exploiting the GB render loop timing to create visually appealing warp effects; background layers scrolling at different speeds to create the illusion of floating water; and more.

Recent GB ROM disassembly projects, such as *Pokémon* and *Links Awakening DX,*[10] provide insight into how these tricks were implemented. I can imagine developers were over the moon when the 2001 32-bit Game Boy Advance (GBA) finally allowed them some wiggle room and, more important, to program in C.

The Game Boy systems are fondly looked back on. Recent open source cross-compilers such as GBDK and devkitPro make programming on older hardware a little more pleasant, with a C compiler for the GB and a C++11 compiler for the GBA. The GB and GBA even occasionally see new commercial game releases, such as *Deadus, The Shapeshifter,* and *Goodboy Galaxy.* If you're inclined to sharpen your Assembly skills, dip a toe into the source code of *µCity,* a *Sim City* clone for the Game Boy Color, available at https://github.com/AntonioND/ucity.

> **NOTE**   For more information on Game Boy programming, see https://github .com/gbdk-2020/gbdk-2020 and https://devkitpro.org/wiki/Getting_Started. If you're scared of CLI and Makefiles (you call yourself a programmer?), GB Studio (https://www.gbstudio.dev/) is a great integrated alternative that enables visual game building without requiring any programming knowledge.

Teaching hardware/software co-design

At our local faculty of engineering technology, the GB(A) devices are used as welcome pedagogical tools to teach students low-level programming (pointers to memory-mapped IO in C), high-level programming (OO in C++), and hardware architecture (CPU implementations).

---

[10] See https://github.com/zladx/LADX-Disassembly.

Using a game device in class obviously piques motivation, but the most interesting part about a 30-year-old 8-bit device is that *everything* can be explained and understood. This is simply impossible to do with modern hardware as technology nowadays dictates too much specialism.

It's always entertaining to see students struggle with the tight hardware constraints. "Why can't I display this photo onscreen?" Perhaps because you unconsciously overflowed the GBA's 96 KB VRAM? "How big is your photo?" I then ask. "Oh, this one is really small, like 2 megs!" We're spoiled brats who, as hardware evolved, got very lazy.

4.4.4 Limited (fantasy) consoles

It would be naive to deny the influence of nostalgia on the recent GB game releases. Childhood memories are not the only reason why game developers are still attracted to Nintendo's retro consoles: self-imposing hardware constraints facilitate the creation of unusual and original games. Any limited environment would do.

Lexaloffle Games understood the creative appeal of self-imposed limits well. In 2015, it created a Lua virtual machine that can run in the browser and includes an 8-bit sprite and map editor, calling it the PICO-8, Lexaloffle Games' 1980s "fantasy video game console." Its specs immediately remind me of console hardware of yore: a resolution of 128×128 pixels with 16 colors, 32 KB cartridge size, and maximum 256 8×8 sprites. Lexaloffle Games' philosophy states:

> *The harsh limitations of PICO-8 are carefully chosen to be fun to work with, to encourage small but expressive designs, and to give cartridges made with PICO-8 their own particular look and feel.*

"Cartridges" are easily shared thanks to the cart browser called SPLORE, available at https://www.lexaloffle.com/pico-8.php. The convenience of an integrated toolkit combined with the creative environment makes the PICO-8 an often-picked development platform in game jams and on https://itch.io/. The original version of *Celeste*, the critically acclaimed and very challenging 2018 2D platform game, was made in just four days in PICO-8 during a game jam.

EXERCISE See if you can figure out what to do with the following code:

```
switch(timeToSpareInDays) {
  case > 5: downloadDevKitProAndCrossCompileForGBAYourself()
  case > 2: downloadGBStudioToDesignA2DJRPGAdventure()
  case > 1: downloadPICO8AndCreateA2DPlatformer()
  default : throw "Drop this book and get back to work,
      this ain't gonna work"
}
```

You'll be surprised how much can be done—and how much fun it is—in just a few hours of fiddling with the PICO-8. Although it is not free ($14.99 at the time of this writing), its official manual and unofficial game development guide are much better maintained than the docs page of its free counterpart, the TIC-80.

To squeeze even more fun out of this exercise, enlist a few friends or colleagues. This also makes for a great hackathon where results can be shared afterward—even if you have zero aspirations to become a game developer. It's a master class in working with constraints (especially if you add a tight deadline like in game jams or hackathon sessions), not necessarily in game design.

Fantasy consoles like the PICO-8 are virtual machines, but new and tangible hardware inspired by old technology also exists. The ZX Spectrum Next, an 8-bit computer released in 2017, is such a device (figure 4.8). It's compatible with all software and hardware for the original 1982 ZX Spectrum, Britain's best-selling home microcomputer from the eighties developed by Sinclair Research.

The original Speccy is similar in power to the Game Boy, also housing a variant of the Z80 CPU running at 3.5 MHz. Compared with its ancestor, the ZX Spectrum Next is a powerhouse: it uses the FPGA technology to faithfully reimplement variations of the 8-bit CPU. This means it can dynamically change its clock speed up to 28 MHz, thus maintaining compatibility with later Spectrum revisions.

Figure 4.8   A rendering of the ZX Spectrum Next, which inherited the sleek design of Sinclair's original but gained a lot of contemporary trinkets, such as an HDMI port and an SD card slot

Next to appealing to retrocomputing fans like me, the goal of Speccy's new old hardware is to "encourage a new generation of creative bedroom coders," according to veteran game programmer and ZX Next co-designer Jim Bagley.[11] The NextZXOS-powered machine ships with an extensive NextBASIC programming manual that encourages aspiring programmers to pick it up and play/code. It's up to you to decide how much constraint to impose: whether or not to stick with the Spectrum's distinct blueish 4-bit RGBI look and whether or not to tap into the Next's Wi-Fi capabilities to produce small multiplayer games, British retro vibes included.

The ZX Spectrum Next produced a slew of creative "new old games" that benefit from the Next's modern hardware trinkets while staying true to the ideas and

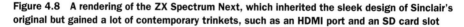

[11] See the interview in MagPi magazine at https://magpi.raspberrypi.com/articles/zx-spectrum-next-raspberry-pi-project-showcase.

limitations of the original Spectrum. And yes, some games developed on the Next were released on cassette tapes that can even be played on your 40-year-old Speccy!

Fans of its competitors at that time—the Commodore 64, the BBC Micro, and the Amstrad CPC—aren't left in the cold: the creative retrocomputing community constantly reinvents classic hardware using FPGAs, opening up these superb pieces of hardware for a new audience to enjoy. Be warned though: its 8-bit limitations take some getting used to.

4.4.5   Limited programming languages

Technological self-imposed constraints don't have to be restricted to hardware requirements: they can just as easily be baked into programming languages. A prime example is Go, the statically typed, C-like compiled language with the added benefits of memory safety, garbage collection, and structural typing. Go was designed to keep the language specification footprint small enough to "hold everything into a programmer's head," according to Rob Pike, one of Go's co-designers. Rob and the Go team share many insights from a language designing perspective at https://go.dev/blog/.

What does that mean, to hold it into your head? It primarily means an *absence* of concepts you might be used to in other languages. For instance, there is no functional `map()`, `filter()`, or `reduce()` utilities; you'll have to make do with a simple `for {}` loop—which happens to be the only way to construct a loop: no `while {}`, no `do {}`. Delightfully boring and liberating at the same time! There aren't even any exceptions built into the language, and there's a very good reason for that: to enforce explicit error handling at the function level, not at the system level.

I love programming in Go precisely because it's that simple. Sure, the ANSI C specification chart also fits comfortably on two A4 pages, but C's age and thus lack of first-class functions and any composition pattern combined with endless `malloc (sizeof(x))` and `free()` statements make it a bit of a drag.

Don't take my word for it. Go started appearing in many "Top 10 Most Popular Programming Languages" lists—it's even the fifth-most-loved language of 2020, according to Stack Overflow, beaten by Kotlin, Python, TypeScript, and Rust.[12] C takes fifth place on the "Most Dreaded" list. I doubt it'll ever dethrone VBA.

Go is slowly but surely gaining traction in the enterprise software development world. Code formatting and test-driven development tools are built into the language, parallelism is cheap and easy to do, and Go enthusiasts (better known as *Gophers*) proved that "simple" languages such as Go excel at readability, drastically reducing communication mismatches, code review disagreements, and, ultimately, project costs. Because of its limitations, Go can be seen as boring, but boring is the new exciting.

Furthermore, Go's (self-)imposed limitations also spark creativity. Simply take a look at recent Go projects—and their source code—that are lauded for their high efficiency and original feature set: PhotoPrism, an AI-powered app for browsing, sharing, and organizing your photo collection; Navidrome, a personal music streaming server;

---

[12] See https://insights.stackoverflow.com/survey/2020.

Gitea, a "painless" self-hosted git service; Drone, a continuous integration platform; Hugo, a blazing fast and flexible static website generator; Listmonk, an easy self-hosted newsletter solution; Commento, a privacy-aware comments widget; and so on.

4.4.6   *Crack intros and the demoscene*

A long time ago, I messed around with keygens. Don't worry; I'm clean now, although I couldn't quite shake the catchy 8-bit chiptune music. A keygen program, or a cracked executable that removes the copyright protection, usually came with custom intro sequences to inform the defaulter which cracking crew they were dealing with.

Since a crack involves intricate hacking in assembly (imposed constraints), the intros, too, started involving creative and often-undocumented tricks with the equipped CPU and GPU (self-imposed constraints). Sometimes, the crack intro was even more complex than the cracked software. Crackers sure found a clever way to show off their hacking skills!

Eventually, cracking evolved into what Eurogamer calls an "interactive art experience,"[13] thankfully leaving the illegal part behind. The demoscene subculture comes with many implicit rules, such as emphasizing originality (what they label *creativity*) over ripping works or assets of others.

Typical coding competitions mandate intro binaries of only 64 KB—or sometimes even 4 KB. It takes plenty of creative effort to pull together such a feat. The demoscene is a masterclass in constraint-based programming. Search on YouTube for "64k intro" and judge for yourself. If that gets you in a hacking mood, indie game website Itch.io also frequently hosts 4 KB game competitions.

In 2020, Finland accepted the demoscene on its national UNESCO list of intangible cultural heritages of humanity, followed by Germany in 2021. It is the first digital subculture to make it to a cultural heritage list. Without rigorous adherence to self-created bounds, these small intros wouldn't be considered digital art. In the demoscene, rigorous self-imposed constraints pave the way for original visualizations and chiptune music that would never see the light without creating and adhering to your own roadblocks.

> **EXERCISE** Next time you're in a creative rut, try self-imposing *more* constraints instead of wrapping your head around the existing ones. For example, what if you were to write that piece without using loops? Or without that client-server round trip? Or without querying the database? The imaginary application of invented constraints is sure to spark an idea or two for the actual problem—it doesn't even have to be implemented.

4.5   *Hitting that sweet spot*

Constraints are the fertile ground for creativity. But what happens when you add too much fertilizer to your vegetable garden? Tomato plant roots get burned. Add too little,

---

[13] Dan Whitehead. Linger in shadows: Scene but not heard. Eurogamer, 2008. https://www.eurogamer.net/articles/ linge r-in-shadows-hands-on.

and your precious *Cœur de bœuf* will more likely resemble a sour cherry tomato. Add too much, and the plant dies. The same is true for constraints: Michael Mose Biskjaer talks about the *sweet spot*.[14] Time for another inverted U-curve, as shown in figure 4.9.

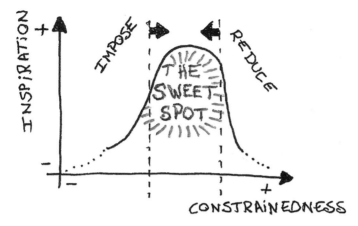

Figure 4.9   **The constrainedness sweet spot, representing perceived potential for creativity.**

The sweet spot sits comfortably between underconstrainedness and overconstrainedness, not unlike Mihaly Csikszentmihalyi's concept of flow. Too little flow equals repeating boring tasks over and over again. Too much of it and the task at hand is perceived as too difficult, impeding the learning process.

The y-axis denotes the level of inspiration, also varying between too little (there won't be any idea to work with) and too much (chaos and no time to Catch 'Em All, even though you Gotta). Note that Biskjaer writes about *sources of inspiration*, hinting at our personal knowledge management system—or the inspiration *engine*—unveiled in chapter 2.

To deliberately reach the sweet spot and increase the x factor, induce self-imposed constraints. To alleviate constraint pressure and decrease x, reduce constraints, for example, by temporarily removing or ignoring them. It's all about striking a balance.

In practice, the sweet spot concept as a theoretical model never completely resembles its paper definition. Novices and creative experts will more than likely handle constraints differently. Bear in mind that, as with all things creative, constraint limits are personal and inherent to constant change.

A team-based sweet spot value might not even begin to approach your individual golden mean—or might exceed your personal limit. Being well attuned to the project constraints and figuring out a shared sweet spot again puts emphasis on the communication concepts introduced in chapter 3.

---

[14] Michael Mose Biskjaer, Bo T Christensen, Morten Friis-Olivarius, Sille JJ Abildgaard, Caroline Lundqvist, and Kim Halskov. How task constraints affect inspiration search strategies. International Journal of Technology and Design Education, 2020.

4.5.1   *Facilitating abstraction with the right amount of constraints*

What if just the right amount of constrainedness could improve your ability to abstract when problem solving? Abstraction plays a key role in both efficient and creative problem solving. Australian computer scientist Cruz Izu developed a classification for abstraction by studying how students tackle programming problems.[15] She presented students with a simple case that can be approached from different angles: the "Egg Cartons" problem (see sidebar).

> **The Egg Cartons problem**
>
> There are two possible egg carton sizes: one contains 6 eggs and another 8. You want to buy exactly N eggs. What is the minimum number of cartons to buy? If it's impossible to buy exactly N eggs, return -1. In other words, implement `minCartons(N int) int`.
>
> For example, `minCartons(20)` returns 3: we buy two cartons of 6 eggs and one of 8. `minCartons(7)` returns -1 since we can't buy an odd number of eggs. See if you can figure this out for yourself before reading on!

Suppose we're not worried about constraints for a minute. What would be the easiest way to approach such a problem? Right, a *brute force* approach: all potential solutions are tested for feasibility. Izu calls this "Level Zero": you haven't discovered interesting properties of the problem yet that could simplify the approach.

What if I told you to first look for specific cases and handle those differently? Enter constraint number 1 and abstraction level 1: the problem space is somewhat adjusted to the assignment using special cases. For our Egg Cartons problem, are there any upper or lower bounds to take into account? Yes! Since we want to buy *exactly* N eggs, anything lower than 6 won't generate a feasible solution. There's another special case, but before spoiling it, I'll let you think about that for a while.[16]

Okay, you've got your basic brute force loop and a few special cases set, but we can do better. Here's constraint number 2: solve a few examples by hand with pen and paper. Can you spot a pattern that way? All right, we reached abstraction level 2! Take a look at the following sequences:

```
12 {6, 6} -> 14 {8, 6} -> 16 {8, 8} -> 18 {6, 6, 6}
20 {8, 6, 6} -> 22 {8, 8, 6} -> 24 {8, 8, 8} -> 26 {8, 6, 6, 6}
```

Do you notice anything unusual? The pattern can be summarized in two steps:

1 If there is a 6-egg carton, replace it with an 8-egg one.

2 If not, replace two 8-egg cartons with three 6-egg ones.

---

[15] Cruz Izu. Modelling the use of abstraction in algorithmic problem solving. Proceedings of the 27th ACM Conference on Innovation and Technology in Computer Science Education, 2022. The Egg Carton example is taken from the paper.

[16] We know odd numbers are problematic, but is there an even number without a solution as well? (Hint: 10)

These two steps can then be easily translated into code. All that remains is to check if our discovered pattern works for all numbers, for example, by testing the logic with a large multiple of 8.

We're not done yet. The Egg Cartons problem can be solved without a single loop—there's constraint number 3. Can you figure out how? Perhaps the introduction of the third constraint pushes you beyond your personal sweet spot, and if that's the case, that's totally okay! Abstraction level 3 is called *mathematical abstraction*—if a discovered pattern is regular, it can usually be described mathematically in a model instead of generating values step by step. Whether or not this leads to easily maintainable code is another question.

For the Egg Cartons problem, the remainder of `n/8` can be used to determine the amount of 6-egg cartons to use. This is possible because `minCartons(22)` and `min-Cartons(24)` both return 3: after all, we're only interested in the total number of cartons.

A possible solution using portions of levels 1 and 3 could be as follows:

```
func minCartons(n int) int {
    switch {
            case n < 6 || n == 10: return -1
            case n % 8 == 0: return n / 8
            default: return n / 8 + 1
    }
}
```

I would never have discovered this solution without explicitly having to come up with an implementation that does not involve looping (constraint number 3).

Another technique that you're perhaps inclined to reach for is writing unit tests first that cover every possible scenario. This can also be considered a (self-imposed) constraint that pushes you toward the sweet spot. By considering test cases, you almost automatically uncover patterns that can be put to good use in the production code.

4.5.2   *Sweetness or bitterness?*

As sweet as the victory of overcoming limitations can be, that sweetness might leave a bitter aftertaste. The constrainedness sweet spot may not necessarily be sweet. Creativity may be severely painful and a formidable struggle.

History books burst with tales of suffering artists and authors who went through processes of artistic creation heavily intertwined with periods of misery. Vincent van Gogh's schizophrenia and bipolar disorder that caused him to cut off his own ear; Virginia Woolf's declining mental health that ultimately led to her suicide; and August Strindberg's constant struggle with mental illness are a few.

The constraint sweet spot is *highly desirable*, rewarding the right amount of creative freedom. It doesn't mean it's an awesomely good deal. Some artists go as far as cultivating both curiosity and misery to optimize their creative process. Hervé Guibert, a French writer and photographer and a close friend of philosopher Michel Foucault, neatly summarized it as follows: "Must the artist not have left a foot in his childhood, and projected the other one into his grave?"[17]

Guibert succumbed to AIDS just before turning 36. Is romanticizing death a way to induce a constraint that can facilitate creativity? At the danger of becoming too macabre: perhaps. Artists have shown that thinking about the inevitable end benefited their work. The symbolic saying *Memento mori* ("Remember that you die"), typically depicted in paintings as a flower, a skull, and an hourglass—life, death, and time— serves as such a reminder.

Medieval artists perhaps took this concept a bit too far by creating *vanitas* paintings, showing the worthlessness of life and the futility of pleasure. It also provided a moral justification to paint skulls, books, and withering flowers instead of typical Christian scenes.

The morbid connection between creativity and mortality motivated researchers to dig up the scary-sounding "terror management theory," supporting the notion that creativity plays an important role in the management of existential concerns. Having one foot in the grave boosts creativity, and creativity boosts our resistance to existential anxiety.[18] Creating something that outlasts our feeble bodies can be seen as an attempt to aim for immortality.

Creative people are sometimes obsessed with their work, which can have detrimental effects on mental health, including the mental health of those close to them. Please remember that work is only work: there's more to life than the constant dopamine rush of the creative flow.

> **EXERCISE**   Some problems are more easily solved when one explicitly ignores certain constraints by taking the problem outside of its hardware and software context. For example, consider programming the tile-based dominoes game. Its rules (matching pairs) still count as constraints, but thinking about how to solve a game without a computer won't encumber you with recursion, backtracking, and stack overflow memory problems. Once the concept of a solver has taken form, *only then* translate it into code to face additional challenges. Congrats, you've hit that sweet spot!

4.6   *Working with constraints in practice*

How do you transcend the many intrinsic, imposed, and self-imposed constraints that come with a software development project? The constrainedness sweet spot suggests imposing or reducing constraints if inspiration is running a bit low. There are a few practical ways to do this, of which we'll explore divergent thinking and naivety in the following sections. More examples will be interwoven in the coming chapters.

---

[17] Hervé Guibert. The mausoleum of lovers: Journals 1976–1991. Nightboat Books, 2014.

[18] Rotem Perach and Arnaud Wisman. Can creativity beat death? A review and evidence on the existential anxiety buffering functions of creative achievement. The Journal of Creative Behavior, 2019.

4.6.1 Divergent thinking

In the seventies, when academic creativity research was a brand-new field, researchers thought that the only way to overcome constraints was by thinking outside of the box. At that time, researcher Paul Torrance developed the Torrance Test of Creative Thinking or TTCT.[19] Academics are always looking to measure and quantify things, including creativity. A high score on the TTCT was assumed to be an excellent indicator of high creative potential, while in fact all it measures is your divergent thinking skills—a small subset of what psychologists nowadays consider as defining creativity.

Unfortunately, the vast majority of computing education researchers and educators still cling to outdated concepts such as the TTCT, as it's one of the most commonly cited and readily available creativity measurement tools.[20] Remember that there's more to creativity than a dull brainstorming session.

Divergent thinking is in fact (imposed) constraint-based thinking. It's improvising and coming up with a lot of original uses based on tight constraints. For example, in the TTCT that shape you're given a basic starting shape, such as a circle, and asked to use or combine that shape with a picture. If you see a circle and draw a smiley or the world, like thousands did before you, that's not very creative. On the other hand, if you decide to draw a coconut tree out of circles, like I did in figure 4.10, that could be considered more creative.

Figure 4.10   A TTCT test in action. I hope I did well! You can assess multiple factors here: how many unique drawings can you come up with, and how many of these deviate from the average drawing?

The question here is, are we really testing *creativity* here, as a systemic and sociocultural concept? I highly doubt it. Yet when we asked developers how they assess creativity—for example, in job interviews—they unanimously answer with a divergent-thinking

[19] E. Paul Torrance. Predictive validity of the Torrance Tests of Creative Thinking. The Journal of Creative Behavior, 1972.

[20] Wouter Groeneveld, Brett A Becker, and Joost Vennekens. How creatively are we teaching and assessing creativity in computing education?: A systematic literature review. Proceedings of the 2022 ACM Conference on Innovation and Technology in Computer Science Education, 2022.

technique. Of course, seeing how somebody performs at improvisation exercises is much more tangible than how well the person is connected within their liquid network(s).

Many tech interviews include behavioral questions that gauge creative potential by asking how you handle imposed constraints. GitHub is sprawling with curated lists of interview questions that might be worth looking into if you're curious.

During our interviews, one developer mentioned the card game *Black Stories* by Holger Bösch, which has you thinking outside the box to resolve dark and morbid riddles. Each card tells the story of a tragic murder you'll have to solve using just the title and one sentence to set the scene. Then, it's up to the group to come up with an original and fitting cause of death. The back of the card describes the solution, which can sometimes be a bit far-fetched.

Black Stories has been published by more than 18 companies and, the last time I counted on BoardGameGeek.com, has 21 different versions. Perhaps this isn't that shocking: people are drawn to mysteries, the game is very easy to play, there are virtually no rules, and everybody loves blurting out extreme death scenarios. It's even easy to adapt to the world of programming! How about this:

Title: **The Blog**.[21]

Wouter pushed his latest blog post to his Git repository, expecting it to be picked up by the build system to be published. Five minutes later, Wouter's blog was offline.

EXERCISE Can you come up with other possible, less exceptional and perhaps more plausible causes of the sudden outage? Think of at least five different things that technically could be the culprit. How about another five causes?

I might go ahead and produce 50 of those, calling it *Crash Stories*. Don't you dare try to beat me to it!

4.6.2   *Naivety and constraints*

A dangerous overabundance of constraints can cause creatives to reject ideas that are otherwise worth exploring further. Have you ever attended a brainstorming session where ideas were crossed out as soon as they were posed because "It's just not possible" or "The server is not up to it"? In that case, a certain amount of naivety helps. Instead of immediately thinking of the existing system and its constraints, pretend you know nothing and simply generate ideas. Decide which ideas to implement after they have been gathered.

Researchers rarely recognize naivety as an important ingredient of creativity. Psychology researchers John Gero and Mary Lou Maher state that creativity is seldom the result of naivety, but rather it results from the ability of a highly intelligent person to

---

[21] The solution: the data center where Wouter rents a virtual private server was on fire. Yes, this actually happened. And no, I did not have backups of everything. Lesson learned!

Figure 4.11   A *Black Stories* card. Left, the story: "Because the moon was at full strength, Heidi did not find out who the murderer was." Right, the solution: "Heidi was lying on the beach reading a detective story when she fell asleep. She was still sleeping when the tide came in and swept the book away forever." *Black Stories* card, © Holger Bösch, published by Moses and others.

put different ideas together and recognize their value.[22] Luckily, that outdated early-nineties definition of creativity is recently starting to be refuted by academics who do see the potential of naivety.

Academic philosopher and creativity critic Caterina Moruzzi mentions naivety next to problem solving and evaluation as an important feature of creativity.[23] She relates naivety to various aspects that in the literature have a place among the core traits of creativity: spontaneity, unconscious thought processing, challenging domain norms, and independence from rigid structures of thought.

Naivety can be a childlike, playful trait of creativity. It can also denote a lack of previous exposure to the properties of the situation at hand, leaning into ignorance. Sometimes, ignorance is bliss! We'll briefly explore two cases of naivety where constraints were overcome thanks to these interpretations.

---

[22] John S. Gero and Mary Lou Maher. Modeling creativity and knowledge-based creative design. Psychology Press, 2013.

[23] Caterina Moruzzi. Measuring creativity: an account of natural and artificial creativity. European Journal for Philosophy of Science, 2021.

4.6.3   *A naive but legendary poet*

Hilde Domin, a renowned German poet interviewed by Mihaly Csikszentmihalyi, talks about her difficulties in getting accepted in the manly world of poetry. She thinks she persisted because she wasn't fully aware of the hidden literary power struggle that took place near her:[24]

> *I was very naive. I don't know why, but that's how I was. I did not believe in literary intrigues and that sort of stuff, a literary mafia. To me, work was work, and it still is.*

It took six years before one of her poems was published. It was very difficult as a woman to make a successful living in the literary world of the fifties, especially since Domin was patronized by her jealous husband who at first couldn't accept the possibility of her being more successful. The then-young Domin was very susceptible to the vulnerability of women in the art world.

The romanticized scenario where the genius always breaks through, regardless of the setbacks the artist has to face, was and still is more fiction than reality. But instead of giving up because of the setbacks (or constraints), Domin naively persisted, and eventually she became one of the most important German-language poets of her time. She continues: "Mallarmé says that a poem is like a rocket: it just lifts off. Maybe he's right. But it of course can be sabotaged. By jealousy. I think that's the right word."[25]

4.6.4   *A naive James Bond*

Naivety can sometimes yield groundbreaking results. Another superb example in the software world is the 007-themed Nintendo 64 game *GoldenEye*. Rare's 1997 first-person shooter (FPS) pioneered body-specific hit reactions through motion capture, sniper rifles and dual-wielding guns, environmental reflection mapping, and split-screen death matches—all features that would become standards in the shooter genre. The game shifted a staggering eight million copies, breaking into the Top 3 Nintendo 64 games, next to behemoths *Mario 64* and *Mario Kart 64*—even beating Nintendo's iconic *The Legend of Zelda: Ocarina of Time*!

As the majority of Rare's 007 team then had no prior development experience whatsoever, they were completely unaware of the notions of what was and wasn't possible in game design or on the Nintendo 64's hardware. If they thought of a good idea, they just tried implementing it.

In a *Retro Gamer* interview, producer and director Martin Hollis admits that a bit of naivety and inexperience might have helped shape *GoldenEye*'s future. When asked if there was an advantage to *GoldenEye* being their first game, that the team didn't know what they could and couldn't do, Hollis replied:[26]

> *Oh certainly. I didn't know what we couldn't do either. It was supposed to be a three person project and take nine months or something. No one told me it would take three years and about ten people because no one knew.*

---

[24] Mihaly Csikszentmihalyi. Creativity: Flow and the psychology of discovery and invention. HarperPerennial, 1997.
[25] Ibid.
[26] See Retro Gamer's *100 Games To Play Before You Die: Nintendo Consoles Edition*, p. 144.

Figure 4.12 A hectic *GoldenEye* death match in four-player split-screen action. Imagine lots of swearing and couch jumping—possibly even controller throwing and ducking. That is the unintended but real legacy of *GoldenEye*!

Multiplayer madness

The multiplayer addition to *GoldenEye* that many gamers so fondly remember was an afterthought that almost didn't make it into the game: it was worked in just six months before the release date. Lunchtimes at Rare were spent playing *Bomberman* and early prototypes of *Mario 64*, sparking the idea of frantic split-screen shooter action. The team didn't know whether it would work until they started developing it, almost immediately hitting frame-rate constraints—only partially solving the problem by mostly limiting the multiplayer maps to small low-poly areas. More seasoned game developers would probably not even have tried. If Rare hadn't, I doubt *GoldenEye* would have been fondly remembered.

GoldenEye evolved the FPS genre that *DOOM* popularized: from collecting colored key cards in puzzle-like maps and shooting monsters to more Bond-like gadgetry approaches and story-driven objectives. Without the team's naive approach to implementing ideas that might have been dismissed otherwise, there would be no memorable *Half-Life* and other big FPS hits.

Naivety can get you further than you think. Even if you are aware of the constraining factors of a given project, it might pay to adopt a naive mindset to discover what is possible in the unexplored areas of the constrained design space.

4.6.5   *Naive algorithm implementations*

Over the years, many implemented algorithms start out too complicated because we, as programming experts, are immediately thinking about possible consequences that, in practice, (almost) never occur. Our previous failures still haunt us, so this time it better be resilient! By not adopting a naive mindset, solutions are quickly overengineered: two layers of caching are introduced "just in case," a piece of code suddenly becomes yet another dependency instead of a copy because "it might be reused," servers are load-balanced without testing the load because "you never know." Sound familiar?

Algorithms usually come in different shapes and forms, of which the naive approach is usually the simplest and most readable. Of course, sometimes the implementation doesn't pass the stress test. As a simple example, consider the Fibonacci sequence. Each number is calculated by adding the two preceding numbers, and the sequence starts with 0 and 1. $0 + 1 = 1$, $1 + 1 = 2$, and so forth. A naive but still highly useful recursive implementation would be as follows:

```
func Fibonacci(n int) int {
    if n <= 1 return n
    return Fibonacci(n - 1) + Fibonacci(n - 2)
}
```

Simple and readable: exactly like we want our functions to be. Except that if we put in a big number, like 50, the result (1,258,626,9025) will take a minute because the stack exploded in size since we constantly recalculate already known Fibonacci numbers. Possible solutions would be to optimize the function with a technique called *memoization* or *tail recursion*:

```
func fibonacciTail(n, a, b int) int {
    if n <= 1 return b
    return fibonacciTail(n - 1, b, a + b)
}
func Fibonacci(n int) int {
    return fibonacciTail(n, 0, 1)
}
```

This is arguably still readable but a lot less simple, even though we dramatically improved the performance of our Fibonacci function: it now only increases the stack n times. The danger of starting with those optimizations—because of pressure from various constraints or nightmares from the past—is resulting in needlessly complicated solutions or, worse, no solution at all, because we're stuck in a certain way of thinking. The takeaway here is this: to get the creative flow going, always start with a naive approach. Only then take a step back and consider improving things.

> **EXERCISE**   What if you could bring a bit of healthy naivety into your daily programming practice by not immediately following your expert judgment? Next time when facing a problem, pretend you don't know the constraints and let your imagination run wild. This might yield more interesting approaches to tackling the problem.

Summary

- A taxonomy of beneficial constraints that aids our creative problem-solving skills consists of intrinsic and imposed constraints (incidental) and self-imposed constraints (essential).

- The harsh intrinsic hardware constraints that seem to work against you can actually be put to your creative advantage when working with them instead of against them.

- Even when stumbling about in old Visual Basic brownfield projects, adhering to modern software development best practices and ideals is possible. You just have to find a way to massage the imposed constraints.

- Keeping quiet about identified constraints is never a good idea. It might affect your team, your software, and ultimately your clients.

- In the same vein, never shoot down an idea too soon because "it can't be done" before figuring out if it can't be done.

- There is a sweet spot for constrainedness. Drowning in constraints will prevent you from reaching your creative potential. Be mindful when self-imposing constraints that might race well past that sweet spot.

- Self-imposing constraints not only gets you closer to a creative solution; it also battles boredom and mediocrity.

- The naive excitement of your inner child should not always be oppressed. That voice might help you tackle that particularly difficult constraint.

- Divergent thinking can also help when working with constraints. Just be sure not to pay too much attention to various divergent-thinking tests. Creativity is much more than just lateral thinking.

Critical thinking 5

The chaotic mixture of loud voices and fragrant spices marks yet another busy day at the agora, the hub of the ancient Athenian empire. Shopkeepers are engaged in a fierce bidding war to get rid of their dried fish, olives, sandals, dirt on local politicians, amphorae, goat milk, lawsuits, givers of evidence, figs, and bread. You want something; they've got it. In the midst of the yelling and cursing, a stocky and aging man—barefooted and flat nosed, almost unkempt—felt right at home. Socrates peppered every single being he encountered with annoying questions during his daily strolls in the vicinity of the agora. His motto was "Know what you don't know."

On the other side of Athens, sophist teachers specializing in subjects such as mathematics, music, philosophy, or—the gods forbid—a craft were busy teaching virtues to the few wealthy Greeks who could afford it. Sophists, traveling experts and skilled talkers, had one thing in common: whatever they did not know, they pretended to know to impress or persuade their audience. A few sophists even claimed to have the answers to all questions.

Whom should one turn to when in dire need of knowledge: a weird old man pretending to know nothing, posing question after question, or a deceitful wordsmith assuring you he's got all the answers? Socrates' "Know what you don't know" was, during his lifetime, mostly met with disdain. Athenians were easily seduced by the many (and almost exclusively manly) rhetorical speeches of the sophists. Even Socrates at one point admitted to being less skillful than some genuine sophists, sending one of his pupils off to learn from them. Plato would later depict the sophists as stingy instructors who taught nothing but deceit.

Twenty centuries later, the hollow clunks of empty bottles carelessly pushed against each other fill an otherwise-silent laboratory in Paris, France. Louis Pasteur, preoccupied and bent over a small cup of souring wine, would need just a few more weeks before summarizing his thoughts on alcoholic fermentation, or the lack thereof, in sterilized and sealed flasks. Instead of agreeing with fellow chemist Justus von Liebig, who thought fermentation was simply the result of "organic decomposition," Pasteur proved it was the naturally present yeast that produced alcohol from sugar.

During the 1850s, the existence of microorganisms such as yeasts and lactic acid bacteria was up for heavy debate. How can something we cannot see nor smell be part of fermentation, an ancient and important phenomenon once attributed to the gods? Louis Pasteur and his sterilized bottles shook up the 19th century's surprisingly sophistic and narrow-minded way of thinking by demonstrating the process, ultimately winning countless awards and financial support, enabling him to expand his laboratory into the Pasteur Institute it is now. Pasteur's demonstrations succeeded in convincing people, where others, many years before him, had not.

People unwilling to believe in microorganisms weren't the only ones to partake in (self-)deceit. The now-legendary genius Louis Pasteur also had dirty secrets to hide, trusted only to his laboratory notebook, which was kept private for another century, until Gerald L. Geison published *The Private Science of Louis Pasteur*.[1] This work revealed several misleading and deceitful tricks Pasteur used to keep ahead of his adversaries, including stealing ideas and discoveries. This resulted in a lifelong plagiarism battle with Antoine Béchamp, a chemistry professor in Montpellier, who (of course) regarded himself as the first discoverer of the role of microorganisms in fermentation.

Let's fast forward another century. The almost-hypnotizing hum of several heavy-duty computer fans slowly but steadily fill a nondescript office with heat. The computers and employees of Grove Street Games, stationed in Gainesville, Florida, are working overtime to meet the very tight deadline of their upcoming game *Grand Theft Auto: The Trilogy—The Definitive Edition*, in association with Rockstar Games. Textures are increased, meshes are cleaned up, lightning is improved, and superior weather effects are introduced.

---

[1] Gerald L. Geison, The private science of Louis Pasteur. Princeton University Press, 2014.

However, the efforts, mainly automated by AI upscalers,[2] produced uglier textures, too many meshes to run fluidly, harsh contrasts that break the game's atmosphere, and rain effects that look like God spilled a few jugs of milk. The remastering of classic *Grand Theft Auto* (*GTA*) games (*GTA III*, *GTA Vice City*, and *GTA San Andreas*; see figure 5.1) by porting assets from RenderWare into Unreal Engine 4 was initially met with high expectations. Messing with nostalgia can have devastating consequences—as can neglecting to critically review the 100,000 AI-powered upscaled assets.

Figure 5.1   See that bolt ("nut") to the right of the donut in the original *GTA San Andreas* screenshot? It somehow became a tire, killing the "Tuff Nut" joke in the process. Whether this is the result of the AI upscaler or a distracted designer who simply saw rough edges in dire need of rounding remains unknown. Screenshots courtesy of *RockmanBN*, ResetEra.

The game was reportedly in development for more than two years before it got slammed with negative responses, both from gaming critics and from gamers themselves. The *Definitive Edition* turned out to be far from definitive. Worse yet, Rockstar Games decided to pull the original *GTA* games from online stores, leaving gamers with fond memories of cruising cars on the beach while listening to the eighties-inspired *Flash FM* with no choice but to scour the secondhand market. Tuff Nut indeed.

5.1   *Creative critical thinking*

What is the greatest common divisor between Socrates' overabundant (self-)questioning and the sophists' lack thereof; the critical but wrong reception of microorganisms after their discovery; and Grove Street Games' failure to critically review the generated assets of their video game, resulting in a total bust? All three examples showcase various degrees of critical thinking—or a total lack thereof.

New inventions or ways of doing things are usually first met with skepticism. Athenians found Socrates' endless questioning method weird. It took a long time before the arrogant attitudes and accumulated wealth of the sophists led to resentment of their practices. Louis Pasteur wasn't the first to discover living microorganisms, and

---

[2] See The Gamer interview with Rockstar producer Rich Rosado at https://www.thegamer.com/gta-remastered-trilogy-rockstar-interview/.

yet once again denial was the easier option. Once his genius was finally acknowledged, it turned out that he was more of a con man, stealing creative ideas from others.

Grove Street Games' reliance on imperfect AI tech, probably combined with hefty deadline pressure from Rockstar, caused them to release an unfinished game that was universally destroyed by critics. A lot of creative effort by the development team showed potential that was never fully realized thanks to the uncritical insistence on the release date. Another month of intensive play-testing might have given *GTA Trilogy* the polish it very much needed. One day after its release, gamers posted videos of silly bugs, ruined jokes like the one depicted in figure 5.1, and random crashes, proving these problems weren't that hard to find.

Creative thinking alone is not enough: both *creative* and *critical* thinking are requirements to reap the fruits of creative labor. Creative thinking is needed to generate original ideas, to validate or reject ideas, to make timely adjustments to the creative process, to ask for and correctly interpret feedback, and to overcome the many cognitive biases formed in our heads. To better understand the relationship between creativity and critical thinking, let's take a more in-depth look at the typical creative process.

> **EXERCISE**   Is there a Socrates on your software development team who frequently questions the actions and roads taken? If not, shouldn't there be one? If so, is that person perceived as annoying because your team is afraid of the answers or because the modern Socrates incarnation exaggerates in their role as a coding critic?

5.2   *The creative process*

Both Pieter J. van Strien and Mihaly Csikszentmihalyi, well-respected creativity researchers who were introduced in the previous chapters, agree with the five stages of a creative process first identified by Graham Wallas in 1921 (figure 5.2):[3]

1   *Participate*—No creative product is the result of a sudden flash of insight: it's more likely the result of 90% transpiration through lengthy preparatory work and 10% illumination.

2   *Incubate*—A variable period where the creator takes distance (from the participation) and interrupts the process, speeding up insight unconsciously.

3   *Illuminate*—This will never happen without the sweat and tears from step 1.

4   *Verify*—Recognizing the fruit of the encounter: does it work? Is it worth it? If not, bin it, and restart.

5   *Present/Accept*—Only after the creation has been presented to and accepted by peers can it be called genuinely creative (see the sociocultural definition of creativity in the introduction).

Although a numbered enumeration usually hints at a sequential process, the creative process is anything but that: it is *recursive*. At any given time, a creator might jump

---

[3] Graham Wallas. Creative process. New American Library, 1921.

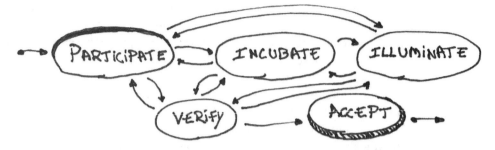

Figure 5.2   The five steps of the creative process. An overabundance of arrows emphasizes the interrelatedness among the steps. Participation is usually step 1, but a sudden idea might just as well put the process in motion. Rejection is not necessarily the end, provided enough energy remains to rework the concept.

back and forth between steps 1 to 4. Got a great idea (step 3)? Get back to it (step 1) to try it out. Stuck in a rut? Have a break (step 2), move on to something else, walk the dog, go for a run. But take Post-Its™ with you in case a lightbulb is turned on (step 3). Time to compile and execute the unit tests (step 4)! Didn't work? Back to square 1. The last step is obviously applicable only after verification.

Many people think that creativity is a matter of developing a single huge insight. Instead, it is about the subtle but constant interaction between all of the steps just described, as indicated by the arrows in figure 5.2. One measly "*Eureka!*"—or, aptly called by German psychologist Karl Bühler, an "*Aha-Erlebnis*"—won't get you very far. It probably wouldn't even drag me through the writing of the introduction of this book.

In a way, Wallas's nonlinear creative process is reminiscent of the test-driven development cycle: red (steps 1–3), green (step 4), refactor (steps 1–3). Nobody executes the `git push` command (step 5) with failing tests—or worse, with none at all. I imagine all readers dutifully nodding in agreement. Please don't let me down.

The first part of the process, participation, includes preparation by gathering data (chapter 2). Without the needed wonder and curiosity (chapter 6) to look into things, the process would prematurely end here. Knowledge of constraints (chapter 4) helps in building solutions relevant to the task at hand.

Having the right creative state of mind can facilitate the incubation and illumination process (chapter 7). Others also play a large part in this, opening up your mind and world, increasing the chances of cross-pollination of ideas (chapter 3).

5.2.1   *Verifying critically*

Where does critical thinking fit in the creative process? Csikszentmihalyi suggests that *verifying* the insight equals taking a step back to take a critical look at the creation so far:

> *When the insight has presented itself, you have to check whether the connections made are indeed correct. The painter takes a few steps back to view from a distance whether or not the composition is good, the poet re-reads his verses with a critical mindset and the scientist makes calculations or executes experiments. The most beautiful insights become ugly as soon as the shortcomings become clear under the cold light of reason.*

He didn't interview programmers, but if he had, he probably would have written something along the lines of "The programmer presses F10 to execute their unit tests, cursing in agony if they fail." Our own interviews with software developers confirmed that the verification step plays an important role in the lives of creative programmers.

I can still vividly remember a pair programming session with an ex-colleague, lecturing me on my decision-making process, which he thought was too quick. "Why didn't you persist with this collection?" he'd ask. "Oh, that's simple; this is the aggregated root, right, so saving this object auto-cascades this second parameter here," I'd respond. Then the head-shaking began. "Don't just assume things! Did you inspect the code? Where are your integration tests? Does it do what you think it does?" A period of silence on my part usually indicated denial. "Don't *ASS*-ume! You'll make an ASS out of U and ME."

The "ass" part stuck with me for a long time: fun ways of teaching to verify your assumptions are always remembered as more lively. We became good friends afterward, and I owe him a lot. But seriously, don't assume. Place a few breakpoints and inspect memory regions to verify their contents. Step through unclear code to break up the fog. Write unit tests to cement those verifications for your colleagues and your future self. Grab an oscilloscope and inspect voltage waves, if you must. Just be sure to check, check, and triple-check. And if it doesn't check out, no worries; the creative process is recursive. Perhaps you need more caffeine or a good jog to walk it off and incubate some more.

> **Cameratas facilitate verification**
>
> As mentioned in chapter 3, mutual learning happens within a social group of like-minded people trying to achieve a shared goal. Various cognitive biases (see section 5.4) sometimes complicate the verification of our own ideas.
>
> In cases like that, the critical feedback of your peers can be of great value, provided you're willing to accept and process the criticism. Treat constructive criticism from others—under close scrutiny—as important pieces of the puzzle when verifying your wild ideas.

5.2.2   Focused thinking

Programming requires focused attention on lines, methods, members, arguments, brackets, gutters of IDEs, constructors, types, exceptions, and so forth. *Knee-Deep in the Code* instead of *in the Dead*, as the first shareware episode of *DOOM* is called.

This self-explanatory thinking phase is called *analytic problem-solving* or *focused thinking*: the eyes on the prize, the mind set on a solution. It involves an incremental and largely conscious process that, according to psychology researchers, is an integral part of creativity.[4] Without focused action, not a single painting will be painted, verse written, or line of code programmed.

---

[4] Claire M. Zedelius and Jonathan W. Schooler. The richness of inner experience: Relating styles of daydreaming to creative processes. Frontiers in Psychology, 2016.

Focused thinking is great for tackling low-level problems, but it can sometimes lead to taking a few shortcuts here and there (e.g., let's just use `static` here; it won't affect the entire system that much), thereby losing the overview (how does this method relate to our client's problem again?), and making wrong decisions, even with ample critical thinking. Therefore, we'll occasionally need to resort to other thinking modes, such as diffuse thinking.

5.2.3   *Diffuse thinking*

Critical thinking isn't always warmly welcomed: it's usually met with heavy resistance. Sometimes, it *should* be met with heavy resistance. For instance, when ideating—coming up with many crazy and unusual ideas—there's little point in immediately shooting down proposals. Barbara Oakley, an engineering professor at Oakland University and McMaster University, calls the ideation phase *diffuse-mode thinking*. She created a Coursera training entitled "Learning How to Learn" in which both focused and diffuse modes are introduced as powerful mental tools to help you master tough subjects (figure 5.3).[5]

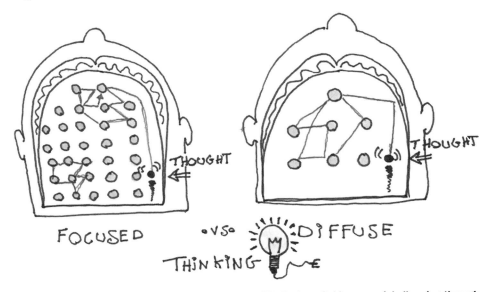

Figure 5.3   Focused and diffuse thinking, represented by Barbara Oakley as a pinball racing through our neurons. The focused pinball machine has a higher chance of hitting perfectly sorted and related bumpers, while a ball in a diffuse machine bounces in all directions, hitting seemingly unrelated ideas.

While focused thinking is about zooming in and analyzing the problem at hand, diffuse thinking is about zooming out and looking at the bigger picture, temporarily letting go of the problem and approaching different aspects of it on a higher level. Diffuse thinking, which is more freely associated with spontaneity, when ideas "suddenly" spring to mind, might lead to more, and relevant, insightful moments that in turn can be

---

[5] See https://www.coursera.org/learn/learning-how-to-learn.

integrated into the solution using more focused thinking. In practice, you're constantly switching between thinking modes, not unlike Daniel Kahneman's fast and slow thinking modes.[6] Kahneman, a researcher interested in the psychology of judgment and decision making, identified a duality between two modes of thought: "System 1," which is fast, instinctive, and emotional, and "System 2," which is slow, deliberate, and logical. Kahneman suggests that we have too much confidence in our own judgment, which we usually do unconsciously by using the wrong thinking mode.

Learning researcher Jonathan Schooler and his colleagues refer to diffuse thinking as *mind-wandering*.[7] Mind-wandering doesn't involve anything special. In fact, it involves nothing: it is an everyday experience in which attention becomes disengaged from the immediate external environment.

A distracted colleague, staring out the window, fooling us into thinking they're inspecting the construction site across the street, is probably mind-wandering. Their peers are probably annoyed. While Schooler's team admits that mind-wandering comes with a social and cognitive cost (to regain focus—more about that in chapter 7), they also measure significant improvements in creative performance—provided you're still hovering around the *incubation* phase.

Too much mind-wandering can be detrimental to your mental health: recently, reports have been popping up that claim to prove a correlation between mind-wandering and a negative mood, which has a lasting effect on one's general happiness level. Too-frequent construction site inspections from afar might be a sign of your job dissatisfaction, not just a way to facilitate diffuse thinking.

5.2.4   *Combining diffuse and focused thinking*

Schooler's research team advocates for an Aristotelian Middle Way between mindfulness (which increases focus) and mind-wandering (which facilitates diffuse thinking), hinting at the combination of the two thinking modes. American bio-chemist and prolific[8] academic publisher Linus Pauling was once asked by a student how to come up with so many good ideas. Pauling answered: "Well, that's easy. You come up with a lot of ideas, and you throw out the bad ones." To do that, you need both diffuse thinking (coming up with many ideas) and focused/critical thinking (throwing out the bad ones).

Pauling's contemporary Jonas Salk developed the first effective polio vaccine (figure 5.4) by smartly combining diffuse and focused thinking. Salk's ideas earned him many Nobel Prize nominations, although, unlike Pauling, he was never actually awarded one. He chose not to patent his polio vaccine, making it an affordable treatment for everyone—and missing out on more than $7 billion. In coding terminology, he released it as *open source*. "Our greatest responsibility is to be good ancestors," said Salk. Sadly, Louis Pasteur's private laboratory notes reveal that creative geniuses aren't immune to greed.

---

[6] Daniel Kahneman. Thinking, fast and slow. Macmillan, 2011.
[7] Jonathan W. Schooler, Michael D. Mrazek, Michael S. Franklin, et al. The middle way: Finding the balance between mindfulness and mind-wandering. Psychology of Learning and Motivation, 2014.
[8] He published 1,200 papers and books combined—that's even more than Niklas Luhmann!

Figure 5.4   Jonas Salk in 1952 at the University of Pittsburgh, proudly showcasing the first polio vaccine. Source: public domain, Wikimedia Commons.

The concept of generating ideas (the *incubate/illuminate* stages of the creative process) and picking the best ones (the *verify/accept* stages) is reflected in many cognitive psychology theories. The duality is also present in cognitive psychology researcher Robert Sternberg's definition of creativity: "Creativity is the decision to buy low and sell high in the world of ideas."[9]

That indicates some form of critical thinking: what to buy and what to sell—and, more important, *when*. To Sternberg, creativity is, in large part, a (risky) decision. Creative thinking without critical judgment tends toward the fanciful (buying high instead of low), the impractical (buying the wrong thing), and the ridiculous (selling the wrong thing).

Overselling code

Buying low and selling high reminds me of a specific code smell: *speculative generality*—that is, overengineering to impress yourself and your colleagues just to be able to call your coding efforts creative. These two date utility methods are bound to be reused; let's release them as a separate utility package to further complicate all our projects' dependency trees! Why aren't you using a mutex lock on this static singleton instance here? Let's refactor it into a thread-safe parallel complex system, because you never know! Lots of selling high; only the market isn't that interested in your Gordian knot.

---

[9] Robert Sternberg. Investment theory of creativity. http://www.robert jsternberg.com/investment-theory-of-creativity/, 2001.

Sternberg's commercialization of creativity suggests the presence of a gambling factor. Eric Weiner calls risk taking and creative genius inseparable, mentioning Marie Curie as an example, as she was well aware of the life-threatening radiation levels but stubbornly continued working with the toxic materials until they led to her death.

Certain amounts of diffuse and focused thinking are called for depending on the situation. Too much diffuse thinking leads to lots of unusual but weird ideas that never get implemented. Too much focused thinking leads to tunnel vision and speculative generality. Remember that the problem space is systemic: everything is interconnected. Frequently switching thinking modes might therefore be the most advisable approach. As we learn from Schooler's research, neatly summarized by Farnam Street (figure 5.5):[10]

> *Mental oscillation is important. If we stay in a focused mode too long, diminishing returns set in and our thinking stagnates. We stop getting new ideas and can experience cognitive tunneling.*

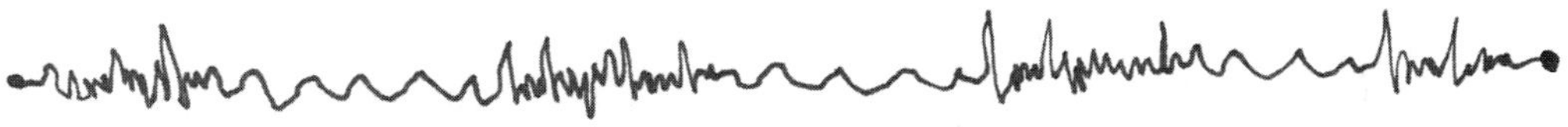

Figure 5.5   Mental oscillation: alternating between focused and diffuse thinking—and resting, of course

EXERCISE   In your daily practice, are you primarily a focused or a diffuse thinker? Does this differ on the basis of the task at hand and, if so, why? Can you identify opportunities to lean more on the thinking process you are less familiar with, or perhaps a timely combination of both?

5.3   *Creativity is the means, not the goal*

It is important to note that *creativity* does not always have a positive connotation. It is possible to come up with extremely "creative" but completely unusable solutions. How about using the Java Native Interface to call a custom Ruby interpreter written in C instead of simply evaluating the script using JRuby—or, even better, migrating the script to plain old Java? I doubt it'll be accepted as a viable solution—although we've all witnessed weird things being hacked together that miraculously work.

While my colleagues and I were discussing the uses of creativity in software development with our interviewees, an interesting thesis surfaced. Someone said, "Creativity is the means, not the goal." Interviewees emphasized the right combination between idea generation and critical thinking, taking into account the context and constraints of the problem. Creativity is more than ideation: it also involves critical reflection. Both concepts are required to solve problems that seem unsolvable using conventional best practices (or to identify and isolate the problem in the first place).

Creativity for the sake of being creative is where we enter the danger zone. Blinded by aesthetics, we suddenly feel the urge to make everything "beautiful," unconsciously introducing even more speculative generality. Is a programmer a craftsman? Many of

---

[10] See https://fs.blog/focused-diffuse-thinking/.

us love to emphasize our pretty coding skills. Not working software, but *well-crafted soft-ware* is one of the values present in the "Manifesto for Software Craftsmanship,"[11] signed by more than 32,000 self-proclaimed craftsmen at the time of writing.

The problem with software craftsmanship is the unbalanced emphasis on aesthetics instead of function. I've "paired" with programmers who've fallen in love with their own coding ways, frantically recrafting every line of code they encounter to "beautify" things, completely ignoring their pairs, deadlines, and team-based code style decisions. These craftsmen seem to forget that end users don't care about the aesthetics of the code: they care whether it works as intended and is delivered on time. If you are interested in the heated debate on software craftsmanship, Dan North's article "Programming Is Not a Craft" at https://dannorth.net/2011/01/11/programming-is-not-a-craft/ is a good place to start.

A healthy splash of critical thinking might bring craftsmen to their senses. Of course, clean code is of paramount importance; I wouldn't dare to deny that. Code is read 10 times more often than it is (re)written. Simple, readable, and clean code is a delight to maintain. Ugly spaghetti code is not. However, differentiating yourself from mediocre copy-and-paste programmers by wielding creativity as a beating stick ends up being just as damaging to the codebase, to your self-esteem, and to your peers. Creativity is the means, not the goal, although it *can* be the goal. The case of *creative coding*, where creativity in coding is used exclusively to express oneself, is such an example. There is no software problem you're trying to solve on behalf of a paying customer: there's only a blank canvas you're trying to fill for the sake of being creative. Creative coding is often used in higher education to promote creative self-expression and spark interest in computing.

Students are introduced to creative coding with the help of Processing (figure 5.6), a flexible software sketchbook and a language for learning how to code within the context of the visual arts.[12] Processing traditionally runs on the JVM, although recently, versions in JavaScript (p5.js) and Python (Processing.py) have emerged.

As fun as filling a canvas with visually impressive scenes is, creative self-expression teaches little about the bigger picture of systemic creative problem solving. Environments such as the p5.js editor are, next to the PICO-8 system from chapter 4, excellent vehicles for teaching constraint-based creative thinking. Unfortunately, most related academic papers I encountered during my literature review limit their use to an intro-duction to computing and a motivational tool to further spark interest in programming.

Creative coding feels like an unlucky choice of words, because in academia it is mostly associated with self-expression. A creative programmer is not a creative coder, but a creative coder can be a creative programmer. Wait, what? Proofreading that sentence sent my head spinning.

---

[11] See http://manifesto.softwarecraftsmanship.org/.
[12] Ira Greenberg. Processing: Creative coding and computational art. Apress, 2007.

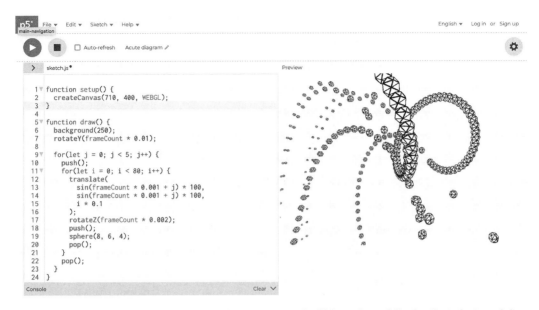

Figure 5.6   **The online p5.js editor running a simple example of colliding spheres following the trajectory of sine waves. Once logged in, projects are easy to share: simply copy the URL. p5.js requires little knowledge of JavaScript since you'll be relying on the well-documented Processing-specific functions, such as *sphere*.**

> **EXERCISE**   When do you think using creativity makes sense beyond the domain of problem solving in the context of programming? Is this done too often or too infrequently by your current development team?

We will continue to discuss creative exploration in chapter 6, where curiosity becomes the main driver of creativity.

5.4   *Common critical thinking fallacies*

"Je pense, donc je suis" ("I think, therefore I am"). Those famous words written by René Descartes laid the foundation for 17th-century rationalism and epistemology, later expanded upon by Spinoza and Leibniz. Philosophy quotes are popular one-liners that seem to promote rational thinking. "*Sapere aude*" ("Dare to know")!

While Descartes' dream theory did prove his existence (*je suis*), other wild ideas by the French philosopher are now met with skepticism. In an attempt to solve the problem of mind–body dualism, he attributed the connection between rational thinking and the immortality of the soul to the pineal gland in the brain. A devout Catholic, Descartes' extreme rationalism had to marry the divine somewhere, leaving the door open for the existence of God.

It is strange to read about such obvious thinking fallacies in the works of one of the most critical thinkers of our civilization. Animal spirits that move through the pineal gland based on God's will, telling us to want and like things? It sure is a creative explanation, I'll give him that. Descartes isn't the only respected philosopher with strange ideas: other examples are Plato's *Republic* doctrines and Aristotle's controversial views on sexism.

These now-refuted views on the world should be approached while taking into account their unique *Zeitgeist*. Still, I somehow find thinking fallacies of the great philosophers reassuring: it proves they were just humans and perhaps gives us humble beings an excuse to be plain wrong from time to time.

Critical thinking—or *rationality*,[13] as cognitive psychologist Steven Pinker likes to call it—is never flawless. Cognitive biases, influenced by our social environment, constantly warp our thinking patterns.

For example, consider the following simple test, administered to undergraduate students at Yale University. A Nintendo 3DS and a 3DS case together cost €110. The 3DS costs €100 more than the case. How much does that case cost? The overwhelming majority of the students answered €10 instead of the correct amount, €5. If the answer was €10, the 3DS would cost €110—€100 more than the case. But the sum of those amounts is €120 and not €110!

Verifying the amount that swiftly popped into your mind might have prevented embarrassment. Pinker accredits this behavior to Daniel Kahneman's thinking mode duality: instead of thoroughly analyzing and thinking about the task at hand (System 2), we quickly blurt out a number, confident that the exercise is too trivial to waste energy-consuming thoughts on (System 1). While System 1 is indispensable for making quick decisions in life-threatening situations, it's hardly competent at critical thinking. According to Pinker, most thinking fallacies befall us when we misuse Kahneman's System 1.

In the next section, I'd like to highlight a subset of cognitive biases we as programmers often fall victim to. This is nowhere near a complete enumeration: Wikipedia lists hundreds of biases, all backed up by scientific research.[14]

If you are interested in more examples related to programming, agile manifesto cocreator Andy Hunt devoted an entire chapter to cognitive (programming) biases in his *Pragmatic Thinking & Learning*, and, more recently, software engineering education researcher Felienne Hermans published a book on the programmer's brain,[15] featuring common thinking mistakes that occur while coding and debugging.

5.4.1 Cross-language clashes

Why is it difficult for developers to learn another programming language? That question was raised by software engineering researcher Nischal Shrestha and colleagues after it was pointed out that most research focuses on beginners (more specifically, students) learning languages, even though expert programmers might also struggle with learning another language.

---

[13] Steven Pinker. Rationality: What it is, why it seems scare, why it matters. Allen Lane, 2021.
[14] See https://en.wikipedia.org/wiki/List_of_cognitive_biases.
[15] Felienne Hermans. The programmer's brain: What every programmer needs to know about cognition. Manning, 2021.

Shrestha's team found that both cross-language interference and facilitation occur.[16] A simple example of facilitation, taken from their paper, is asking a Java developer who is learning Kotlin how to simplify the following expression:

```
val boundsBuilder: LatLngBounds.Builder =
  LatLngBounds.Builder()
```

Sure enough, the developer suspects this declaration is more verbose than it should be, figures out the type, knows about local variable type inference in Java, and comes up with this:

```
val boundsBuilder = LatLngBounds.Builder()
```

There are no big surprises here: Kotlin is built on top of the JVM, so obviously your previous Java knowledge will matter. This is more generally known as *transfer during learning*.

Unfortunately, the trick doesn't always work. I know many Java developers who really struggle with JavaScript, unable to wrap their heads around prototypal inheritance and async functional programming, even though modern Java code finally got rid of interface implementations through anonymous inner classes by resorting to function references.

Cross-language interference can also be a hindrance when learning a new spoken language. Words in one language that resemble words in another might not necessarily mean the same thing. For example, the Spanish word *embarazada* looks like *embarrassed*, but in reality means "pregnant." Too confidently saying *embarazada* will surely lead to embarrassment!

> **EXERCISE** This exercise is adapted from Felienne Hermans' book *The Programmer's Brain*. Think of a new programming language you learned recently. What concepts that you already knew helped you learn the new language? Now think of a situation where you made incorrect assumptions about a programming language that is new to you. Was it because of cross-language interference?

Cross-language interference is not always worth mentioning. Syntactic differences are enough to make anyone trip, but seasoned programmers are usually quick to recover. A difference in fundamental concepts, such as immutability in Scala or Elixir, is much more challenging to overcome.

Other problems that surfaced when interviewing experienced developers about how they learn new languages are "old habits die hard" and "mindshifts are required when switching paradigms." Does the good outweigh the bad? Having experience with facilitation and as a polyglot programming advocate, I'd dare to say yes, although

---

[16] Nischal Shrestha, Colton Botta, Titus Barik, and Chris Parnin. Here we go again: Why is it difficult for developers to learn another programming language? In 2020 IEEE/ACM 42nd International Conference on Software Engineering, 2020.

small case studies suggest that regularly switching could affect human productivity in practice.[17] More on the (dis)advantages of polyglotism in chapter 6. How do we overcome cross-language interference? *Verify, verify, verify.*

Context-switching in class

Regularly switching languages involves context-switching that can sometimes short-circuit the brain—at least, my brain. I teach C/C++, Java, Kotlin, and Python, and I write JavaScript and Go code in my spare time, doing my best to forget my VB6 and PHP past along the way. Clashes are bound to occur. I'm regularly stumped in class, of course at the worst possible time, halfway through a simple demonstration of a for loop, suddenly completely forgetting the syntax. Iterator? Foreach? No wait, this is C, dereference the pointer and then ... then what?

Or how about trying to showcase the correct use of collections, typing `.add()` instead of `.push_back()`, blanking at the compile error. Confusing zero-based indexing with R's one-based arrays, falsely relying on the garbage collector when working with pointers (C++ is not Go), ... My students must think I really suck at programming.

A healthy dose of postcritical analysis instructs me to push aside my overconfidence and properly prepare the demos. Next time, I promise!

5.4.2   *The superior flash of insight*

The illumination step of the creative process might yield insights worthy enough to develop, but remember to first critically verify your "sudden" flash of insight. Insight also comes equipped with bias: ideas gained by unexpected burning lightbulbs are seen as more truthful than ideas gained through a logical step-by-step balance. Behold the divine power of the "*Aha-Erlebnis*!" Treat these ideas as any other idea: *verify, verify, verify.*

5.4.3   *Ignorance and Deliberate Discovery*

In 2010, renowned enterprise software developer Dan North introduced a concept called *Deliberate Discovery* to challenge assumptions around software planning and estimation.[18] Programmers constantly make assumptions while creating software. "This static variable won't affect things that much"; "I'm sure this breakpoint won't get hit while debugging"; "Duplicating this service is faster than creating another one from scratch"; "This button is redundant; our clients don't use it"; and so on. Sound familiar?

The problem with making assumptions is that most of the time they're completely wrong. Most of our assumptions are somehow biased in favor of our prior beliefs and values. This is called *confirmation bias*: ignoring counterarguments and interpreting situations to support our own cause instead of critically investigating the facts.

---

[17] Phillip Merlin Uesbeck and Andreas Stefik. A randomized controlled trial on the impact of polyglot programming in a database context. Open Access Series in Informatics, 2019.

[18] See https://dannorth.net/2010/08/30/introducing-deliberate-discovery/.

Confirmation bias is rampant among programmers, even though logical reasoning comes with the job.[19] Ouch, that's sobering!

Only when something unexpected occurs do we start to truly learn. If all goes according to plan, we'll simply produce the code we've been producing before. You might be fooled into thinking you're learning by doing so, but you're merely getting better at performing an already familiar sequence of actions.

Unexpected behavior causes us to stop and think—and, one hopes, debug. North called this *accidental discovery*. We do not intend for these learning moments to happen: that pesky `NullPointerException` should not have happened in the first place.

Yet we rarely try to turn these accidental learning moments into *deliberate* learning moments. Is that button really redundant? We don't know—why don't we simply ask our clients? What do the access logs tell us? During the lifetime of a project, your ignorance will likely decrease thanks to unexpected exceptions and other accidental moments of learning.

However, ignorance is multidimensional: you can be ignorant of the technology in use, ignorant of other possible technologies out there that might be a better fit, ignorant of colleagues' technical knowledge that might help, ignorant of the wishes of your client, ignorant of the ways your company communicates with clients, and so on.

Although we have touched upon *deliberate* ignorance, or naivety—as a temporary measure to alleviate overconstrainedness—in chapter 4, we're mostly ignorant of our ignorance, and that, in turn, acts as another invisible constraint. According to North, ignorance isn't a constraint to get things moving. It is a constraint to get things moving *in the right direction*. Instead of relying on (un)happy accidents to reduce your ignorance and learn, it might be a better idea to deliberately identify how ignorance is hampering you, your colleagues, and the project.

Socratic "thoroughly conscious ignorance," as Scottish physicist James Clerk Maxwell liked to call it, is the prelude to every real advance in science—the prelude to creative breakthroughs. We used to have fun calling out fake assumptions while pair programming, jokingly throwing the *ass-u-me* joke around as a catchphrase. However, Deliberate Discovery goes beyond the occasional critical inspection when things go wrong. The catchphrase was still mostly used as a result of accidental discovery.

Creative programmers are mindful of their own ignorance. In true Socratic fashion, they know what they don't know, and they actively remediate that if it helps them as they move forward.

> **EXERCISE** This is an adaptation of a typical critical thinking test handed out during interviews. Brain Baking, Inc., released *My Little Baker* five years ago, and it became its best-selling video game. The sequel, *My Little Chocolatier*, became one of the top-five best-selling games. Industrial Bakes, Inc., acquired Brain Baking a few years later because they believed a second sequel, *My Bolder Bakery*, would bring great profits. Is *My Little Baker* Brain Baking's best-selling video game?

---

[19] Gul Calikli and Ayse Bener. Empirical analysis of factors affecting confirmation bias levels of software engineers. Software Quality Journal, 2015.

The answer is, we simply don't know. *My Little Chocolatier* could have outsold *My Little Baker* a few years later, even if it had been only the fifth entry on the best-selling chart at that time. The acquisition is useless information to throw you off guard. Socrates would have answered the question correctly. Know what you don't know!

5.4.4   I am the greatest

Attributing the success of a project to yourself is called *self-serving bias.* Congrats, you! *I did it!* Wait, isn't the expression "*We* did it"? Keep in mind that because chapter 3 explained creativity as systemic, your creative genius is part of a greater ecology. The system influenced you as much as you influenced the system.

Of course, if the project was a big failure, we're usually the first ones to scream "I didn't do it!" Psychologists have identified this behavior as a largely unconscious self-protection mechanism. A possible good way to get out of this bias is by becoming aware of it through the different phases of Christopher Avery's shared responsibility model, introduced in chapter 3.

5.4.5   I am the fanciest

We love to add as many modern frameworks, libraries, and programming languages as possible to our curricula vitae—and our job ads. Our burning desire to work with the latest and greatest results in huge refactoring attempts and technical debt stories that ultimately do little for the end user. But at least we managed to squeeze in React, Redux, and GraphQL!

I was reluctant to drop a few framework names here: by the time this book is published, it'll probably be replaced by something "even better." My yearly attempts to try to keep up to date with https://stateofjs.com always end in depression.

Why are we seduced by the sparkle of the shiny and the new? Why do we keep on rebuilding the same software again and again, only with different technology stacks?[20] I've been involved in many web-based enterprise software products that would have been better off as a fat-client application (blasphemy!), yet most engineers I know continue to—perhaps uncritically—worship complicated cloud-based solutions.

In the West, creativity is associated with *radical inventiveness.* Yet, in the East, creativity is more often seen as cyclical, rooted in decades of tradition. Design researchers ConRong Wang and Qiduan Chen describe Western creativity as the empowerment of human imagination envisioning eternally original artifacts, while Eastern creativity is enmeshed in the nature-in-the-human or spiritual power of Qi inherent in nature.[21] Perhaps our Western culture indoctrinated a *belief bias* that everything has to be shiny and new in order to be innovative.

---

[20] At least these research questions are not new! Technology acceptance and the influences of technology attractiveness have been extensively studied, but I have failed to find a satisfying answer related to software development.

[21] ConRong Wang and Qiduan Chen. Eastern and Western creativity of tradition. Asian Philosophy, 2021.

5.4.6   *First-Google-hit coding*

From time to time, we're all guilty of Google-coding: quickly looking up how to work with an unfamiliar API, heavily relying on the first search result we hit, and accepting its contents without asking further questions. The problem is that sometimes hasty search terms equal incorrect search results. Stack Overflow might have alleviated the problem a little bit by up-voting or down-voting technical answers, although I've seen plenty of "accepted" answers elaborating on something completely irrelevant.

What if your search results yield only two matches? Are you more or less inclined to verify their contents? Relying heavily on only one piece of information instead of cross-checking when making decisions is called *anchoring bias*.

Programmer Brian Provinciano, the creator of the video game *Retro City Rampage* (figure 5.7), whom we initially met in chapter 4, also struggled with this problem. As he was looking into porting his game to the now-ancient DOS environment, he noticed that most of the technical information had been lost. For starters, in 1990 the internet wasn't around like the way we know it now. Special DOS VGA instruction manuals have gone missing. Many current-generation programmers don't even know what a floppy disk looks like. Only a few obscure retro programming forums provide hints here and there that, as Provinciano attempted to implement them, proved to be dead wrong.

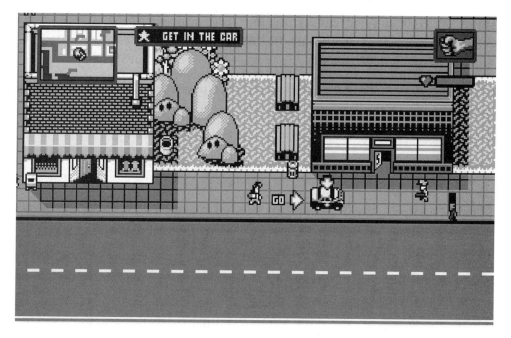

Figure 5.7   The DOS port of *Retro City Rampage*, made possible by cleverly working around constraints and cross-verification of programming forums and manuals. Note the absence of a logo on the gray bricks of the left store: it was cut to fit in one 3.5-inch floppy disk. The now open source and fully documented Open Watcom C/C++ toolkit used to compile the game was also used by *DOOM*, *Duke Nukem 3D*, and *Full Throttle*.

Here is an incorrect example of how to detect the presence of a co-processor, posted as a correct solution:

```
finit
mov cx,3
.wait:
loop .wait
mov word [test_word],0000h
fnstcw word [test_word]
cmp word [test_word],03FFh
jne .no_fpu
```

The poster assures us that the 8087 FPU co-processor initializes `test_word` to 03FFh. It's easy to see why most programmers would just copy and paste this snippet: cryptic and old assembly code renders correct interpretation of these statements almost impossible. According to Provinciano, the `cmp` statement turned out to be failing to successfully detect the presence of a co-processor in some cases.

> **A generational technology gap**
>
> A few years ago, I restored my father-in-law's 80486 IBM PC to its former glory. I even upgraded the 30-year-old machine by adding an authentic ISA SoundBlaster card (these things cost at least €80 nowadays!) and socketing in an AMD 486DX2-66 CPU. Proud of my creation, I hauled it to our faculty to showcase it to a close hardware engineering colleague, who is a few years older than me.
>
> The mechanical keystrokes and beeps and bloops from the OPL3 chip attracted the attention of some PhD students a few aisles away. I opened up the case to let them inspect the motherboard. "What is that?" they asked, pointing at an 8-bit ISA slot. "What is that?" they asked, pointing at the VLB controller card. When the blue BIOS screen tested the extended memory region of 7424 K, their jaws dropped. "Whooww!" They were lucky I didn't bring a Tandy 1000 SX.

The Internet Archive Digital Library is a blessing for people like Provinciano who are on the lookout for digitized versions of classic Borland International books. The *C++ Programmer's Guide: Borland C++: Version 5.0* book[22] even contains *Part II: Borland C++ DOS Programmer's Guide* on page 291! BIOS interrupt 13h, here I come! How to overcome anchoring biases? Cross-check using multiple information sources, and then *verify, verify, verify.* Typing this is getting repetitive.

5.4.7   *A long list of novice programming misconceptions*

Of course that `string` gets converted to an `int` when concatenating these variables! The boxing effect in this loop with big numbers is causing us performance troubles; there's no need to measure—I just know. We need to change that parameter name; it's the same as our field, and that does not compile. That while loop will stop as soon as the condition is `false`, so I need to repeat my logic below it.

---

[22] See https://archive.org/details/cprogrammersguid00borl/page/n9/mode/2up.

All these misconceptions are part of Teemu Sirkiä and Juha Sorva's research. They identified more than 100 common programming misconceptions in undergraduate students learning their first few programming languages.[23]

Some misconceptions are deeply rooted in students' beliefs and are very difficult to rectify. Some stay suspicious even after you have proven them wrong. In that case, a mind switch is needed to gain a new understanding of the concept. Sometimes, *unlearning* takes as much time as *learning*.

Preventing students from learning the wrong thing is difficult if they attend class preprogrammed with beliefs and misconceptions based on prior experience with mathematics, statistics, or basic (but wrong) programming skills. Instead of teaching students endless methods within the JDK API, thereby falsely convincing ourselves they're competent Java devs once awarded a grade, it might be better to teach them how to interrogate their assumptions. Oh yes, we teachers are also burdened with a bunch of misconceptions!

5.4.8 Converting prejudice into insight

What do you do when someone flat-out says, "In our tech, this can't be done"? Do you accept their expertise, or do you rebelliously reject it and show them how it's done? Perhaps the smarter alternative is to first try to understand why this person says it can't be done. Was it effectively tried before in the same context, or is this an academic statement? Is the conclusion originating from a dislike of the current technology stack, or was it uttered because others said it couldn't be done?

This predicament is not merely a case where critical thinking can be applied: it's first and foremost a delicate communication problem. Proving a person wrong won't convert their prejudice to insight, but it most definitely will portray you as arrogant, further complicating future conflicts. It might be better to clear up any misconceptions before letting your creative urge run wild.

Our brain's fight-or-flight system is very good at dishing out quick but often wrong judgments. Helping others to convert their prejudice into insight is best done by stepping into their shoes and, in the case of software development, pair programming.

> **EXERCISE** Make a list of common critical-thinking fallacies you've spotted in your team while writing code. Which pitfalls are commonplace, and which happen less often? What action will you take to prevent future mistakes? Keep the list updated to track progress. Remember not to point the finger but to use this as a way to move forward!

5.5 Too much self-criticism

Sometimes, a creative rut is the result of too much critical thinking when it comes to our own work. Artist and teacher Julia Cameron describes in her worldwide bestseller *The Artist's Way* how to scramble out of the valley and conquer our inner creative

---

[23] Teemu Sirkiä and Juha Sorva. Exploring programming misconceptions: an analysis of student mistakes in visual program simulation exercises. In Proceedings of the 12th Koli Calling International Conference on Computing Education Research, 2012.

critic.[24] According to Cameron, freeing the inner artist is simply a matter of dealing with our own criticism:

> *Many artists have an inner critic, me too. I call mine Nigel—a stern British interior designer. When I'm creating an artwork, Nigel immediately yells: "It's too boring, too childish, too crappy!" I then say "Nigel, thank you for sharing," and keep on working.*

Nigel feeds on consistent negative remarks we have to endure, either by ourselves or by a bad teacher. "Give up already; you'll never get it!" or "Try another hobby; programming just isn't for you"—sound familiar? Cameron teaches us to learn to be self-nourishing: "We must become alert enough to consciously replenish our creative resources, as we draw on them," she writes. Nigel's constant nagging can be mentally draining, slowly depleting our creative energy until all we can do is comply and throw out our work.

According to Cameron, the most important instruments for creative recovery are writing daily *morning pages* (unfiltered brain dumps as soon as you're awake) and *artistic dates* with yourself (treating yourself to a trip of a few hours to get inspired). These techniques saved Cameron's creative life and keep on saving the lives of millions of *Artist's Way* readers.

Feel free to replace Cameron's classic suggestions (expositions, galleries, concerts, watching a sunset, etc.) with things that spark your coding imagination (talks, browsing through cool GitHub repositories, reverse engineering Yamaha OPL sound chips, playing games, tearing up C++ books, disassembling Game Boy cartridges, etc.).

The Artist's Way, generously filled with spiritual vagueness, does not particularly attract logical-thinking programmers like you and me. Still, its message is a powerful one: sometimes, we're too hard on ourselves. Creativity researchers Darya Zabelina and Michael Robinson discovered similar results: self-judgmental individuals display lower levels of creative originality.[25] Although their study was limited to the assessment of 86 undergraduates' creativity by the Torrance Test of Creative Thinking (see chapter 4), a growing body of academic literature seems to agree: do less listening to your inner Nigel and more creating.

How many times have you blindly resorted to a Stack Overflow code snippet because "it was probably too complicated for you to understand anyway"? How many times have you accepted implementation proposals by your peers without thinking it through because "they're smarter than you"? I bet many of you even skipped the PICO-8 constraint exercise from chapter 4 because "you're no good at creating pixels" or "you don't know how to program in Lua." Don't let your inner Nigel beat you to it. In other words, take a critical look at your own work *and* at Nigel's remarks.

EXERCISE   The *morning pages* exercise is a powerful and unfiltered way to get out ideas floating in your subconscious. Try out the technique for an entire week. Each morning, even before breakfast, write down anything that comes

---

[24] Julia Cameron. The artist's way: a spiritual path to higher creativity. 30th Anniversary Edition. TarcherPerigee, 2016.

[25] Darya L. Zabelina and Michael D. Robinson. Don't be so hard on yourself: Self-compassion facilitates creative originality among self-judgmental individuals. Creativity Research Journal, 2010.

to mind, including "I don't want to do this," "I have nothing to say," or "I don't want to get up." After a few minutes of writing, you'll manage past the initial heavy resistance. Write for at least 15 minutes without stopping. Only *after* the exercise is Nigel allowed to critically assess the words to separate the wheat from the chaff.

5.6   *Why others' critical thinking matters*

This chapter has mostly revolved around (self-)criticism to sharpen your own or collective thoughts and creative ideas. I also briefly mentioned the advantages of sharing ideas with others, revealing an important link between critical thinking and communication.

Feedback from others to iterate on your creative idea isn't the only reason why the critical thinking of others matters. Philosopher and creativity critic Caterina Moruzzi writes about the relevance of the *understanding* of creativity besides the development of creative abilities.[26] She exclusively talks not only about the person developing the idea but also about the people around that person. Remember that creativity is a sociocultural verdict: without someone recognizing your work as creative, it won't be perceived as such. That also means the critical evaluation and verification of others are relevant to the acceptance of our own work—well past the idea-development phase. This isn't an invitation to apply pressure and extort people; instead, look at it this way: if nobody understands your code, perhaps you should consider simplifying things. Feel free to insert *you're doing it wrong* memes here.

When it comes to creativity, there's a thin line between conventions and nonconformity. It's up to you to decide how far you're willing to take it—in either direction. Just be prepared for the critical responses: creativity does not exist in a void.

> **EXERCISE**   Revisit the first exercise in this chapter. Has your opinion changed about having the need for a modern Socrates (and not a Nigel) on your team who, at unexpected moments, asks the right critical questions?

Summary

- A typical creative process contains the following interrelated steps: *participate, incubate, illuminate, verify,* and *present/accept.* Thus, critical thinking by verifying ideas and implementations is a vital component of the Creative Programmer.

- The creative process requires different modes of thinking at different stages of the process: diffuse and focused thinking, and, perhaps ideally, a good mixture of both. If you ever find yourself out of ideas, try switching modes.

- In the context of software problem solving, creativity is usually used as the means, not the goal. However, creativity *can* be the goal: to self-express, to beautify, to explore and play with new technologies. Be well aware of the boundary between creativity as the means and creativity as the goal. Do not craft beautiful code just because of the code instead of the product.

---

[26] Caterina Moruzzi. On the relevance of understanding for creativity. Philosophy after AI, 2021.

- Knowing the existence of many critical-thinking fallacies will certainly help you overcome even the most stubborn ones. As Socrates would have said: know what you don't know.
- Critical thinking can lead to being too hard on others or on yourself, ultimately diminishing the creative flow. Remember that creativity is systemic and that you're part of a mutual learning ecology.
- Do not limit critical thinking to your own work: others' creative work is in need of feedback, too. It might be a good idea to first consider how the feedback will be received. Consequently, adopt an open mindset when receiving critical feedback from others.

Curiosity

The never-ending murmur of the scouring sand that spans the ancient Egyptian desert has little effect on the traveler's mood. Equipped with nothing but a walking stick and a light backpack, the stranger defies turbulent seas, sandy deserts, and dusty roads, only to arrive at yet another half-deserted village. He calmly rests his walking stick against a palm tree, shakes the sand from his clothing, and, without hesitating, strikes up a conversation with a local. After a long chat and a shared but meager meal, he unrolls a partially finished manuscript and starts writing, beginning with the iconic words: "I was told that . . . ."

That man was Herodotus, and he was on a mission: to record the history of the world. His work *Histories* is now regarded as one of the first meticulously detailed investigations of cultural, geographical, and historical events, in particular, the Greco-Persian wars. Herodotus is the world's first true fearless historian, willing to travel long and far, whatever the risks. *Histories* records the worldview not just from the viewpoint of his beloved Greece but also from the Persian Empire, where he was born.

Herodotus' curiosity about what was happening to the ordinary inhabitants of his era, combined with his wit and keen senses, sprouted literature that was considered essential reading material—and nowadays still should be. Three hundred years later, the systematic investigation of anthropological excavations thoroughly impressed Cicero, who called Herodotus the "Father of History."

Twenty centuries later, the chaotic but everyday maelstrom of masts creaking, sailors yelling, and waves sloshing indicates a ship is about to set sail. The *Beagle*, under the command of Royal Navy officer and scientist Robert FitzRoy, was tasked with charting the coastline of South America. A 22-year-old Brit managed to persuade FitzRoy to join the crew as a naturalist. That young man was Charles Darwin.

The captain sent Darwin ashore to investigate the local geology while the *Beagle* itself continued surveying and charting the coasts. Darwin's curiosity wasn't limited to geology; it was the perfect excuse for him to explore and collect samples of local fauna and flora, making extensive notes while back on the ship—not only on what he saw but also on theoretical speculations.

Darwin wasn't an expert in biology: he knew only a little bit about geology and had the odd beetle collection back home. He was a novice in all other areas, but his curiosity wasn't diminished because of it: precisely the opposite happened. Despite suffering from prolonged periods of seasickness, he still managed to write down anything that piqued his interest, which was almost *everything*—at least, until he ran out of paper.

In 1836, the *Beagle* finally returned to Plymouth after a journey of five years. Six months after the grand adventure, Darwin slowly but surely started connecting the dots. The result of his endless curiosity—a huge body of evidence collected in notes—reworked into papers and his journals, gradually revealed that "one species does change into another." His seminal work, *On the Origin of Species*, eventually published in 1859, would still be a long way off (23 years!), first requiring several more essays; conversations with befriended scientists; more revisions; and very long, thoughtful walks.

One hundred sixty years later, the sizzling of molten tin, accompanied by small circles of smoke, fills a small office space in Colindale, London. The floor is littered with DIY-printed circuit boards and unscrewed *Tetris* Game Boy cartridges. A couple of software and electronics engineers are hacking together a Game Boy development kit by reverse-engineering *Tetris*.

Jez San, the founder of British video game developer Argonaut Games, crossed paths with Nintendo's Game Boy during an electronics fair in 1989. He immediately decided to redirect programming efforts from the Spectrum and Amiga to the peculiar new handheld device. However, Nintendo was very stingy about handing out official development kits, especially outside of Japan. The seeming impossibility of developing for the Game Boy could have driven San to give up on the idea. However, his curiosity fueled his drive to push forward and overcome the severe constraints by hacking together a development kit from scratch, connecting wires from a cartridge to chips on a homemade circuit board.

New programming recruit Dylan Cuthbert was tasked with the development of Argonaut's first Game Boy game, which would become *X*, or *Ekkusu* (figure 6.1). Jez San thought it would be cool to develop a 3D space simulator for the Game Boy—something that had already been achieved on other platforms with the *Starglider* series. However, the limited Game Boy technology housed a variant of the meager Z80 CPU, running at 3.5 MHz. Even worse, it could display only four shades of gray. Luckily, Cuthbert proved to be up to the task. The fully 3D-rendered meshes in the game even impressed Nintendo, who invited the team to Japan.

X would be the beginning of a shared history between Argonaut Games and Nintendo. Nintendo's interest in British boldness got Argonaut and Cuthbert heavily involved in the development of the Super FX RISC coprocessor, powering *Yoshi's Island* (2D sprite scaling), the *DOOM* Super Nintendo port (Binary Space Partitioning), and, of course, *Star Fox* (true 3D polygons), also developed by Argonaut. Cuthbert's 3D hardware experience landed him a job at Sony, helping developers unlock the power of the first two PlayStation generations. He eventually started his own company, Q-Games, based in Japan, a development studio well known for the *PixelJunk* series.

Figure 6.1 *X* on the Game Boy, released in 1992. Note all those cool-looking UI borders, which cleverly further reduce the resolution to land at an acceptable frame rate.

6.1   Curiosity jump-starts creativity

What is the greatest common divisor between Herodotus' herculean effort to meet people and write down their stories, Charles Darwin's extensive notes on geology and biology, and Argonaut Games' soldering hack to peek inside a *Tetris* cartridge? All three examples showcase a lot of curiosity: about the tales of others and the history of empires, about the evolution of nature and the origin of species, and about the inner workings of a piece of hardware.

If it weren't for the curiosity and persistence of these people, we would have lost even more ancient Greek and Persian knowledge, we would still have no idea how nature evolved when sea life crawled upon land, and a Super FX chip might never have been released on time to prolong the life of the Super Nintendo (figure 6.2). Perhaps SEGA might have won the 16-bit console war!

Figure 6.2   The PCB of the PAL version of *Yoshi's Island***, with the beefed-up SuperFX (GSU-2) chip in the middle, flanked by the 2 MB ROM on the left and the 256 kB frame buffer and save game SRAM on the upper right**

In Mihaly Csikszentmihalyi's many interviews with creative geniuses, *curiosity* and *perseverance* are identified as the two most important personality traits for creative success. Without curiosity, there is little motivation to learn or build something. Without perseverance, there is little chance of effectively finishing the work. Creativity is not creativity without the initial curiosity that gets everything started.

Although we may never know whether curiosity stems from genes or from stimulating experiences in our youth, it is important to acknowledge its existence and cherish it, giving it the opportunity to grow into a creative life. Csikszentmihalyi's emphasis on creativity and perseverance lead me to believe that curiosity is where the creativeness of the programmer begins.

6.2   *Growing wonder and wanderlust*

As Charles Darwin proved, the best kind of curiosity is an all-encompassing curiosity. Wondering how something works evolves into genuine curiosity, which, in turn, is the primary driver of motivation. How does one get started as a Creative Programmer? First and foremost, you must cultivate interests. Otherwise, the *participate* step in the creative process explained in chapter 5 will yield few intriguing new experiences and information. To generate novel ideas by connecting the dots, you first need to collect them—and persist them to your *system* from chapter 2.

Sometimes, we're in a rut, and our mood prevents us from discovering new and exciting things. Sometimes, our anxiety imprisons our wanderlust. Sometimes, our tunnel vision fixates our interests. Fortunately, there's a way out: it's called cultivating a *growth mindset*.

6.2.1   *Fixed and growth mindsets*

After decades of research on achievement and success, the renowned psychologist and sociologist Carol Dweck concluded that the power of unlocking our full potential lies in the mind. Her studies on the mindset of top performers revealed that our mindset can be roughly categorized into two camps as shown in figure 6.3: the fixed mindset and the growth mindset.[1]

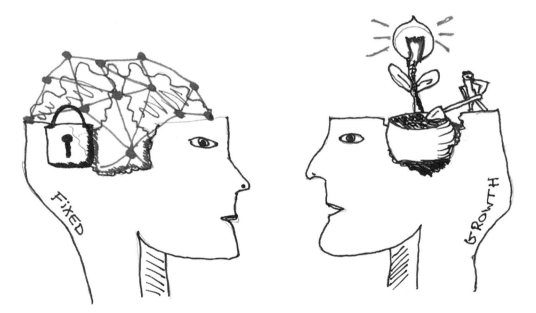

Figure 6.3   Fixed and growth mindsets. Would you rather buy a padlock to protect (limiting) or get fertilizer to grow (freedom)?

---

[1] Carol S. Dweck. Mindset: Changing the way you think to fulfill your potential. Revised edition. Robinson, 2017.

A *fixed mindset* is the belief that your talent and abilities are set in stone. Either you're creative, or you're not. Fixed mindset people usually either envy others because they see a quality they lack and will never master, or they are arrogant and disdainful toward others whom they think lack a quality and will never master it. A fixed mindset equals fixed traits. Their motto is "Smart people succeed."

A *growth mindset* is the belief that your talent and abilities can be cultivated and grown over time through effort. Growth mindset people recognize they are not *yet* creative; they just need a little bit more practice. A growth mindset equals malleable traits. Their motto is "People can get smarter."

In practice, these two opposite ends of the spectrum are purely indicative. Between the black and white, there are hundreds—no, wait, 50—shades of gray. You might think you can still develop your cooking skills to become a competent chef but also be convinced that you'll never be more than a shabby coder. According to Dweck's research, whatever mindset you have in a particular field will guide you in that area. Are you convinced that you'll never be good at coding? Then you never will be.

Embracing criticism as valuable feedback is one of the key traits of a growth mindset. Eric Weiner's travels around the world to chase the odd geographical clusters of dead geniuses revealed that these people thrived on negative feedback: it only added more fuel to their creative burn. Criticism is indeed never fun to receive, but it is up to you to decide how to deal with it. Are you really going to throw in the proverbial towel just because some fixed mindset told you that you suck at this?

The stimulating or damaging influence of teachers

It is remarkable that many creative geniuses have either no recollection whatsoever of a special bond with a teacher in school or a very intimate one. I've read about the damaging effects of teachers carelessly criticizing children for their bad performance, and I've read about teachers being fondly remembered as genuine curiosity promoters. Even some Nobel Prize winners rate their high school teachers negatively across the board.

I honestly can't blame them. When I was in high school, I eventually switched to a trade school where only the truly excellent students move on to a local college. I was the only one to enroll in a computer science degree at a university—against the advice of all my teachers. "You'll never make it there," they warned. Four years later, I graduated. As I type this, I'm finishing my PhD. Perhaps I should send them my copy of Carol Dweck's *Mindset*.

6.2.2   *Believing is doing*

Dweck calls a growth mindset "a passport to new adventures." I'd like to alter the expression to "a free pass to creativity," a pass handed out by ourselves, to ourselves, to remind us to lead a creative life—provided we believe in it. Dweck teaches us that how we view our lives drastically affects how we lead them: "For twenty years, my research has shown that the view you adopt of yourself profoundly affects the way you lead your life."

Anyone can lead the life of the Creative Programmer. There are no high-IQ requirements, and there is no need for friends in high places. Sure, the ability to rapidly process information helps, as does surrounding yourself with inspiring people, as we saw in chapter 3. But Dweck tells us that the most important thing is to believe in ourselves. This simple yet incredibly powerful message takes a lot of guts to realize. That belief influences how we cope with setbacks and often marks the difference between excellence and mediocrity. Even Leonardo da Vinci instinctively knew this when he wrote (*The Notebooks of Leonardo da Vinci*, Richter, 1888), "Obstacles cannot crush me. Every obstacle yields to stern resolve. He who is fixed to a star does not change his mind."

6.2.3 Growing out of your comfort zone

Sometimes, we're simply afraid to learn new things—to jump down the hole. I might as well stay in the Java world where I know most of the gotchas. People might think I'm a fraud. I'd rather not get involved in this new JavaScript stuff. I'm not a philosopher; I'd rather read some fiction. My colleagues respect me for my domain knowledge; there's no way I'm switching to a new project. I studied computer science, so there's no point in reading up on psychology (guess what you're doing right now?).

All these statements reek of a very fixed mindset. Cultivating a growth mindset involves facing and defeating our fears of the unknown. The research of my colleagues and myself indicates that creative software engineering students get out of their comfort zone more often than noncreative students.[2] In an open programming assignment, the creativity of the end product was evaluated by a group of expert judges using Amabile's Consensual Assessment Technique (CAT), as explained in chapter 1. A survey that collected contextual information revealed that significantly higher-performing students didn't limit their implementation to what we taught them. Instead, their curiosity pushed them out of their comfort zone, initially fumbling and failing but carrying on and eventually submitting a more original and creative design. Interestingly, the more creative a project was deemed by the judges, the more clean code problems a static code analysis tool revealed. Perhaps not unexpectedly, exploring unknown code territory with a tight deadline seemed to cause students to skimp on the code quality.

In another ongoing study, our software engineering students had to work together with students from the design faculty of another university to code a visually appealing digital piece of art. Many students mentioned in postproject interviews that their partner had made them explore more than usual and get out of their comfort zone. One student testified to this:

> I had the feeling that my partner made me start exploring more [implementation options]. Usually I'd stay comfortably within [the knowledge of] my group. The interaction [with] my partner made me really get out of my comfort zone.

---

[2] Wouter Groeneveld, Dries Martin, Tibo Poncelet, and Kris Aerts. Are undergraduate creative coders clean coders? A correlation study. Proceedings of the 53rd ACM Technical Symposium on Computer Science Education, 2022.

This positive feedback loop ties in nicely with the findings discussed in chapter 3, where the influence of communication on creativity was explored. Other students noted that getting over the initial discomfort of getting to know another person came at the cost of precious project time. They didn't manage to finish what they intended, but the core concept they aimed for certainly was more grandiose compared with a conventional programming project limited to the engineering faculty. In this study, the self-reported creativity of the engineering student who was paired with the design student again was rated higher compared with that of the control group, in which engineering students were paired with other engineering students.

A conclusion could be that getting out of the comfort zone can be refreshing for the creativity of the programmer. The problem with yelling "Get out of your comfort zone!" is the vagueness of that zone (figure 6.4)—what, exactly, does it entail? For one person, it might mean carefully exploring the possibility of switching to another development team to learn more about the frontend instead of the backend of the system. For another person, it might mean giving a presentation and sharing knowledge.

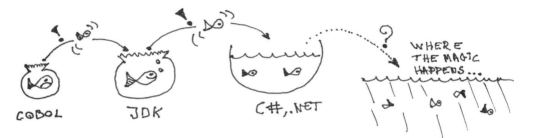

Figure 6.4   Good job at getting out of your comfort zone! But wait—did we just swap fishbowls?

Many programmers tout having thwarted their inner fears by making the switch from Java to C#. The internet is littered with mediocre articles that clickbait people in with fancy titles such as "Programmers, Don't Stay in Your Comfort Zone," "The Power of Stepping Out of Your Comfort Zone When Coding," or the very daring "Lessons Learned by Stepping Outside [the] WordPress Comfort Zone."

I'll be blunt here: switching languages, teams, technologies, and sharing knowledge are everything but getting out of the *programming* comfort zone. Both research and practice indicate that those attributes are becoming the minimum requirements for calling yourself a competent programmer. By limiting the interpretation of a comfort zone to technical programming knowledge, we risk turning a blind eye toward a much more fertile pool of cross-pollinating ideas. Creative Programmers do a lot better than that.

6.2.4   *Growth mindsets and creativity*

Why is developing a growth mindset relevant to creativity? Because a growth mindset embraces challenges rather than avoids them, persists in case of setbacks rather than giving up, sees effort as a way towards mastery rather than a waste of energy, learns from criticism rather than ignores it, and finds inspiration in the success of others rather than being threatened by it. All these feedback loops are an integral part of the creative process.

Robert Sternberg polled 143 creativity researchers and concluded that there was wide agreement on the number-one ingredient of creative achievement.[3] Although Sternberg used the term *persistence*, it was, as Carol Dweck noted in her work, "exactly the kind of perseverance and resilience produced by the growth mindset."

Dweck's publications are among the most cited in psychological research. More recently, countless studies investigating creativity seamlessly integrated the growth mindset concept. Behavioral psychologists Jean Pretz and Danielle Nelson identified mindset as one of the key factors that can positively or negatively affect creativity.[4] In another example, the motivation to be creative was related to having a growth mindset by undergraduate students who had declared an education major. Their perceptions of a creative other were positively related to their growth mindset of creativity.[5] The most promising part of their study is the following conclusion:

These findings point to promising creativity motivation strategies, including the cultivation of a malleable view of creativity and of creative role models, that may, in turn, promote creative achievement by encouraging students to do, learn, and accomplish new things.

If you show students—or, in our case, programmers—that creativity is a skill that can be learned and thus is not fixed, their creativity blossoms. I'd be more than happy if this book somehow managed to cultivate that malleable view in the minds of its readers. If not, feel free to send criticism my way!

Responsibility and the growth mindset

Fixed mindset people constantly feel the need to prove their worth. When things go wrong, admitting mistakes isn't part of the plan. "I didn't do it!" or "It's their fault!" responses are typical fixed mindset behavior. Denying or laying blame also stand in the way of sharing responsibilities, as shown in chapter 3.

Intellectual abilities can be developed, and so can creativity, yet we need to be open to the idea of the development of creativity just as with any other skill. In a recent study of the relationship between mindset in higher education computing students and their study performance,[6] researchers Mikko-Ville Apiola and Erkki Sutinen discovered that

---

[3] Robert J. Sternberg. Handbook of creativity. Cambridge University Press, 1999.

[4] Jean E. Pretz and Danielle Nelson. Creativity is influenced by domain, creative self-efficacy, mindset, self-efficacy, and self-esteem. The Creative Self. Elsevier, 2017.

[5] Pin Li, Zhitian Skylor Zhang, Yanna Zhang, Jia Zhang, Miguelina Nunez, and Jiannong Shi. From implicit theories to creative achievements: The mediating role of creativity motivation in the relationship between stereotypes, growth mindset, and creative achievement. The Journal of Creative Behavior, 2021.

[6] Mikko-Ville Apiola and Erkki Sutinen. Mindset and study performance: New scales and research directions. Proceedings of the 20th Koli Calling International Conference on Computing Education Research, 2020.

mindset on computing was growth oriented but that mindset on creativity was the most fixed of all scales. This means that computing students either think they are creative or think they are not, but they are not open to the idea of nurturing creativity. As the authors concluded,

> *This is interesting and alarming at the same time. As computer science is inherently a creative domain, and building technologies requires creativity, one could presume that a fixed mindset on creativity might have negative consequences in building future technologies.*

The question remains whether we can extrapolate these results to more experienced programmers. Research on mindsets in computing is still in its infancy. A few pilot studies have reported successes while deploying growth mindset interventions in an effort to increase programming performance in first-year computing students.[7] One intervention comprised three parts: lectures to promote the fundamentals of developing a growth mindset and testimonials, case studies drawn from Dweck's work, and frequent feedback loops.

However, the average mindset did not change significantly. An intervention of a single semester might (slightly) increase grades, but a mindset is not so easily changed. This again shows the importance of continuously rerouting the fixed mindset into an open mindset, not only in the context of intelligence but also, and especially, when it comes to creativity.

EXERCISE   When was the last time you were forced to get out of your comfort zone related to your programming work? What was it, exactly, that made you dip a toe into the unknown? What was the creative result like—for yourself, for the project, and for possible future ventures into the unknown?

6.3   *Staying on the curious course*

Perseverance is, along with curiosity, identified as a major creative characteristic. Without curiosity, Charles Darwin would not have collected as much compelling information in his notebooks. But without the perseverance to keep on connecting, digging, reworking, and reviewing his collected notes, he would never have written *On the Origin of Species* 23 years after his journey aboard the *Beagle*.

6.3.1   *Persistence and grit*

Carol Dweck's mindsets are perspectives that alter the way you perceive your learning abilities (and those of others). A growth mindset focuses on both cultivating curiosity and persevering in the face of adversity. The research of psychologist Angela Duckworth picked up where Dweck left off. She coined the term *grit*, a special blend of passion and persistence that she calls the secret to success.[8] Just like the growth mindset,

[7] Keith Quille, Susan Bergin. Promoting a growth mindset in CS1: Does one size fit all? A pilot study. Proceedings of the 2020 ACM Conference on Innovations and Technology in Computer Science Education, 2020.

[8] Angela L. Duckworth, Christopher Peterson, Michael D. Matthews, and Dennis R. Kelly. Grit: Perseverance and passion for long-term goals. Journal of Personality and Social Psychology, 2007.

grit is backed by scientific evidence telling us that it can grow. Forget talent—just keep on bashing your head against the wall: eventually, you'll break through.

The link between grit and academic success has been established by numerous studies. The same is true for programming courses, which are notorious for their high failure rates: researchers James Wolf and Ronnie Jia found that grittier students earn higher grades compared with less gritty students.[9]

Of course, grit can take you only so far. Innate factors, described as IQ or talent, still matter as measures of potential. I don't want to linger on this for too long because it is an unresolved and heated debate in the field of psychology.

Grit and the growth mindset both show clear signs of curiosity and perseverance. Passion can evolve from curiosity, and nobody keeps on bashing their head against code problems without a tiny bit of passion. By the 23,954th bash, passion might have evaporated and turned into a severe headache.

When Angela Duckworth was interviewed by Farnam Street, she also emphasized the importance of asking for and correctly processing feedback:[10] "Feedback is a gift, but most of us don't know how to unwrap it. And don't want to receive it." Grit can be seen as a part of the broader growth mindset in the form of a trait defined by a set of characteristics: courage, conscientiousness, resilience, and endurance. What stands out is that both Dweck and Duckworth urge us not to always look for a new challenge when the going gets tough. Like Albert Einstein said, "It's not that I'm so smart, it's just that I stay with problems longer."

Most of us struggle with direction versus determination. We take another direction as soon as things go awry, hastily covering up our mistakes. Instead, grit teaches us to learn from them and continue pressing on. Darwin suffered from severe seasickness. Why would any sane person deliberately cope with seasickness on and off for five years? I know I wouldn't—the thought alone makes my stomach churn. Darwin must have scored very high on Duckworth's Grit Scale.

Bill Gates on grit

There are countless success stories of perseverance in the programming world, of which perhaps Bill Gates' is the most famous. As a young boy, he began to show interest in computer programming. Back then, programming was done on terminals that interface with a central machine: computer time was expensive and thus limited and shared. When his time was up but his curiosity wasn't satisfied yet, he exploited a glitch to obtain more computer time. When his rights were eventually revoked, he kept on hacking into his school's scheduling program just to learn how the internals worked.

---

[9] James R. Wolf and Ronnie Jia. The role of grit in predicting student performance in introductory programming courses: An exploratory study. Proceedings of the Southern Association for Information Systems Conference, 2015.

[10] Listen to the interview at https://fs.blog/knowledge-podcast/angela-duckworth/.

(continued)

In the 1970s, before founding Microsoft, Gates and his partner Paul Allen created software for traffic counting. The project, Traf-O-Data, was considered a failure, yet instead of giving up the business and going to study something serious, he dropped out of Harvard and eventually made billions.

In an interview with Angela Duckworth, Bill Gates revealed that when he used to screen applicants for Microsoft, he selected the most gritty candidates. In tough programming assignments, he preferred candidates to keep on trying rather than give up in frustration.

6.3.2   *Willpower is a depletable resource*

In theory, developing growth mindsets and increasing your grit sound easy enough. In practice, it requires a lot of willpower to swallow our pride when dealing with negative feedback—especially if that same day our mood has already plummeted because of an unlucky combination of a flat bicycle tire and a sudden downpour. "It's just one of those days," you think later that night after indulging in too much chocolate.

It's not just one of those days: it's called *willpower*, and social psychologist Roy F. Baumeister discovered that it is a finite resource.[11] Most decisions we make secretly consume a little bit of willpower. Big and scary decisions or events, like coping with a sudden downpour and negative feedback, gobble up a lot of it. At the end of the day, there won't be anything left to keep you from snacking.

Creative geniuses instinctively knew this. Sigmund Freud and Immanuel Kant both adhered to a strict daily schedule. Einstein and da Vinci wore the same clothes day in and day out. Even the president of the United States does not choose which clothes to wear; his staff does: one fewer decision to make equals a little bit more willpower for creative or important life-threatening decisions. This sounds ridiculous, but all the little bits do add up. What Baumeister calls *ego depletion* can make you lose control (performance control) and give in to cravings (impulse control).

Self-control, at the cost of willpower, is indispensable when it comes to perseverance and switching from a fixed to a growth mindset. A mindset change is not about picking up a few pointers here and there; it's about continually investing in seeing things in a new way. Nobody ever said it was going to be easy! Thankfully, Baumeister shows that willpower is like a muscle: given enough training, it can gradually do more heavy lifting. He concludes his book *Willpower*, written with John Marion Tierney, with a few tips on how to increase willpower and how to avoid wasting it, such as creating habits, finding a beacon to hold onto, and challenging yourself by setting goals.

---

[11] Roy F. Baumeister and John Marion Tierney. Willpower: Rediscovering the greatest human strength. Penguin, 2012.

EXERCISE Take the Grit Scale by filling in responses to 10 questions at https://angeladuckworth.com/grit-scale/. The result is a grit score on a scale between 0.0 and 5.0. How do you feel about that score—does that reflect the current you? Which questions evoked a bit of resistance? That might be interesting to work on in the near future. Note that the result is not set in stone!

6.4 *From curiosity to motivation*

Wonder is the source of all learning. Wonder can evolve into motivation to keep on learning. But how about that classic intrinsic-versus-extrinsic motivation debate, and where does creativity fit in? Let's take a closer look.

6.4.1 *Intrinsic motivation*

Becoming motivated to do something (such as being creative) by yourself, without an external source that pushes you to do it, is called an *intrinsic* motivation. As first mentioned in chapter 1, feeding Umberto Eco's *creative urge*, which lives within us, is most likely an intrinsic decision. We're creative because we want to be. Vincent van Gogh painted because he wanted to paint, not because he was driven by the promise of wealth. If that was the case, he would have followed in his father's footsteps, who was a minister of the Dutch Reformed Church. In fact, van Gogh's initial desire was to become a pastor.

Studies by cognitive psychologist Teresa Amabile have shown that intrinsically motivated students produce more creativity. One group of students was told that their work would be evaluated by artists, while the other group was told to just have fun. The results were astonishing: the "just have fun" group scored significantly higher on CAT tests compared with the control group. Amabile calls it the *intrinsic theory of motivation*: "People will be more creative when they feel motivated primarily by interest, enjoyment, satisfaction, and the challenge of the work itself—not by external pressures."[12]

So far, so good. I don't think the outcome of that study surprises anyone. This intrinsic theory, however, doesn't always bode well in the real world.

6.4.2 *Extrinsic motivation*

External sources telling you to do something are called *extrinsic* motivation. This can be an assignment tasked by your employer or the promise of money or power. That call from your bank pushing you to start investing your money could have been made because the caller was on commission.

Amabile's experiments are limited to undergraduate students. In other words, she picked out novice creators with little experience. Would the inclusion of experienced creators have mattered? Other studies say yes.[13] All we need to do to prove it is to take

---

[12] Teresa M. Amabile. Motivational synergy: Toward new conceptualizations of intrinsic and extrinsic motivation in the workplace. Human Resource Management Review, 1993.

[13] Barry Gerhart and Meiyu Fang. Pay, intrinsic motivation, extrinsic motivation, performance, and creativity in the workplace: Revisiting long-held beliefs. Annual Reviews, 2015.

a look at the highly competitive world of renowned scientists. Remember the jealousy of Louis Pasteur from chapter 5? He did everything he could to keep his adversaries from earning more fame and money in the form of grants. Nobel Prize winners James Watson and Francis Crick said they were motivated by the Nobel Prize itself.

Extrinsic competition clearly motivates skilled scientists. Even without the influence of the "publish or perish" system, the allure of a reward seems to positively affect creative work.

By now, you should be familiar with systems thinking. We can't talk about motivation without also considering its environment. Furthermore, extrinsic pushes come in many flavors: constant, external, performance monitoring obviously impedes creativity. More about the environment in the following chapters.

6.4.3   *Combining intrinsic and extrinsic motivation*

But wait a minute—ample software systems and artworks have also been produced on commission. Is the decisive factor intrinsic or extrinsic motivation? The answer is, of course, a little bit of both.

For example, Mozart was both extrinsically and intrinsically motivated. He performed miracles only when someone demanded it. It was only after the contractor kicked his butt into action and the creative process bootstrapped, that the exceptional musical compositions flowed. Mozart is well known for his greed and loved to take part in commercial politics. The Renaissance contains similar examples. Countless marvelous creative artworks and buildings were commissioned by the Church and the de Medici family. Filippo Brunelleschi's eye-catching cathedral dome in Firenze was built because of gold, not because of intrinsic motivations.

Sometimes, the project starts as a boring coding job that gradually fuels motivation and ends up becoming a big-passion project. I know a programming consultant who offers his services a few days a week to a company that, according to him, "makes really boring .NET stuff." Yet, when I ask him why he's still doing that, the answer is twofold: "It pays well and the company allows for a lot of creative freedom where I can go wild, even though the software itself isn't exciting. It's like I'm being paid to experiment!" Another ex-colleague explicitly requested to be transferred to the C++ maintenance team that everybody dreaded, just to learn the ropes of C++ and smart pointer usage. That's what I call dedication.

Sometimes, it's the other way around. Two ex-colleagues of mine were bored with enterprise Java development and started dabbling in the Play Framework to learn Scala and Akka. To have something tangible to build after working hours, they created a seating reservation system for the local choir. A good year later, they quit their jobs, launched it as a start-up with the help of a sales specialist, and have been evolving their own cloud-based product ever since.

Software entrepreneurs Jason Fried and David Heinemeier Hansson like to call this phenomenon "scratching your own itch."[14] Basecamp, originally designed as a way to internally manage client work, is such an itch that was thoroughly scratched. First, build for yourself (intrinsic), and then expand it to others (extrinsic). The "scratch your own itch" mantra can be very powerful in boosting your creative curiosity as you're initially making something cool for yourself.

It is interesting to note that although some software systems start out as intrinsic passion projects, as time goes on, that motivation can gradually wane, and hence the added boost of extrinsic motivation won't hurt. After all, how many of us would still be cracking programming problems without getting paid? How many of us would still be enthusiastically coding away while getting severely underpaid? Prestige, competition, and money apparently motivate experienced creators but inhibit inexperienced ones. There, this is your free pass to ask for a raise.

> **EXERCISE** When it comes to programming, do you have a *creative urge*? For instance, do you maintain a lot of pet projects? Which of those could evolve into something production ready that can be deployed and effectively used? Or are you more easily enticed by extrinsic means? If so, can you identify intrinsic means at your current job that help you deal with the mundane?

6.5   *Multipotentiality*

Truly creative people rarely limit their curiosity to only one discipline. Does this sound counterintuitive? Maybe you're thinking about the lifelong dedication of people like Sigmund Freud, founder of the field of psychoanalysis. Don't these people heavily specialize—in this case, in psychology? The Dreyfus model and the magical 10,000-hour rule might certainly apply to Freud, but we mustn't forget that he was also an amateur archaeologist. Freud loved collecting unique and ancient pieces to decorate his office. It was his love of archeology that gave him the idea for "excavating the mind"—an idea that was crossbred into psychology.

Freud was *diversifying experiences*, which is proven to enhance cognitive flexibility.[15] Systems thinker Nora Bateson (see chapter 3) compares limiting curiosity to only one domain with agricultural monocultures: endless fields of wheat, soy, or almond trees, that have devastating long-term consequences for biodiversity. *Mental monocropping* (figure 6.5) has the same toxic effect on one's cognitive health.

---

[14] See The Rework Podcast from 37signals. Scratch your own itch. https://www.rework.fm/scratch-your-own-itch/.

[15] Simone M. Ritter, Rodica Ioana Damian, Dean Keith Simonton, Rick B. van Baaren, Madelijn Strick, Jeroen Derks, and Ap Dijksterhuis. Diversifying experiences enhance cognitive flexibility. Journal of Experimental Social Psychology, 2012.

Figure 6.5　Imagine this as a photo of your brain instead of a huge wheat field. *Reap what you sow*: **wheat, wheat, and more wheat. Great for baking bread, disastrous for cultivating ideas. Photo courtesy of Bence Balla-Schottner, Unsplash**

6.5.1　Multiple true callings

The textbook example of a creative individual is Leonardo da Vinci. His Mona Lisa attracts millions of tourists to the Louvre. He wasn't merely a skilled painter and drawer: he studied anatomy, physiology, engineering, and biology; he designed contraptions; he theorized about flying UFOs; and he applied scientific rigor to every single idea he had. Da Vinci was the archetype of the *polymath* or *Renaissance man*: someone whose knowledge spans multiple domains that can be brought together to solve complex problems or come up with novel connections.

Living up to the expectations of the true *Uomo Universale* might be stretching it a bit too far. That is why creative generalist Emilie Wapnick came up with her own word for a person with multiple interests: a *multipotentialite*.[16] After studying law, building websites, and trying to get into arts, she got bored and moved on to yet another interest. Frustrated with never being able to answer the "What do you do?" question posed at every cocktail party, she discovered that she was a *multipo*—a generalist.

Wapnick discovered something more troubling: our current society does not easily accept multipotentiality. It puts specialism on a pedestal and shoves aside people with multiple interests. Even worse, people like Wapnick are left wondering what is wrong with them after blurting out "baker" and "programmer" and "philosopher" to answer "What do you want to be when you grow up?" Our culture expects a single silver bullet, not a scattershot.

Multipos have several advantages over specialists. The following is a summary from Wapnick's work:

---

[16] Emilie Wapnick. How to be everything: A guide for those who (still) don't know what they want to be when they grow up. HarperOne, 2017.

- *Idea synthesis*—Creativity happens in between domains, not safely within one.
- *Rapid learning*—Generalists are used to being beginners and excel at learning new things.
- *Adaptability*—Different situations call for different approaches, which are best tackled by adapting to them.
- *Big picture thinking*—Specialists tend to develop tunnel vision while generalists keep a wider view.
- *Relating and translating*—Because of their familiarity with many domains, it is easier for generalists to relate to other areas of expertise they know.

Emilie Wapnick is not an academic, but her ideas are echoed in many papers I've encountered during my research. Wapnick isn't the only nonacademic writer who subscribes to the idea of generalism, as journalist David Epstein proves with his recent book, *Range: Why Generalists Triumph in a Specialized World.*

Restarting from scratch can be quite daunting. Why would one leave a comfortable position as an expert in photography to become a total newbie in a professional kitchen? The following quote from Shunryu Suzuki, a Buddhist monk who founded the first American Zen monastery, might help: "In the beginner's mind, there are many possibilities. In the expert's mind, there are few."

Remember *GoldenEye, the* naively programmed *James Bond* video game from chapter 4? Rare's game-developer newbies saw possibilities that experts assumed were impossible to implement. This suggests that multipotentialites might also be better at working with constraints.

Nathan Myhrvold, the former CTO at Microsoft who completed a PhD in mathematics, applied his engineering experience, scientific rigor, and love of food photography to create the ultimate bread-baking bible, *Modernist Bread* (The Cooking Lab, 2017). In this enormous encyclopedic work, he meticulously deconstructs everything we know about bread baking: the microbiological process in the dough, the chemical process in the oven, and the psychological process in our brain when we munch on a delicious slice of bread. Myhrvold ticks a lot of Wapnick's boxes.

I know a few other engineers who have reinvented themselves as bakers and took advantage of their experience to fine-tune the baking process. Consider Justin Liam, for example, who built a fermentation-monitoring system for his sourdough starter using computer vision on a Raspberry Pi.[17] Or how about the software and hardware duo Fred Benenson and Sarah Pavis, who invented Breadwinner,[18] a smart sourdough tracker with a companion mobile app and intricate web-accessible dashboard? Without their adaptability, idea synthesis, and relating and translating multipotentialite traits, that product would never have existed.

In case you don't plan on quitting your coding job any time soon to become a baker, adopting a more generalist view might open up more creative and commercial

---

[17] See https://www.justinmklam.com/posts/2018/06/sourdough-starter-monitor/.
[18] See https://breadwinner.life/.

doors within the programming domain. This is exactly what Adam Tornhill set out to do. Adam is a programmer who managed to squeeze out everything from his combined degrees in engineering and psychology. He is the creator of CodeScene, a code analysis tool that, unlike many other static code analyzers, such as PMD, does not simply return potential code smells. Instead, based on Adam's psychological experience and collaborations with criminologists, it detects hidden social patterns in code. CodeScene—Code as a Crime Scene—is a behavioral code analysis tool that would not have existed if it weren't for Adam's combined interests.

6.5.2   *How to approach multiple interests*

Not every multipotentialite directs curiosity the same way. For some, sequential deep diving works wonders. Wapnick calls this the *Phoenix Approach*: serial specialists who stick with an interest longer than others to dig deeper but do move on after a while to broaden their horizons.

Other possibilities include these:

- *The Slash Approach*—The parallel processing of interests. I'm a baker/programmer/ teacher/researcher/writer; Adam Tornhill is a psychologist/programmer.
- *The Group Hug Approach*—Having one multifaceted job that hugs together various disciplines. A software developer in academia might be involved in multiple scientific domains, teaching didactics, coding to analyze data, writing to help publish the results, and so on.
- *The Einstein Approach*—Combining a stable but boring day job with creative discovery at night. This provides financial stability while at the same time enabling the freedom to scratch your own itch without the compromises required in most day jobs.

And as always, hybrid solutions that draw from several of these approaches might work best for you.

The dark side of creativity

Original thinkers can be more dishonest, concluded social psychology researchers Francesca Gino and Dan Ariely.[a] They discovered that a creative mindset can promote individuals' ability to justify their behavior, which, in turn, can lead to unethical behavior. Students who rated higher on a creative personality scale were also more likely to cheat during an experiment. Furthermore, students who were primed to think creatively were more likely to behave dishonestly than those in a control condition.

Your creative programming skills should never trump your responsibility toward coworkers, clients, and other stakeholders. Be wary of the path to the Dark Side, my young Padawan!

---

[a]Francesca Gino, Dan Ariely. The dark side of creativity: Original thinkers can be more dishonest. Journal of Personality and Social Psychology, 2012.

6.5.3 Does specialism kill creativity?

In his book *The Geography of Genius*, Eric Weiner laments the increasing pressure to specialize, which, according to him, stifles creativity rather than propels it to new heights. Every field has become so complex that it is now nearly impossible for a single mind to grasp all aspects. I have no problem explaining all the 0s and 1s inside the 1989 Game Boy, but don't ask me to explain how the 2020 M1 chip in my MacBook works (figure 6.6). I could invest a lot of time in trying to figure it out and still fail to truly grasp every tiny detail. The same is true for programming: on the Game Boy, each assembly line is simply an instruction that the CPU literally interprets. But what actually happens when we execute `Collections.sort(myClientList, Collections.reverseOrder())` inside the Java Virtual Machine? Convenience has indeed abstracted away complexity, but when things go wrong, debugging and pinpointing the problem can prove to be real challenges.

Figure 6.6 **Apple's M1 System on a Chip (SoC): 16 billion transistors, up to 8-core GPU *and* CPU coupled with fast cache and DRAM via a unified memory architecture (UMA). Reading that makes me feel like Manuel from *Fawlty Towers*: "¿Qué?" Compare that with the 8-bit Game Boy's Z80 CPU variant, which houses roughly 10,000 transistors. Wow. At the same time, it's impossible to deny its creative genius, but the point is that conceiving this requires hundreds of highly specialized hardware and software engineers (and tons of money).**

The rise of specialism isn't visible only in computing. Consider a job in the baking world, for example. Usually, a job ad titled "baker wanted" would suffice. That person would end up baking bread, leavening pastry treats and tarts, cooking pudding, inventing new praline flavors, and so forth. But that's not how it works. Even small bakeries employ dedicated bread bakers and pastry chefs: a strict separation of concerns that allows for fancy specialties but leaves little wiggle room to combine both.

There is nothing wrong with taking pride in specializing as a sourdough bread baker or chocolatier. The problem is that specialization does not stop there. Most job ads in large-scale baking industries call for either engineering experts as operations managers or ask for "mixers." Don't confuse a mixer with mixing equipment, though: a mixer is a person dedicated to mixing dough. That's it. It is a highly specialized and completely mind-numbing job in an assembly line. That is where the road to specialism is taking us.

British political activist Ken Robinson left little to the imagination with his books and TED talk "Education Kills Creativity."[19] Robinson argued that by educating people out of creative capabilities, we also rob them of the ability to cope with the uncertainty of the future. In high school, you're served carefully wrapped packages of math, history, biology, Latin, and informatics. Teachers do everything they can to safely stay within the bounds of the subject at hand while learning (and interest) occurs in between these packages.

Promoting specialization in higher education makes it even worse. University programs tout "interdisciplinary studying," which unfortunately rarely happens. It is a lot more challenging to study biology, anthropology, *and* history—like Gregory Bateson did in his cybernetics and systems thinking work from chapter 3—than to specialize in a single field, where the pathway to scientific mastery is much more straightforward. If there is no clear path, the curious and the gritty, and those with multiple interests, will thrive where others might fail.

In 2008, Belgian universities added a fifth year to the master's degree program in computer science to encompass more specialist courses to teach expertise demanded by the industry. Discussions to do the same for all engineering degrees are ongoing. Meanwhile, the retirement age keeps on climbing, and the years wasted in school do not count as work experience.

The number of doctoral students—the prototype of specialists—has quadrupled in the past century. When it comes to creativity, owning a PhD won't get you far: it apparently even statistically *decreases* your chance of a creative breakthrough! This was cited in Weiner's work, but I was unable to locate the source. Some dissertations surely can be creative products, but unfortunately they rarely draw from different fields.

6.5.4 *Generalism vs. specialism in tech*

Every programmer knows the tech world is highly specialized. Almost 90% of Pragmatic Bookshelf or Manning books help programmers specialize instead of generalize. Specialization in tech is a risky business because that world is also very volatile, forcing programmers to continually reinvent themselves. Specialism combined with volatility is a sure way to waste a lot of painfully gained skills and knowledge unless we find ways to transfer them to other domains. However, the cross-language clashes explained in chapter 5 teach us that knowledge transfer isn't exactly a cakewalk.

The best creative programmers are multipotentialites, yet technology companies keep on flooding the market with demoralizing job ads such as "Java Specialist," "BI

---

[19] Ken Robinson and Lou Aronica. Creative schools: Revolutionizing education from the ground up. Penguin Books Limited, 2015.

Expert," or "Oracle Database Manager." Specializing in the database syntax of Oracle is certainly a legitimate way to earn a good living, provided after five years the company doesn't switch to MS SQL.

According to the Stack Overflow Annual Developer Survey,[20] technology experts are even paid better compared with full stack developers. It's a gamble at best. The graphs in figure 6.7 illustrate that while the expert can easily outperform the generalist at very specific opportunities, they are useless at other jobs, making them not the best job fit.

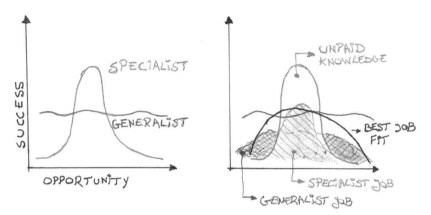

Figure 6.7   Overqualification can happen to specialists. You can't get paid for the value you can't add. This figure is based on the IT skills discussion by Ivan Pepelnjak at https://blog.ipspace.net/2015/05/on-i-shaped-and-t-shaped-skills.html.

Companies might be looking for specialists, but in reality, the best job fit is a combination between specialization and generality. All it takes is a mind switch for a Java expert to become a C# expert—the differences are surprisingly small. And yet, I've had colleagues who swear by one technology and make fun of the other. It is not only our pride and fears that stand in the way of discovery; (company) culture is also often to blame.

Does the advent of the full stack developer save us from specialism hell? Not really. What's the first thing you think of when you encounter the term *full stack*? "What kind of stack?" An Angular JS frontend and a Spring Boot backend? Or something entirely different, the Phoenix framework with a few RESTful Elixir endpoints? Of course, there are different levels of generalism and specialism. Mastering fundamentals—in this case, HTTP, JS, HTML, and REST—will make sure you'll more quickly pick up specialized frameworks, in this case, Angular or Phoenix. The problem is not stepping back to generalize one's Angular/Phoenix knowledge, making the transition between stacks more difficult.

---

[20] See https://insights.stackoverflow.com/survey/.

The best way to stay on top of the game is to pay close attention to the trends in the industry with the help of a Technology Radar as encountered in chapter 3. Be open to new experiences and try not to get yourself stuck in a highly specialized job.

If all else fails, it is never too late to chase other interests—or to combine them to arrive at novel products, such as the Breadwinner. When Mark Ferrari's (see chapter 4) 2D pixel art career was put to a grinding halt by the advent of 3D modeling, he moved on to write fantasy novels instead. His colored pencil work now proudly decorates his books.

> ### The dangers of certification
>
> In an effort to educate their employees, companies organize workshops and send people to expensive specialization courses. Even worse, many consultancy companies oblige their programmers to get certified. I'm a Zend Certified PHP Architect, a Sun Certified Java Developer, and a Certified Scrum Master. Great! Now my employer can charge more for my services while I'm stuck in the PHP/Java lane.
>
> Specialization by certification does little to launch your career except filling the pockets of others and padding your CV with a lot of terms. I got that PHP certificate to prove to my boss that my interests are broader than enterprise Java development. It didn't work: I was never handed a PHP project. In Belgium, in the Brussels area, Java consultants have much higher daily wages (of which, of course, I saw little).
>
> Certificates, just like degrees, can have their value. Just try to diversify and be mindful of what the ultimate goal of that certification is—a personal or a company benefit.

EXERCISE Does your company culture support generalism or prefer specialism? Think about competency matrices, your job title, team compositions. Do they promote specialism (senior Java engineer working in the backend team) or generalism (senior programmer working in the product-something team)? How about the preference of your colleagues and yourself?

6.6   *Serendipitous discoveries*

Have you ever found something interesting in a book or record store without looking for something specific? Then you'll know what serendipity means: finding things you were not necessarily looking for. I love these happy accidents. We're in luck: engineering serendipity is (partially) possible. By fine-tuning our system (see chapter 2) to actively listen for these moments, we can increase the number of joyful discoveries.

Sudden innovation at chance encounters of people being at the right place, time, and moment is shrouded in mysticism. Newton's accidental apple did not make him discover the laws of gravity. Archimedes' accidental "Eureka!" was not only due to his bath. Nonetheless, research has shown that the myth is at least somewhat true. Casual water cooler chats are more often thought provoking than forcing people into a meeting room. This is what Steven Johnson meant with his liquid network that we encountered in chapter 3.

6.6.1 *How to stumble upon things*

According to law professor Cass Sunstein, serendipitous discoveries are what newspapers should produce.[21] The headline of a story is designed to draw you in, hoping to capture your focus and draw you into a story you didn't know you were interested in but that gives you information that changes your worldview. Unfortunately, the modern news industry is more interested in clicks and your data than in providing genuinely interesting information. This is where your RSS filter from chapter 2 comes in!

Wikipedia has a "Random Article" link. Obsidian has an "Open Random Note" button. I can't believe there isn't a JetBrains IDE plugin to open a random source file. Imagine starting with that at the beginning of your coding session! DEVONThink suggests related but unlinked documents in the See Also pane. Discuvver, an alternative to the once-popular StumbleUpon, sends random useful sites to your inbox weekly. The IndieWeb Discovery page (https://indieweb.org/discovery) mentions "serendipitous methods" for finding content, websites, communities, or people. Remember webrings from the nineties, before Yahoo acquired GeoCities, when search and social media algorithms didn't rule the world? Without invisible algorithms dictating what appears in your timeline, some of the more obscure but equally interesting content still has a chance of being discovered, whereas now, you're just being fed more of the same—or, even worse, only the most popular or paid content.

Heterogeneity facilitates serendipity. Replacing traditional news sites with user-generated news aggregators like Reddit might lead to interesting stories, but they're hardly surprising, serendipitous discoveries. The Reddit user base is still overwhelmingly male, employed in tech, and from the United States.[22] This means that certain stories are more likely to be upvoted than others. We won't delve into the details of homophily here, but the message is clear: don't put all your serendipitous eggs in similar baskets. Read this book, *The Creative Programmer*, as well as *Art as Therapy*, *The Go Programming Language*, and *Sophie's World*. Follow the blogs *The Pragmatic Engineer*, *The Marginalian*, *Programming Digressions*, and *Farnam Street*.

6.6.2 *Openness to experience*

Applying for a programming job at big companies can involve taking some kind of personality trait test, likely the Big Five test that was popularized as a job performance assessment by psychologist Sebastiaan Rothmann and his colleagues.[23] The Big Five personality traits are *conscientiousness*, *extroversion*, *agreeableness*, *neuroticism*, and *openness to experience*.

Although the Big Five model has been criticized for its limited scope and wonky theoretical and methodological basis, it remains widely used in industry and in creativity

---

[21] Listen to a dialogue about the architecture of serendipity at https://bloggingheads.tv/videos/1615.

[22] Distribution of Reddit users worldwide as of January 2022, by gender. Statista. https://www.statista.com/statistics/1255182/distribution-of-users-on-reddit-worldwide-gender/.

[23] Sebastiaan Rothmann and Elize P Coetzer. The Big Five personality dimensions and job performance. SA Journal of Industrial Psychology, 2003.

research. Multiple studies investigating possible correlations between creativity and one of the five traits indicate "a medium to small positive relationship between openness to experience and ratings of creativity associated with participants' [work]."[24] Here, the creativity was again rated using Amabile's CAT system.

In the context of our quest to define the Creative Programmer, studies like the aforementioned are suggestive at best. They either adhere to Kaufman and Sternberg's obsolete definition of creativity from chapter 1; use a measurement metric, like the Torrance Test of Creative Thinking, which predicts only divergent thinking; or limit their test subjects to undergraduate students because they're easy to come by. Remember the difference in intrinsic and extrinsic motivation based on the level of experience of the person? Undergraduates are novices. Results from such studies can be indicative but cannot be easily generalized to the entire programming population. That is why we turned to the industry to explore the role of creativity in software engineering by conducting surveys, focus groups, and interviews. The result is a stack of academic papers and a more practical guide: this book.

Still, it makes sense that a combination of certain personality traits facilitates creative work. Being an unreasonable jerk won't help to get you into a Camerata. The same is true for openness to experience: lack of appreciation for others' experiences doesn't exactly scream curiosity.

> **EXERCISE**   Next time someone talks about their hobby, show genuine interest—especially if it's not your thing. Even if you're not an avid reader, at the next opportunity, pop into a bookstore. Run your fingers over the spines of some of the books. Let yourself be influenced by color, typography, and title. Perhaps you'll walk home an experience richer and $40 poorer.

Serendipity demands a certain amount of openness to experience. Try to appreciate the randomness of encounters. Browsing the Amazon web store does *not* count: clever algorithms that suggest related articles are handy but have little to do with serendipity.

6.7   *About having fun*

When we asked programmers how to assess whether their colleagues are being creative, some answers were very surprising: "I'd just look at body language." "Are they happy, and making a lot of jokes?" "Are they in the zone ?" The last statement was rejected by other participants as they claimed one can also be very much in the zone by simply sticking stamps. I guess I must have interviewed a philately enthusiast. After some discussion, the conclusion was as follows: do programmers pause now and then, perhaps thinking? If the pause is too long, they are stuck. If there is no pause, it is likely to be assembly work and not creative work. Measuring productivity (something clearly visible) is something other than measuring creativity.

---

[24] Jason Hornberg and Roni Reiter-Palmon. Creativity and the Big Five personality traits: Is the relationship dependent on the creativity measure? In The Cambridge Handbook of Creativity and Personality Research. Cambridge University Press, 2017.

That second statement is much more intriguing. Why would cracking jokes be an indicator of creativity? Participants weren't sure, but they were onto something. Fun counterbalances repetition and boredom, uplifts the spirit, and increases motivation.

In 1976, behavioral psychologist Avner Ziv asked a group of adolescents to listen to a record of Israel's most popular comedians. Afterward, they had to complete the Torrance Test of Creative Thinking. The group that didn't listen to the record performed significantly worse.[25] Teenagers with the loudest laughs produced the best creative results. We've seen in chapter 4 that the Torrance test isn't all encompassing, but more recent studies have successfully replicated the effect: a laughter response to humorous stimuli increases creative thinking. Even if its effects are limited, the contagious effect of humor is a great way to increase group cohesiveness—which, in turn, plays an important part in creativity.

Cognitive and creativity researcher Beth Nam even discovered that jokes can be used as an unconscious trigger to prime insight.[26] Humor comprehension has been shown to provoke greater activation in language and semantic-related brain regions as well as the temporal and prefrontal regions in both hemispheres: the same brain regions used to develop insight.

So, two bytes walk into a bar. Byte `11111111` asks byte `11101111` "You don't look so well; are you ill?" to which the other byte responds, "No, man; I'm just feeling a bit off." A *bit*—get it? No? Avner Ziv also wrote something about the quality of jokes that matters; perhaps that's the problem. Truly funny jokes (I'll leave that to the professional comedians) are funny because they convey an unexpected but logical element, which is related to serendipity and creative insight.

6.7.1   *Fooling around*

Creativity for the sake of creativity (as we saw in chapter 5), is a great way to learn: simply having fun by fooling around. Insight is welcome, but not the goal. I love how a Mastodon[27] user on the `weirder.earth` instance expressed enthusiasm for "just doing it":

> *I think one of the best ideas to hold in mind is "Go down the rabbit hole"; when you get interested in doing something just go down the rabbit hole. That's how you end up making your own fantasy emulators, toy languages, cool graphics stuff and just having fun with the computer instead of helplessly trying to "stay productive."*

Following the White Rabbit just to chase the rabbit with no real purpose other than having fun can be a great way to stumble onto new things that cascade into even more curious discoveries. That is how I got into bread baking, Game Boy development, philosophy, creativity research, fountain pens, and blogging. Come to think of it, that is also when I felt the most whole and alive.

---

[25] Avner Ziv. Facilitating effects of humor on creativity. Journal of Educational Psychology, 1976.

[26] Beth Nam. Hacking the creative mind: An insight priming tool to facilitate creative problem-solving. Creativity and Cognition, 2021.

[27] Mastodon is a decentralized alternative to Twitter that puts privacy and control first. See https://joinmastodon.org/.

Creative tinkering is an excellent vehicle for discovering interests that, in turn, feed the creative urge. There is only one problem: taking the leap requires guts—which brings us right back to Carol Dweck's growth mindset.

Rabbit chasing is not yak shaving

Chasing down a rabbit sounds an awful lot like yak shaving: the refactoring of seemingly random code, deemed necessary to solve a problem which solves a problem, which, after several levels of recursion later, solves the *real* problem you're working on.

Rabbit chasing inevitably results in chasing down other ideas and getting distracted; only this time that is exactly the purpose, and there is no real goal except to learn and have fun. Shaving a yak is bad only if you're trying to solve a problem.

6.7.2 *Just for fun: A bad guy bonus challenge*

Ready to go down the rabbit hole? Here's an interesting brain teaser. Figure 6.8 contains two examples of nine people, of which some are "good guys" and some are "bad guys." We're interested in identifying the bad ones.

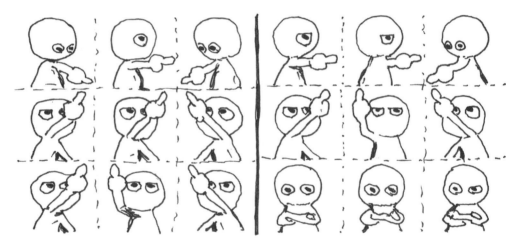

Figure 6.8 Who are the two bad guys? These are two separate puzzles. This idea is based on puzzles by LEVEL 5 Interactive.

If a good guy has one or more bad guys next to him, the good guy will point to one of the bad guys; otherwise, he'll cross his arms. A bad guy always points to someone, whether good or bad. Find the two bad guys!

That was fun, wasn't it? Okay, now for the real work: let's convert that into code and program a solver. We could translate the picture into a 3×3 matrix where the pointing is modeled with an arrow. The two situations in figure 6.8 can be described as follows:

```
1->5,2->3,3->5
4->2,5->3,6->2
7->5,8->5,9->5

1->2,2->3,3->5
4->2,5->2,6->2
7,8,9
```

The expected output would produce two numbers for each situation, identifying the bad guys. Don't forget to enjoy enjoying—we're just fooling around. Does your solver work with the above input from figure 6.8? Great, but that's hardly a challenge since you could have hardcoded the results. How about writing a puzzle input generator for it? If you limit the matrix size to 3 × 3, it won't be too difficult.

You know what else could be fun? Reimplement it in another programming language. Perhaps a performance analysis (by timing how long it takes to solve 100 puzzles) will reveal opportunities for optimizations. If you're still into it after that, a web interface or app to challenge friends won't hurt.

Looking for more puzzle challenges? Try playing the *Professor Layton* series on the Nintendo (3)DS and Switch, on which this puzzle is based. It's always fun to try to implement a solver in code, you know, *because*!

If puzzles aren't your thing, there's always a cool random maze to code. Programmer Jamis Buck dedicated a whole book to generating mazes because "it's fun—remember when programming used to be fun?"[28] While working for Basecamp, Buck wrestled with burnout, and after taking a year off, he never thought he'd write code again—until he rediscovered his motivation by just coding silly things, such as a maze. As Buck wrote, it is "the best medicine for programmer's block, burnout, and the grayest of days." Coding just for fun is a great way to take the edge off, discover interesting approaches to algorithmic problems, and ultimately feed those ideas back into your daily programming routine.

Summary

- Safely sticking to what you know will be of little help when you are trying to come up with a creative solution to a challenging programming problem.
- The same is true for giving up after trying to wrap your head around something without much success. Remember that a combination of curiosity and perseverance will get you much further.
- Make time to wander and wonder instead of always rushing through and moving on to the next problem. Do you know *why* that solution works the way it does?
- The concepts introduced in this book can, of course, also be applied outside of the field of programming. Follow your curiosity. Pursue new interests. Just make sure to stop now and then and think about how that new interest could be cross-pollinated into a potential programming solution.

---

[28] Jamis Buck. Mazes for programmers: Code your own twisty little passages. Pragmatic Bookshelf, 2015.

- Creativity as a skill can be grown, just like knowledge. Remember that next time you say, "I'm not that creative"—you might *not yet* be. The moment you realize it can be developed, you're shifting from a fixed mindset to a growth mindset.

- Embrace criticism as a way to further increase your skill set. It is never fun to deal with, but it is up to you to learn something from it and, again, to grow as a creative programmer.

- Don't wait until you're forced outside of your comfort zone. Acknowledge that, by doing so, you might encounter new people and techniques that could end up in your toolkit. This could be as simple as switching programming languages or pursuing a new hobby.

- Some people thrive as generalists, or what Emilie Wapnick calls *multipotentialites*. Those who do are usually better at, among others, rapid learning, idea synthesis, and adapting. Perhaps you can use an approach such as Phoenix, Slash, Group Hug, or Einstein to embrace multiple interests.

- You *can* excel at multiple things. Try not to limit your programming experience to just one language: the more, the better. Heavy specialization can narrow your field of view.

- The best way to keep the motivation flowing is a combination method that incorporates both intrinsic and extrinsic means. Being aware of what currently motivates you (or what doesn't) might help better focus your creative efforts.

- Don't always take things too seriously. Programming should also be fun! Coding for fun is a great way to discover interesting approaches that might even help you conquer tough problems in your daily programming job.

Creative state of mind

"Eureka, eureka; I've found it!" cried Archimedes, while running around naked in the streets of Syracuse. The ancient Sicilians didn't mind; they were used to turning a blind eye to naked lunatics. Archimedes rushed back home, grabbed something to write with, and got to work—or, rather, continued working. According to the Roman author Vitruvius, Archimedes was tasked by King Hiero II to find out whether his newly made crown was truly crafted of solid gold, without damaging the crown itself. Every time Archimedes pondered a difficult problem, he took a bath, and this time he noticed that the level of water in the tub rose as he got in. Could the submerged crown displace an amount of water equal to its volume? Eureka!

The "Eureka!" story reached its legendary status in modern retellings. Strangely enough, there is no mention of a golden crown in Archimedes' treatise *On Floating Bodies*. We'll never know whether it is true. What is true, however, is that the same king, Hiero II, commissioned Archimedes (figure 7.1) to build a gigantic ship, a

Figure 7.1 Domenico Fetti's *Archimedes* or *Portrait of a Scholar* (1620) Source: public domain.

ship capable of carrying more than 600 people, a gymnasium, and multiple temples. It truly was the *Titanic* of the ancient Greeks.

"*Mon Dieu, c'est ça!*" (that's it!) thought Henri Poincaré 20 centuries later, while boarding a public bus in the neighborhood of Coutances in Normandy. Poincaré's efforts to solve a difficult mathematical problem had been fruitless for weeks. Frustrated by the lack of progress, he called for a break and joined a geological excursion near his then-hometown, Caen. The expedition bus unexpectedly inspired the proof for his equation, but Poincaré was a man steeped in logic: he did not turn to the divine when searching for an explanation for the sudden illumination. In true scientific fashion, he was determined to uncover a pattern, so he formed his own theory on the creative state of mind, concluding that the act of creation involves a period of conscious work followed by a period of unconscious work. After that, more conscious work is required, as what the unconscious mind produces isn't a complete solution but rather a hint in the right direction. Some of those hints might seem elegant and alluring but fall flat during thorough analysis.

After developing his theory on creativity, Poincaré was regularly found walking around the bluffs in Normandy or around the campus of the Sorbonne, where he later taught. He was preoccupied, like any other professor—except that Poincaré's distraction was a deliberate attempt to bootstrap the unconscious processing of his conscious work. It was in those thinking–nonthinking states that he conceived intricate proofs, ideas, and theses on arithmetic transformations of geometry.

"Wow, time sure flies!" Philip noted after hearing his twin brother Andrew's stomach growl. Before they knew it, the Oliver twins were working late yet again, completely absorbed by the flow of programming their next video game, *Fantasy World Dizzy*. The third *Dizzy* game (figure 7.2) was released by Codemasters in October 1989, just six weeks after the twins wrote their first line of code.

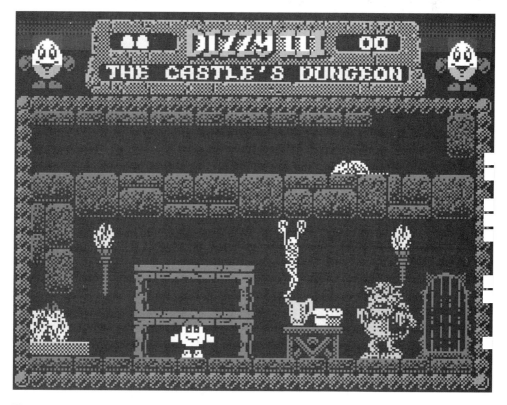

Figure 7.2 *Dizzy III: Fantasy World Dizzy* on the ZX Spectrum

The iconic British egg-headed character was initially drawn as a distraction in between creating various animations for another game, *Ghost Hunters*. Philip tried to get the most facial expressions out of a restricted sprite set of 24 × 32 pixels. There wasn't enough room for arms and legs, so crude-looking red boxing gloves had to do. Satisfied with the result, Philip stashed the character away and resumed developing *Ghost Hunters*.

A few months later, the Oliver twins invented *Dizzy*, a unique blend of arcade and adventure games and an instant bestseller for the Amstrad CPC and ZX Spectrum. Philip and Andrew would eventually release 25 Amstrad, 17 Spectrum, and 11 NES games in a five-year period—enough for Guinness World Records to award them the "Most Prolific 8-Bit Videogame Developers" title. When they were in front of a computer, they were fully engrossed in code, and time seemed to lose its meaning.

Still, the brothers regularly encountered roadblocks on the way to success. When out of ideas, they deliberately took breaks by watching television shows, playing other games, experimenting in their sprite editor, and reading classic fables and tales. *Count Duckula*, *Zork*, *Philosopher's Quest*, *Jack and the Beanstalk*, and *Gauntlet* all influenced various *Dizzy* games.

7.1 Getting in the right creative mood

What is the greatest common divisor between Archimedes' relaxing bath-time moments that helped him think, Henri Poincaré's illuminations on random bus rides and long walks, and the productivity of the Oliver twins? All three examples showcase a certain creative state of mind: alternating pondering with relaxing, letting the unconscious mind work after the conscious one, and taking breaks that inspire when in a rut.

Henri Poincaré (1854–1912) was a polymath and excelled in the fields of mathematics, physics, engineering, and philosophy. By putting his "subliminal self" to work, he was also a master of staging the creative state of mind:[1]

> *The subliminal self is in no way inferior to the conscious self; it is not purely automatic; it is capable of discernment; it has tact, delicacy; it knows how to choose, to divine. What do I say? It knows better how to divine than the conscious self, since it succeeds where that has failed.*

By locking themselves up in their bedroom-turned-office space, the Oliver twins got a lot done in little time.[2] Once they started concentrating on the code, time seemed to speed up. And if things got too rough, a bit of fooling around was all it took to get back on track and keep the flow of ideas going.

Creativity cannot happen without getting into the right state of mind. Running around naked, crying "Eureka!" requires conscious effort: that "aha!" moment will not pop up without previous intentional work and preparing your mind to be receptive to it.

In this chapter, we'll revisit many previously encountered concepts and combine them into a description of what I like to call a *creative state of mind*. The software

---

[1] Henri Poincaré. The foundations of science: Science and hypothesis, the value of science, science and method. Reissue edition. Cambridge University Press, 2014.

[2] The story is based on interviews with Retro Gamer, Retro Gamer Reviews, and Voletic.

developers my colleagues and I have interviewed made a clear distinction between an individual state of mind (being in a creative flow, using productivity tools, having "aha!" moments, shower thoughts) and a collective one (the influence of the environment should facilitate freedom and flexibility). Let's start by examining what it takes to lose control over time while you are happily coding away.

7.2   The flow of deep work

Have you ever been (un)pleasantly surprised by the speed at which the working day flies by? The unbearable slowness of the day where seconds crawl by according to the tenth glimpse at your watch? Or the amazing flash that was the day when hours felt like minutes? We've all been in both situations, and when it comes to work, nothing is more terrible than the illusion of a time stop.

7.2.1   The optimal experience

Psychologist Mihaly Csikszentmihalyi calls this phenomenon the *optimal experience* or, in other words, *flow*.[3] In his interviews with hundreds of successful people in sports, science, business, engineering, and art, he noticed that these people weren't simply good at something. They *excelled*—and somehow deeply enjoyed it. After transcribing, analyzing, and applying the necessary statistics, Csikszentmihalyi distilled the following nine principles of flow:

- One has a clear goal in mind.
- Every activity is immediately followed by feedback.
- There is a balance between challenge and skill.
- Action and awareness are one.
- Distractions are banished from consciousness.
- One is not afraid to fail.
- There is little to no self-awareness.
- The sense of time is confused.
- The activity becomes autotelic (internally driven: programming for the sake of programming).

Csikszentmihalyi's famous work on flow preceded his interest in creativity, and according to numerous studies, his hunch was correct: both concepts are heavily intertwined. We've seen traces of the nine principles in previous chapters: embrace feedback from others, challenge yourself, don't be discouraged by failure, use focused thinking to ban distractions, give your curiosity free reign. We can now add "be in the zone" to that list!

Flow seems to trigger deep enjoyment, creativity, and a total involvement with life. Csikszentmihalyi goes as far as calling flow one of the ways to add meaning to life. But how does one achieve it? Experiencing flow requires three things: realistic goals, skills that match the opportunities for action, and a complete focus on the activity. When

---

[3] Mihaly Csikszentmihalyi. Flow: The psychology of optimal experience. Harper Perennial Modern Classics, 2008.

your skill level is too high for the challenge offered by the task, you'll become distracted and bored. When the activity is too difficult, you'll become anxious or frustrated and give up. Csikszentmihalyi's flow model, which depicts different mental states surrounding flow, is illustrated in figure 7.3.

Figure 7.3   High skill levels and high challenges lead to the mental state of flow. Easier challenges lead to less satisfaction, and lower skill levels can cause anxiety. The depicted mental states were brought together in this flow model by Mihaly Csikszentmihalyi.

Would you be inclined to call on your creative programming skills for a trivial challenge? Of course not—that problem has been solved 10 times before. It's just a matter of repeating the implementation and requires little creativity. On the other hand, a real challenge does call for a creative approach, provided your creative skills are up to snuff, which, by now, they should be!

People love sinking their teeth into difficult problems at work. Csikszentmihalyi mentions that 54% of the participants experienced flow at work, while only 18% did so during their leisure time. This perhaps isn't surprising given that leisure time usually equals downtime. People at work who feel skillful and challenged also feel happier, stronger, more creative, and more satisfied.

Csikszentmihalyi teaches us two important things: flow can be controlled, and flow is not the exclusive domain of masters or spiritual leaders. If you don't feel skillful, you can simply start learning more. But what if you don't feel challenged? Perhaps then it's time to change the job itself.

More flow equals more creativity. When we asked programmers what they needed to be creative, one of the respondents answered thus:

I am creative if really everything feels right. That means the atmosphere, you know, the feeling that you're really in the flow, that, so to speak, you no longer have to think to get something done, to do something.

When encouraged to elaborate, the respondent continued:

For me personally, it is when I can put focus on something, alone or with several people, but in a very relaxed atmosphere, without the pressure of a deadline, and not having the feeling that the deadline is there.

Too much pressure turns flow into worry and anxiety.

Recent studies have discussed "joyous exploration," concluding that flow links each of the dimensions of curiosity with creativity.[4] Perhaps joyous exploration is what Darwin felt when he encountered new species in the Galápagos Islands. Next time you look at your watch and wonder where the last three hours went, pat yourself on the back: congrats; you've experienced flow!

> **EXERCISE** When was the last time you experienced flow while programming? What exactly was it that made you enjoy the task? This question can also be reversed: when was the last time you weren't in the zone at all? Is there a way to increase the occurrence of flow in your life based on your reflections?

7.2.2 Deep work

While Csikszentmihalyi calls losing yourself in the moment *flow*, Cal Newport calls a state of deep and focused concentration *deep work*.[5] Deep work is crucial if one is to make a difference. Newport, a computer science theorist and productivity critic, places our work activities into two groups: shallow work (noncognitively demanding, logistical-style tasks) and deep work (cognitively demanding activities that push us to our limits). Deep work generates value, while shallow work just ties up loose ends.

The problem almost all information workers, including programmers, face is *distraction*. Distractions and interruptions cause us to tackle cognitively demanding tasks the same way we tackle shallow work. As you can imagine—and have probably experienced yourself—this has devastating consequences on both productivity and creativity. Both shallow and deep work keep us busy, but don't confuse activity with productivity—or productivity with creativity!

> **Deep work vs. flow**
> What's the difference between deep work and flow? Aren't people in flow also engaged in a cognitively demanding task (yes; see figure 7.3) without distraction (yes; see the nine principles of flow)?

---

[4] Nicola S. Schutte and John M. Malouff. Connections between curiosity, flow and creativity. Personality and Individual Differences, 2020.

[5] Cal Newport. Deep work: Rules for focused success in a distracted world. Grand Central Publishing, 2016.

(continued)
According to Newport, deep work is an activity well suited to generate a flow state. In other words, deep work does not guarantee a flow state, but being in the zone also means working "deeply." Flow is about the fulfilling experience, while deep work is the part that enables long periods of focus.

In essence, Cal Newport's *Deep Work* book is a mix of cultural criticism with actionable advice on how to minimize environmental noise and interruptions. We all know that more meetings aren't going to solve that difficult problem, and we're all well aware of the destructive nature of push notifications, open mailboxes, and the strategic placement of smartphones on office desks. But we do absolutely nothing about it. If anything, as technology advances, we seem to be making it worse. And yet, academia yells, "Publish or perish!" and industry yells, "Not producing is not thriving!" Newport tries to shed light on this work culture paradox:

> *The ability to perform deep work is becoming increasingly rare at exactly the same time it is becoming increasingly valuable in our economy. As a consequence, the few who cultivate this skill, and then make it the core of their working life, will thrive.*

Focused thinking, from chapter 5, is deep work—provided you manage to banish all distractions.

What is the best way to get started with deep work, besides turning off message notifications? Newport recommends transforming good practices that increase focus into a simple habit. Observant readers will hardly be surprised. We've already discovered in chapter 6 that willpower is a finite resource. Roy Baumeister's willpower research has proven that good habits will ultimately sink into our unconsciousness, consuming less willpower and leaving more energy to ban annoying distractions.

Do a little bit of deep work each day, embed it into a habit, and try to gradually increase the amount of time spent in that concentrated state. Before you know it, you're writing a book!

As cheesy as the saying "What gets your attention is what grows" is, it is true, and there's even scientific evidence for it, neatly summarized by introspective writer Winifred Gallagher in her work, *Rapt*.[6] Our brains construct our worldview on the basis of what we pay attention to. Gallagher concludes: "The skillful management of attention is the sine qua non of the good life and the key to improving virtually every aspect of your experience."

The management of attention includes creativity. Would Archimedes still be regarded as one of the leading scientists and engineers in classical antiquity if his thinking bath times were constantly interrupted? Would Henri Poincaré have found proof for his theorems if his university didn't allow him to spend time walking in deep-thinking mode? Would the Oliver twins have booked much success if the time they spent on *Dizzy* development was carefully monitored by managers? Would Thomas

---

[6] Winifred Gallagher. Rapt: Attention and the focused life. Penguin, 2009.

Edison have persisted in trying to come up with a good way to bring electric light to the masses if he got distracted by loads of pointless administrative and newsletter mail? Would Linus Torvalds have had the time to design and fine-tune the Linux operating system if the comp.os.minix newsgroups from the early nineties had been replaced by our modern, intrusive, instant messaging systems? I don't think so.

7.2.3   Deep work and flow on the move

Does the environment matter when engaging in flow? Our software engineering respondents said, "Yes, of course." In one interview, a respondent said he solved all difficult problems in his car: "What that often is is that my thinking was already done in the car and when I arrive at work, all that is left to do is type for an hour or so."

Other participants murmured their agreement, suggesting that the thinking part is the creative part and the typing work is just "getting it out there." Next, they proceeded to talk about other activities that are likely to foster a creative state of mind: walking, taking a shower, sporting in the local indoor swimming pool. One group jokingly discovered a way to spot creative individuals when driving: "Maybe if the car behind always has to honk when the light turns green."

It seems that Poincaré's subconscious theory of creativity wasn't far off! Csikszentmihalyi's interviews with creative geniuses suggest the same, claiming that "their car is a 'thinking machine,' because only when driving do they feel relaxed enough to reflect on their problems and to place them in perspective."[7] He continued:

> *One person we interviewed said that about once a month, when worries become too pressing, he gets into his car after work and drives for half the night from Chicago to the Mississippi. He parks and looks at the river for about half an hour, then drives back and reaches Chicago as the dawn lights up the lake. The long drive acts as therapy, helping him sort out emotional problems.*

The subjectivity of a workspace

Where to best do your creative thinking work is highly subjective. This sounds obvious, but it needs to be repeated. A few employers ago, it was "recommended" that I extend my daily commute to a round trip of three hours. "Hey, that's a great opportunity to do some real work on the train!" my manager enthused. My protests fell on deaf ears, and in the end, I dutifully obliged.

I never produced anything worthwhile on a train except a crazy story for National Novel Writing Month. I'm susceptible to motion sickness, and I don't like working while being crammed in a small train seat. Even worse, the Belgian railway system is never punctual. Playing kids on the rails, frozen cables, roadsides on fire, suicides, or just plain ol' malfunctioning: I've heard it all.

Creative work on a train is my personal nightmare. If it works for you, great! But never try to convince me to do long commutes by calling it "productive."

---

[7] Mihaly Csikszentmihalyi. Creativity: Flow and the psychology of discovery and invention. Reprint edition. Harper Perennial, 2003.

Cal Newport and Seth Godin romanticize long flights as ideal opportunities to do some really deep work. However, getting productive and creative should not be done at the expense of Mother Earth. Poincaré wasn't the only one to promote zero-carbon-footprint thought walks. Ancient Greek philosophers loved discussing, thinking, and walking at the same time. In fact, these philosophers loved thinking and walking so much they named a whole school after it: the Peripatetics, as also encountered in the introduction to chapter 3. Famous Enlightenment thinker Immanuel Kant gained much insight into the outside world while walking around his hometown of Königsberg, Germany—and never once leaving it. Kant was so famous for the regularity of his daily walks that he was nicknamed "the Königsberg clock."

Perhaps the most interesting walking state of mind is that of philosopher Friedrich Nietzsche. He'd walk 8 to 10 hours a day,[8] wading through the thick German Black Forest, composing thoughts that he would later jot down on paper. His timeless works are steeped in a philosophy of walking:[9]

> *We do not belong to those who have ideas only among books, when stimulated by books. It is our habit to think outdoors—walking, leaping, climbing, dancing, preferably on lonely mountains or near the sea where even the trails become thoughtful.*

Walking became the centerpiece of his philosophy. "Sitting still is a real sin against the Holy Ghost," concluded Nietzsche. French contemporary philosopher Frédéric Gros writes in *A Philosophy of Walking* that "a long walk allows us to commune with the sublime."[10] The striking similarity to Poincaré's conversations with his subliminal self is no coincidence!

Recent studies have confirmed that walking boosts creative ideation, both during a hike and shortly after. Marily Oppezzo and Daniel L. Schwartz suggest that "walking opens up the free flow of ideas" and is a great way to increase both creativity and physical activity.[11] That said . . .

> **EXERCISE** Get up and take a walking break in solitude. Bring along a pen and a piece of paper. Think about what you've read so far and how it could be applied to your daily work routine as a programmer. Go on, I'll wait.

7.2.4   *Walking support or the lack thereof*

If you didn't dare to perform the walking exercise at work, no worries: you're probably not alone. Employers love seeing *productive* employees: they get a kick out of programmers clutching their dual-screen setup, jamming away at that deafening mechanical keyboard. "Wow, they sure must be hard working! Good job, everyone!" What they hate to see is an employee in creative *thinking* mode, just wandering around

---

[8] Nietzsche's progressive dementia that caused insanity might have something to do with his growing obsession with lonely walks.

[9] Friedrich Nietzsche. The gay science: With a prelude in rhymes and an appendix of songs. Vintage, 1974.

[10] Frédéric Gros. A philosophy of walking. Verso Trade, 2014.

[11] Marily Oppezzo and Daniel L. Schwartz. Give your ideas some legs: The positive effect of walking on creative thinking. Journal of Experimental Psychology: Learning, Memory, and Cognition, 2014.

in the hallways or, even worse, team members who suddenly disappear into the wild for a few hours.

It is very sad to see that thought walks are generally met with suspicion. Even at my university, I see little evidence of modern incarnations of Kant or Poincaré: academics are instead swamped in busywork, also known as administrative "bullshit jobs," as the late anthropologist and anarchist David Graeber liked to put it.[12]

A few years ago, a colleague and I were racing to get an urgent hotfix released. Indeed, it was the kind that requires certain "creative workarounds." We worked non-stop, skipping our breaks, and finally managed to come to a workable solution. After patting ourselves on the back, we decided to take a short break by playing cards in the cafeteria. Five minutes in, our boss walked by. He was furious—it was 3:00 p.m., and we had the nerve to play cards?! We conceded and quietly returned to our desks. Our late lunch break made us look like slackers while, in fact, we had worked harder—and more creatively—than usual. It just did not comply with the conventional working rules.

Pretending to be productive

In *Bullshit Jobs*, David Graeber included both entertaining and unsettling stories of employees pretending to be productive to please their bosses. For example, someone installed Lynx, the command-line browser. This made him look like an expert scripting away at a terminal when, in fact, he was editing Wikipedia articles all day long.

Too many managers at tech companies still think programming is a desk job that requires little creative freedom, even though they claim to totally support it. If the Oliver twins got stuck, they watched television shows and played other video games. That was both inspiring *and* relaxing. What do you think would happen if they'd had to work in cubicles and were quickly ushered back to "work"?

That's why independent makers are usually the most creative ones. Although they still work with deadlines and publishers, nobody is around to tell them what can and cannot be done. Independence has long been recognized as a developmental contributor to creative skills. In the seventies, psychologist Joy Guilford mentioned independence next to curiosity and reflection as a characteristic of creativity.[13] Two decades later, creativity researcher Mark Runco noted a positive correlation between independence and divergent thinking in students gifted with a high IQ.[14] Every recent paper on the same subject seems to either mention "freedom," "autonomy," or "independence."

In the world of software development, most of the complex problems are not solved while one is behind a computer or inside a meeting room: they're solved in gyms and in cars and while walking. Of course, implementing the solution still requires a keyboard.

---

[12] David Graeber. Bullshit jobs: A theory. Simon & Schuster, 2018.

[13] Joy P. Guilford. Characteristics of creativity. Illinois State Office of the Superintendent of Public Instruction, 1973.

[14] Mark A. Runco. A longitudinal study of exceptional giftedness and creativity. Creativity Research Journal, 1999.

How can you increase support for creative freedom? Invite your boss to join *The Creative Programmer* reading group! We will delve deeper into the influence of company culture in section 7.5.

7.3   *Interrupt!*

In computer architectures, an interrupt serves as a request for the processor to halt running instructions so that an event can be processed instead of having to wait for the current program to finish. For example, Serial Link Interrupt `0x0058` halts the Sharp LR35902 CPU to announce incoming network data—provided the interrupt flag is turned on. If there's an interrupt handler defined, the CPU temporarily evaluates that function, after which it resumes executing the instructions of the interrupted program.

A creative state of mind works similarly. Sometimes, our current work is unexpectedly interrupted, either by internal ideas that suddenly take form in our own minds or by a multitude of external queries. Elizabeth Gilbert from chapter 2 would say to catch it while you can, before our brains decide to resume our previous task and the idea that interrupted our work is permanently lost, as illustrated in figure 7.4.

Figure 7.4   A crashing stream of thought illustrating the potential loss of ideas

Just like a CPU, we have to recognize that an interrupt is pending, identify the type and source of the interrupt, decide what to do with it, context switch efficiently, and eventually resume our interrupted work. What was I doing again?

Sudden interrupts can break our train of thought—to the extent that the train might derail. Think of it this way: interrupted nontransactional relational database write operations have a chance of losing data. What could be possibly worse in knowledge work than losing a creative idea?

A wreck doesn't just crash your train of thought, scattering its cargo (precious ideas); it also requires a thorough cleanup. The train tracks are covered in debris. If you'd like to receive more ideas, that debris needs to be cleaned up, fast. This is exactly what happens when we're context-switching from task to task: a cooldown period of about 20 minutes is needed to get us back on track.

In a study that investigated software developers' perceptions of productivity, almost all of the 379 interviewees said they found their days to be productive when tasks were completed without significant interruptions or context switches.[15] Yet, according to the second part of the study, which involved observational work, an awful lot of interruptions and context switches occur daily. The context-switching effect is even worse when creative work is involved. Also, switching away from a creative task for which more focus is required is more expensive than switching from a routine task.

Every developer knows that programming "depends on being able to juggle a lot of little details in short-term memory all at once," as Joel Spolsky, cocreator of Stack Overflow, once wrote on his tech blog.[16] When it comes to interruptions, we're in danger of hurting not only our productivity but also our creativity! Most books on programming mention the negative effects of interruptions on productivity but remain silent on creativity, where interruptions can truly wreak havoc. The question then becomes, how can we better prepare ourselves for the inevitable train wrecks?

7.3.1 Increasing your awareness of interruptions

The aforementioned study by André Meyer and colleagues concludes with a discussion of opportunities to better manage and improve developers' work, thereby achieving higher productivity levels. The researchers identified three opportunities.

The first opportunity is *tools for retrospective analysis*. Monitoring programming activities might reveal interruption patterns that can be anticipated. Awareness is always the first step. Simple and popular tools such as Pomodoro apps, time-tracking software, and Fitbit activity-tracking devices are worth trying out.

> ### Kitchen timers that increase coding productivity
>
> With the Pomodoro technique, you use a classic kitchen timer—preferably one in the shape of a *pomodoro*, or tomato—to split your work into intervals of around 25 minutes in length, separated by breaks of 5 to 10 minutes. After four so-called pomodoros, a longer break follows. The technique helps reduce the negative side effects of interruptions of flow and even comes with its own ways of dealing with internal and external interrupts.
>
> It was first introduced as a time management method in the late eighties but more recently has amassed a popular following among programmers.[a] Of course, there are also plenty of tomato-shaped apps available to help you focus on coding work, some of which even disable distractions and your internet connection.

[a]Staffan Nöteberg, Pomodoro technique illustrated: The easy way to do more in less time. The Pragmatic Bookshelf, 2009.

The second opportunity is *reducing context switches*. According to the interviewees, quick context switches, such as reading an email while waiting for a build, did not affect productivity, while context switches that require a change in thinking are much more costly. I'm a bit reluctant to believe that, since the email is likely to cover a topic

---

[15] André N. Meyer, Thomas Fritz, Gail C. Murphy, and Thomas Zimmermann. Software developers' perceptions of productivity. In Proceedings of the 22nd ACM SIGSOFT International Symposium on Foundations of Software Engineering, 2014.

[16] See https://www.joelonsoftware.com/2000/04/19/where-do-these-people-get-their-unoriginal-ideas/.

other than the thing you're building, and hence a change in thinking might be required to answer it. Of course, keeping your email inbox closed circumvents the problem entirely. Or having faster build times. Or no builds at all?

The third opportunity is *setting goals*. Goal-setting combined with self-monitoring has been shown before to be effective in motivating behavioral change. However, some participants rightfully mentioned that (corporate) goals usually come with more (strict) monitoring and thus more overhead instead of less.

7.3.2   *Preparing for interruptions*

The simplest solution to the interruption problem—besides avoiding them entirely—was, strangely enough, not mentioned in the study: write stuff down! If you see a train coming in, full speed ahead, try to catch a glimpse of its contents, quickly get that down, and *then* let it crash.

Try not to become a disaster tourist, though. Regular train crashes will destabilize the train tracks. Research has shown that long-term frequent interruptions can be detrimental to working memory and even to mental health.

Research and my own work experience also suggest that vital information in your working memory is lost when you are interrupted. Therefore, resuming work can be hard: what was I doing again? Which test did I intend to write? What idea was forming in my head? As mentioned before, this warmup and cooldown period can take up to 20 minutes!

In her book *The Programmer's Brain* (see chapter 5), Felienne Hermans devoted a chapter to interruptions and how to handle them. Her advice is simple and effective: write stuff down. Store your mental model before allowing anyone else to interrupt you. Leave breadcrumbs   for yourself: quickly dump your brain on a screen or on paper. Type out everything you were thinking about and were planning on doing, even if that does not compile. Don't bother with syntax or spaces. This will get you back on track much faster.

The problem with hastily written sticky notes is the lack of context. Remember from chapter 2 that ideas in your personal knowledge management system should be self-contained. Rereading those TODO items a few days later is a sure way to lose their meaning despite the attempt to retain them. I've made this mistake time and time again by jotting down a few keywords too quickly, going back to something else, and not being able to decipher the note later.

Be sure either to immediately continue working on the item after the interruption has been dealt with or to add enough context. Advice from famous novel writers teaches us the same: never end your day with a clean slate. If a chapter is done, write a few sentences on the next. This persistent mental state will give you a head start the next day. More practical advice from coders and writers will be discussed in chapter 8.

7.3.3   *Knowing which interruptions to look out for*

Not all interruptions are equally damaging to our creative flow. An instant message on Slack or WhatsApp can be put off for awhile. Your boss yelling at you to promptly fix an urgent matter, probably not. We mostly view interruptions as *external* troublemakers, although that is only part of the story.

In 2018, an interuniversity longitudinal study was published that investigated what makes some interruptions during software development more disruptive than others.[17] In addition to obvious *task-specific factors*, such as priority, *contextual factors*, such as interruption type and time of day, are found to be potentially more damaging! Even though respondents believed that external interruptions were the most disruptive to their flow state, the analysis revealed that voluntary task-switching is more destructive.

In another behavioral experiment, researchers measured the extra time it takes to self-interrupt by closely inspecting pupil dilation. Each self-interruption costs approximately one second.[18] A puny second sounds negligible, but consider this: the researchers measured, on average, five interruptions just for opening and partially reading an email. Imagine how many potentially creative minutes are lost each workday.

> **EXERCISE**   During the next hour-long programming session, keep track of the number of interruptions you experience by tallying the score on a piece of paper. Mark internal and external interruptions separately. Try to be honest in reporting self-interruptions. Repeat the exercise a few times—for example, in the morning and afternoon on a Monday and a Tuesday. What do the results say? Are you surprised? When did you get the most creative work done?

Reducing the number of self-interruptions involves relying on willpower, as explained in chapter 6. Of course, when the mind wanders, it is perhaps time for a break, unless you already did so two minutes ago—in that case, seeking new horizons might perhaps do wonders.

Not all interruptions should be counted as wasteful. When prolific sociologist Niklas Luhmann, whom we met in chapter 2, got stuck, he switched contexts to something else he was working on. Luhmann always had several irons in the fire; this strategy even increased the chances of ideas cross-breeding between different domains.

Deliberately interrupting a coworker to exchange ideas could also be seen as a way to increase productivity, as one of the participants in the 2018 longitudinal behavioral study stated:

> *If someone is working on the same project as I am and we can exchange ideas, that can be a productive task-switching. It's also productive for more fire drill–type situations, like fast bug triage.*

It sounds a bit silly to describe pair programming in terms of interruptions. Perhaps more interesting is the influence of the time of day on the detrimental effect of interruptions. Some developers have a tougher time recovering in the afternoon, while others struggle in the morning.

---

[17] Zahra Shakeri, Hossein Abad, Oliver Karras, Kurt Schneider, Ken Barker, and Mike Bauer. Task interruption. In Software development projects: What makes some interruptions more disruptive than others? Proceedings of the 22nd International Conference on Evaluation and Assessment in Software Engineering, 2018.

[18] Ioanna Katidioti, Jelmer P. Borst, Marieke K. Van Vugt, and Niels A. Taatgen. Interrupt me: External interruptions are less disruptive than self-interruptions. Computers in Human Behavior, 2016.

> **Do Not Disturb Christmas lights**
>
> While working together, it's always a challenge to take these time-of-day preferences into account when deciding to interrupt someone with your questions. At a previous employer, we tried introducing personal "busy lights": if the light is on, it's Do Not Disturb time.
>
> Sadly, the consistent ignoring of the Do Not Disturb lights by management and suspicions of misuse quickly returned the cheerfully lit office landscape to a depressing gray drab.

7.3.4   *Mindfulness increases focus*

Combating self-interruptions with sheer willpower sounds like a feat only Superman could pull off. Fear not. While investigating mind-wandering, as first seen in chapter 5, Jonathan Schooler discovered that focus is just like willpower: it's a muscle that can be trained. The easiest way to do so is through a very old and deceptively simple trick called *mindfulness*:

> *Our results suggest that training to enhance attentional focus may be . . . key to enhancing cognitive skills that were until recently viewed as immutable. Thus, there are good reasons to be optimistic about mind-wandering: it indeed appears that many of its documented costs for perception, cognition, and action can be remedied by applying an age-old antidote known as mindfulness.*

Did we just link mindfulness to creativity? Increasing focus via mindfulness was already mentioned in 2008 by Andy Hunt in *Pragmatic Thinking and Learning*. The ambivalent relationship between creativity and mindfulness spiked recent academic interest. A meta-analysis of 89 published correlations found a statistically significant but weak correlation between the two concepts.[19]

What does that mean? The effect seemed to depend on the measurement of creativity (insight vs. divergent thinking) and the type of mindfulness (observation vs. acting with awareness). Other studies are cautiously optimistic: mindfulness practices improve skills or habits of the mind that *can* indeed support creativity.[20] Note the added emphasis on *can*. Becoming a mindfulness guru is not a guarantee of creative success. It merely increases our attention span. Generating creative insights still involves a lot of hard work.

7.4   *Triggering creative insights*

My wife is obsessed with crime series. She enjoys any show that involves a good murder. The best part of each episode is, of course, the big reveal at the end, when the detective—*of course!*—portrays a sudden flash of insight. Leaving their still-puzzled coworkers

---

[19] Izabela Lebuda, Darya L. Zabelina, and Maciej Karwowski. Mind full of ideas: A meta-analysis of the mindfulness–creativity link. Personality and Individual Differences, 2016.

[20] Danah Henriksen, Carmen Richardson, and Kyle Shack. Mindfulness and creativity: Implications for thinking and learning. Thinking Skills and Creativity, 2020.

behind, they rush off to apprehend the bad guy and unfold the vile plan in front of all involved. This scenario is another classic case of romanticizing insight. We especially recommend the British–French *Death in Paradise* television series, which comes with a twist of humor and nice Caribbean scenery. The show is known for its sudden moments of realization and the gathering of suspects to talk through the evidence.

By now, you should be well acquainted with every stage of the creative process from chapter 5: participate, incubate, illuminate, verify, present/accept. Archimedes, Poincaré, and the Oliver twins underscored the importance of the incubation stage before any illumination is triggered. Poincaré's subconscious theory of creativity insists on the importance of conscious work (participation) before subconscious insight: 90% perspiration, 10% illumination.

Observant crime show watchers closely follow the inspector as he slowly but surely collects and connects different clues (perspiration). Some clues make little sense until they fit into the bigger picture. After alternating periods of preoccupation, it is time for the finale (illumination).

Managers obsessed with time efficiency might easily believe the fairy tale of *sudden* insight coming out of nowhere, but creative programmers aren't that easily fooled. Perhaps the word *progressive* is more appropriate here. As American novelist Jack London said: "You can't wait for inspiration. You have to go after it with a club."

In the following section, we'll encounter a few more considerations to take into account when on the hunt for the Golden Bird called *insight*.

7.4.1 *Alone or together?*

The thought walks of prominent scholars such as Nietzsche, Kant, and Poincaré seemed to take place in solitude. Were these intentional decisions? I doubt that many contemporaries of Nietzsche were willing to hike alongside an antisocial narcissist. With the insights into communication of chapter 3 in mind, we can piece together the many advantages of thought walking. Since modern software development is a collective endeavor, it would make no sense to ponder difficult problems on your own. Even Aristotle and his followers loved strolling around Athens while discussing various philosophical topics, as mentioned in the introduction to chapter 3. Which of the two options will ultimately yield more insight, thought walks by yourself or in good company?

As with all questions in this book, the answer isn't black and white. I hope all the ambiguity isn't getting on your nerves. Let's try to visualize what I mean.

Figure 7.5 illustrates five different ways to represent thoughts. In the first case, *data*, all we have are loose bits and pieces. Sorting through the rubbish evolves data into *information*: some pieces are x, while others are y. Great, we're onto something! Now how about connecting separate pieces through experience and practice? All relational databases express *knowledge* using foreign key constraints.

However, the relations so far are obvious ones: parent-of, child-of. When *insight* occurs, we make a novel connection between seemingly disconnected pieces of information. Finally, when a certain path between different insight nodes makes sense, we've generated genuine *wisdom*.

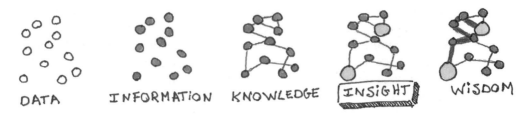

DATA   INFORMATION   KNOWLEDGE   INSIGHT   WISDOM

Figure 7.5   The evolution of seemingly loose data to insight and wisdom. Based on ideas of the Gapingvoid Culture Design Group.

I first encountered a variation of this wonderful illustration on the website of the Gapingvoid Culture Design Group,[21] a group dedicated to helping other organizations transform their company cultures. Gapingvoid uses the drawing to study and explain the signs and processes of company cultures, and we can do the same to explain personal insight.

Admittedly, the drawing is only partially complete—external influences, starting from (almost) nothing, backfeeding could all be added. Think back to the symmathesy concept of chapter 3. Combining both ideas with my limited drawing skills would certainly have resulted in a mess.

Still, the core of the message of figure 7.5 remains intact. To get to a novel insight, we need to do two things:

1 *Collect* the dots.
2 *Connect* the dots.

Collecting the dots requires input—including from others. Lively discussions certainly help with that. Connecting the dots, on the other hand, is a more personal process. Not everyone's thinking train is designed the same way, travels at the same speed, or uses the same tracks. This is a basis for a lot of frustrating pair programming sessions. Putting together expert and novice isn't always the best bet to transfer knowledge. The expert is usually 10 steps ahead and reluctant to explain all the little details they know by heart, while the novice struggles to keep their train up to speed—losing precious cargo in the process.

Collect dots together with others. Connect the dots alone. At least provide enough breathing room for others to think and process new information at their own frequency. I've worked in companies that enforce pair programming all day long. That was both enriching and exhausting. I have never learned so much in so little time. But true insight? That mainly happened before or after working hours. There was simply no time to ponder things through! I had to keep up the pace or risk derailing.

Companies I worked for later applied pair programming only sporadically, leaving enough breathing room to process new knowledge at your own pace. This also comes with its downside: less sense of true camaraderie, slower distribution of best practices,

----

[21] See https://www.gapingvoid.com/.

and so forth. A 100% pair programming job is also devastating for introverts. I'm a big pair programming advocate, but when it comes to the Creative Programmer, the occasional break from each other will definitely be beneficial—for both individuals.

Since becoming an academic researcher, I'm usually left to my own devices, which is a double-edged sword. On the one hand, getting paid to connect the dots feels liberating. On the other hand, regularly overlooking dots that my pair programming partner might otherwise notice makes me feel very lonely.

Remember the interviewee who mentioned flow and focus as two of the traits of being creative, free of the terror of looming deadlines? He was actually quite pessimistic about true creativity on the job:

> *I think that being truly, really creative, that is really limited in our job. . . . For me, it's more about the feeling of getting inside your head, really being in your own world, at that moment.*

What he actually wanted to say is this: creativity involves connecting dots, which requires me-time (or even downtime). Further into the discussion, he mentioned the *aha-erlebnis* as the ultimate proof of creativity—which, according to most participants, does not usually happen while behind a desk.

Every programmer I have talked to puts the 10% illumination on a pedestal. Strangely enough, nobody mentioned the 90% perspiration needed to get there: rooting in the codebase, digging through untested methods, wading through misused pattern after pattern, deciphering bug reports, discussing the same functionality for the sixth time just to make sure, and so on. No dots collecting? No dots connecting.

7.4.2   *Sleep and insight*

Quite a few prominent creators attribute insight to a good night's sleep. Ample empirical support indeed confirms that (good) sleep promotes creativity. When we're asleep, our hippocampus, an area in the brain responsible for the continuity of the self over time and spatial navigation, gets free reign to play with and connect the impressions of the day. Neuroscientist Matt Wilson makes it sound like a deliberate action:[22]

> *During sleep you try to make sense of things you already learned. . . . You go into a vast database of experience and try to figure out new connections and then build a model to explain new experiences. Wisdom is the rules, based on experience, that allow us to make good decisions in novel situations in the future.*

We don't have to passively wait for our sleep to do its thing. Behavioral scientist Simone Ritter and her research team discovered that secretly dispensing odors facilitates creativity.[23] In the evening, prior to sleep, participants were presented with a problem that required a creative solution. A hidden diffuser spread a scent while the problem was presented. During sleep, one group of participants was conditioned with the same

---

[22] M. R. O'Connor. Wayfinding: The science and mystery of how humans navigate the world. St. Martin's Press, 2019.

[23] Simone M. Ritter, Madelijn Strick, Maarten W. Bos, Rick B. Van Baaren, and A. P. Dijksterhuis. Good morning creativity: Task reactivation during sleep enhances beneficial effect of sleep on creative performance. Journal of Sleep Research, 2012.

scent, and one group, with another scent; a third group was not conditioned with a scent. The next morning, when presenting their solution immediately after waking up, the first group was found to be much more creative.

Ritter calls this "task reactivation during sleep." Although the number of participants was very limited and an outdated creativity assessment method from the sixties was used, the message here is clear: our sleep can connect previously unassociated information, and it can be actively triggered to some extent. In case you were wondering, orange-vanilla was the winning scent.

Perhaps Dexter was right when he proclaimed, "Hey, who needs to study? With my genius, I can learn while I sleep!" in an episode of the animated television series *Dexter's Laboratory*. While enjoying his sleep, the "Subconscious Discographic Hypnotator" would induce the needed French vocabulary (http://mng.bz/D4oV). Just make sure the record doesn't get stuck on *Omelette du Fromage*.

7.4.3   *A note on stimulants*

Programmers love their coffee—a conclusion we came to after conducting several focus groups. The effect of coffee on creativity seems to be twofold. First, and perhaps foremost, the act of getting up to take a stroll to the coffee machine or water dispenser can often be enough to trigger a connection, as one participant explained:

> . . . *coffee, in a sense of, you're doing something and you're stuck, and you get up to go drink some coffee and on the way back something comes to mind that might solve the issue.*

Another participant jokingly said drinking lots of coffee also increases the number of toilet visits, which, in turn, might trigger something (besides the act of relieving oneself). Drinking coffee—or any other beverage—is to modern programmers what taking a bath was to Archimedes.

But coffee has another well-known effect: the caffeine "makes your brain work faster," as one programmer mentioned. It indeed increases our focused attention span. What is less known, however, is that too much coffee can lock you out of the diffuse-thinking mode (see chapter 5), an indispensable tool that can help us come up with original ideas.

In a literature review on the links between psychostimulants and creativity in the arts, Iain Smith concludes, "The ability of psychostimulants to boost convergent thinking is the main mechanism at work but this is at a cost as divergent thinking is diminished."[24] Ancient Greeks drank diluted wine to tear down cognitive walls during philosophical discussions. Nicotine and caffeine are often used by writers to put words on paper and to evaluate their creative work. However, when it comes to ideation and pondering, your best bet is a clear head.

The study of stimulants and their influence on the brain is a whole field of research in itself. Summarizing recent findings is well beyond the scope of this book.

---

[24] Iain Smith. Psychostimulants and artistic, musical, and literary creativity. International Review of Neurobiology, 2015.

If you are still interested in delving deeper, I recommend Michael Pollan's *How to Change Your Mind*, a personal journey through the science of psychedelics.[25]

7.5 A corporate creative state of mind

If we are to believe architects, the exterior and interior designs of company buildings matter. If we are to believe our interviewed programmers, working in a stimulating environment—literally—can enhance your creativity. In chapter 3, we encountered modern technology sites that attempt to replicate genius clusters by carefully planning urban and industrial communities. Our workplace environment influences us more than we'd like to admit. Would you prefer to be surrounded by a jungle of lush greenery alternated with strategically placed office desks and pool tables, or would you rather face a gray brick wall every single day?

Designing a perfect office for everyone is impossible. Some programmers prefer the bustle of activity, while others like the privacy of a closed door. Some don't even like playing pool. Let's examine what an ideal corporate creative state of mind should look like.

7.5.1 Environmental creativity

The first thing that probably springs to mind when thinking about creative environmental design is the clash between, on the one hand, open spaces that (in theory) promote serendipitous creativity and, on the other hand, closed office spaces that promote deep work. Open spaces should disrupt structures and boundaries, allowing for unexpected collisions that generate better ideas.

Numerous studies—including those of mine and my colleagues—have confirmed that, in practice, the noise of open offices actually *undermines* creativity![26] On the other end of the spectrum, isolating people in tiny cubicles is depressing. If both open and closed spaces work against creativity, then how should architects design the workspace? The only solution is to compromise.

In *Deep Work*, Cal Newport suggests combining long hallways with clusters of closed subenvironments. This way, bumping into people to exchange ideas happens while walking to the coffee machine, without disturbing the flow of coworkers who are wrestling with implementation details. Coworking spaces can be further subdivided into compartments as teams see fit.

Newport mentions MIT's Building 20 as an example of mismatched departments that shared a building alongside more esoteric tenants, such as a machine shop and a piano repair facility. The space could be rearranged as needed and allowed for both interdisciplinary discussions and solitary moments of concentration.

---

[25] Michael Pollan. How to change your mind: What the new science of psychedelics teaches us about consciousness, dying, addiction, depression, and transcendence. Penguin Books, 2019.

[26] Torkild Thanem, Sara Varlander, and Stephen Cummings. Open space = open minds? The ambiguities of pro-creative office design. International Journal of Work Organisation and Emotion, 2011.

Building 20 was initially created as a temporary overflow space. Since then, other, more systematically planned buildings have showcased the same design philosophy. Newport quotes Jon Gertner's notes on the design of Bell Labs:

> *Traveling the hall's length without encountering a number of acquaintances, problems, diversions and ideas was almost impossible. A physicist on his way to lunch in the cafeteria was like a magnet rolling past iron filings.*

As one programmer we interviewed summarized, office spaces should "have incentives without being disruptive, but must appeal to the imagination." Freud loved to surround himself with archeological marvels that inspired him. Perhaps without these shiny trinkets, his work would not shine as much.

A hybrid coworking space is exactly what Jonas Salk from chapter 5 envisioned when commissioning the Salk Institute for Biological Studies. Architect Louis Kahn opted for a bold light-altering exterior and free-flowing labs that were meant to allow for cross-pollination of ideas without constant interruptions of others' work. The result is a stunning piece of modern art, as you can see in figure 7.6.

Figure 7.6   The Salk Institute courtyard showcasing a mirrored structure containing strategically placed laboratories, utilities, office spaces overlooking the Pacific Ocean, and study areas. Photo courtesy of Adam Bignell, Unsplash.

What, exactly, are the characteristics and configurations of a (hybrid) creative space? Behavioral engineering researchers Katja Thoring and her colleagues tried to answer that by turning to the literature. Most unconventional work environments, like the aforementioned Salk Institute, provide separate spaces for different needs. The following list is a selection of the identified space types:[27]

- Personal/focus space
- Collaboration space
- Making/experimentation space
- Exhibition space
- Presentation/sharing space
- Disengaged/intermission/relaxation space
- Unusual/playful space
- Virtual space
- Incubation and reflection space

Big tech companies love to show off their "playful" spaces in the hope of attracting new talent. I remember a job interview in which the employer proudly mentioned the Xbox tournaments during lunch. I later heard the lunch break is strictly monitored. I kindly turned down the offer. Now, if there was mention of a Super Nintendo. . . .

Some companies go as far as requiring their programmers to not only work but also live on campus. It is interesting to see an incubation space listed as a separate entity in Thoring's paper. Archimedes would have demanded a luxurious bathroom.

Creative environments have lots of boxes to tick: they need to be social, stimulating, engaging, comfortable, healthy, safe, surprising, flexible, accessible, playful, spacious, remote, cozy, nourishing, and informative. On top of that, they should promote chance encounters, reflect the identity of the company, contain ample greenery, evoke wonder with their architecture, contain lots of cafés, and facilitate the exhibition of project work.

No wonder most workplaces fail to live up to these expectations. Eric Weiner puts it bluntly: "Creativity is a response to our environment." (See chapter 3.) The global COVID-19 pandemic abruptly changed that environment by initially mandating remote work. Whether the change has had a positive influence on creativity remains to be seen.

Although our influence on the design of the workspace is perhaps limited, it is not impossible to add a few inspiring objects here and there, just like Freud did. I've seen companies recruit "Chief Happiness Officers" who are co-responsible for the layout and decoration of the workspace. If your company has roles like these, great, get involved, and point them to creativity research or lend them your copy of this book! If your company lacks dedicated people concerned with interior design or the well-being of the workforce, there's an opportunity lurking: step up and help increase awareness of the influence of environments on creative performance.

---

[27] Katja Thoring, Pieter Desmet, and Petra Badke-Schaub. Creative space: A systematic review of the literature. In Proceedings of the Design Society: International Conference on Engineering, 2019.

EXERCISE   Take a look around at your desk, whether it's at home or at the office. Does it scream *boring!*? How about adding a few inspirational books, posters, or plants? Spray-paint an old motherboard or deconstruct an unused iPod to mount on the wall. Craft a mood board full of things that define and inspire you. As always, turn to the internet for more creative examples.

Donning the monk's habit

Sometimes it pays off to temporarily work in another environment. I know of a colleague who retreated to an abbey to finish his dissertation. The constant presence of yelling children at home breaking his creative flow might have had something to do with it.

Mihaly Csikszentmihalyi wrote a large chunk of his *Creativity* book in a secluded cell that looked out over the eastern branch of Lake Como in northern Italy. Each year, The Rockefeller Foundation sends out academics to beautiful but remote areas in the hope that the panoramic views and the historical weight of the nearby ruins produce great outbursts of creativity. They usually do.

7.5.2   *Workplaces as creative workshops*

In the eyes of the uninitiated, workshops of artists are nothing but bright and messy spaces littered with junk. The most important aspect of the workshop—its *context*—is invisible. As with all things systemic, the workshop itself is part of the system that determines and alters the creative product. At the 2021 workshop conference "1 + 1 = 3,"[28] Contemporary Flemish visual artists Jonas Vansteenkiste and Joke Raes talked about how their work developed and formed in relationship with the physical workspace. The logic-defying "1 + 1 = 3" formula refers to what Nora Bateson from chapter 3 calls a *symmathesy*—the sum is greater than its individual parts.

Each workshop has a major effect on the end result. For instance, a shop comes equipped with specific technical options, such as a wood lathe or ceramic materials. The guidance of professional woodworkers or sculptors present at the workshop will also further influence the result.

Joke Raes' art arises from material she happens to stumble upon in and outside her atelier,[29] such as discarded industrial remnants or objects of natural origin (figure 7.7). Her art changes as she changes her environment. She also emphasizes the importance of serendipity. Her work evolves organically, sometimes boosted by sheer coincidence, although she deliberately chooses when to stray from the premeditated path. According to her, there is no single recipe for creative work.

Programming and hardware tinkering are also dependent on physical materials and happen within a physical context. If a few engineers at Argonaut Games from the

---

[28] See https://www.platformwerkplaatsen.nl/nl/werkconferentie-1-1-3.

[29] Artists and designers seem to prefer the term *atelier* over *workshop*. In the context of this section, its meaning remains the same.

Figure 7.7   A peek inside Joke Raes' atelier. The walls are decorated with her sculptures. Ample sketchbooks, manuals, and various materials are within reach, yet enough light and space remain to breathe, think, and work. Photo courtesy of Joke Raes.

introduction to chapter 6 weren't into circuit board printing, they might never have managed to reverse-engineer the Game Boy internals. Suppose their curiosity and persistence eventually failed them, and by ordering parts instead of making them, they still managed to produce the Game Boy game *X*. The end result would have looked completely different.

The programming workplace influences the creative end product. A romantic image of tinkering garages where Google and Apple products were conceived might have popped into your mind. History researcher Katherine Erica McFadden devoted an entire doctoral dissertation to the subject of what she calls *garagecraft*.[30] These garages acted very much like creative workshops:

> *[The garage] has provided a place to play, experiment, [and] commercialize technology, while also providing a space to create new identities and communal standards. What we make and how we make it is, in the end, more about crafting ourselves than crafting objects.*

While Silicon Valley garage tinkering can sometimes sound like a fairy tale, it is indeed hard to deny the influence of the garage/workshop and its contents on the imagination of the tinkerer. Why don't we as programmers build our own private workshop or atelier to which we can occasionally retreat in search of inspiration?

---

[30] Katherine Erica McFadden. Garagecraft: Tinkering in the American garage. PhD dissertation, College of Arts and Sciences, University of South Carolina, 2018.

7.5.3   *Workplaces as a safe haven*

That same workplace should also allow for creative experiments. An interviewee from our focus group study explained:

> *I think that's like motivation. You create the framework in which you can be creative and that means you're allowed to make mistakes and can try out things, that you're supported by that and feel comfortable in that environment. . . . For example, flexible working hours, I think that's important, that you don't have to worry about getting there on time; instead I can calmly think in the car about a problem.*

Workplaces that facilitate creativity are the ones that boost your confidence to try out things, fumble, fail, and try again, without being put on a clock (too much). Again, freedom emerges as an important determinant of creativity. Of course, it also helps if a whiteboard is in the vicinity—or, even better, if the walls can be drawn on, thanks to IdeaPaint or chalkboard paint. The question that remains unanswered is this: what is the ideal equilibrium between constraints and freedom? Perhaps that's a good thinking exercise to end this chapter with.

Summary

- If coding problems while behind the desk aren't directly solvable, perhaps it's a good idea to get away from that desk for awhile.
- Offload your brain now and then, for instance, by playing a game—even while you're in the middle of something that absolutely has to be solved. You'll be pleasantly surprised by what a refreshed mind does to your creative problem-solving skills. Never ignore the signals from your subconscious.
- Agree on a way to respect everyone's flow of optimal programming work experience, both within your team and between different teams.
- In the same vein, see whether you can get your most concentration-intensive work done outside of a typical office landscape. Try to identify tasks as either deep work or shallow work and choose your workspace accordingly.
- A flexible, creative state of mind is easier to maintain with corporate assistance. Lobby your employer for creative support (environmental, flexibility related).
- Continuous, repetitive, unskilled work leads to boredom, completely killing creativity, while frequently taking on work that is too challenging piques your stress levels, also decreasing creative output. This is self-evident, but in the heat of a sprint-planning meeting, everyone tends to forget this.
- Never go for a walk without a way to take notes.
- Instant messages and emails are typical creativity killers. When choosing a communication system for your team, try to keep in mind which messages absolutely have to reach developers at all times and which don't. This system should allow for the checking of email only a few times a day at predetermined moments.
- Being aware of frequent interruptions—either from yourself or due to unexpected questions from colleagues—will help you to better direct your creative

attention. If interruptions are commonplace, try to dump your current train of thought before reacting.

- Show interest in the work of others that could improve your own, even if it has nothing to do with programming.
- Brighten up your desk environment instead of leaving it bare and uninspired. Sometimes, it really is the little things that matter.
- If the pair programming tempo is too high for you to connect the dots, try to process new knowledge at your own pace. Your pair will surely understand if you explain how your personal creative state of mind works.
- A Creative Programmer is a well-rested programmer. Do not ignore the importance of a good night's sleep!

Creative techniques 8

This chapter covers

- The concept of Art-Based Learning
- Borrowing ideas: good theft versus bad theft
- Writing techniques that boost creativity
- An inspection of a Creative Programmer's toolbox

The shadow of death looms over the streets of collapsing Rome. The Antonine Plague, the first-known pandemic in history, hit the Roman Empire in 170 AD and eradicated 15% of the population within two decades. A widespread state of panic caused most survivors to either ransack or flee the city. Yet its emperor at that time, Marcus Aurelius, chose to stay and brave the crisis, reassuring the people that his life wasn't worth more than anyone else's, in stark contrast to so many of his predecessors. When faced with a life-threatening problem such as the plague, Aurelius' Stoic training taught him to look at the whole instead of zooming in on his own situation.

During and after the ravages of the plague, more bad news kept pouring in. The Roman borders were constantly under attack by Germanic tribes, slowly but surely exhausting both its soldiers and its finances. Instead of taking a narrow-minded approach to solving the gaping hole in the treasury—for example, by raising taxes and plundering neighbors—Aurelius did the opposite. He zoomed out and looked

174

at all aspects of the problem. It occurred to him that his predecessors had amassed a lot of shiny trinkets that did nothing but gather dust. Thus, Aurelius made a bold decision: he simply sold all the imperial treasures in the Forum. He later returned the gold to those who brought back the ornaments, without forcing anyone unwilling to do so. His motto was simple, humbling even: "Do the right thing. The rest doesn't matter. Waste no more time talking about what a good man is like. Be one." This statement came from a man who had lost 9 out of 14 children, faced constant war, and because of recurring health problems, presumably succumbed to the plague himself (figure 8.1), thereby ending the 200-year-long Roman Golden Age.

Eighteen centuries later, the scratching of a pen fills an otherwise peacefully silent hotel room somewhere in the western United States. A middle-aged, balding man scribbles notes on a small piece of paper. Many hotel visits later, the ever-growing stack of paper would form the basis of the 20th-century classic novel *Lolita* that the Russian-American author Vladimir Nabokov wrote during his butterfly-collection travels as a lepidopterist.

Figure 8.1 **The Antonine Plague called for creative action from a devoted Stoic to keep the finances flowing. You could say that Aurelius threw a very unusual yard sale during a very unusual time. Engraving by Étienne Picart, based on "Plague of Ashdod" by Poussin. Source: public domain.**

Nabokov didn't approach writing like many others do. Instead, after forming a picture in his mind, he gradually mapped out the entire structure of a novel on index cards.

This allowed him to overcome the infamous fear of the blank page, or writer's block. New cards got filled as he felt inspiration bubbling up, sometimes even during his butterfly hunts. "I do not begin my novel at the beginning. I do not reach chapter three before I reach chapter four, I do not go dutifully from one page to the next, in consecutive order; no, I pick out a bit here and a bit there, till I have filled all the gaps on paper," he says in an interview.[1]

When Nabokov got stuck, or when a part of the story somehow didn't appeal to him, he simply placed the related index cards on the floor[2] to rearrange, add, or remove bits and pieces. After many rearrangements (and reiterations), Nabokov would join the cards by numbering them and then dictate everything to his wife, who acted as a typist, proofreader, and sometimes savior of discarded index cards. Nabokov's jigsaw puzzle–like approach to novel writing earned him a lot of flexibility and efficiency.

The Original of Laura, Nabokov's final novel, was never completed. Thirty-two years later, in 2009, Penguin published it as "a novel in fragments." The 138 index cards, which were faithfully reproduced, complete with smudges and crossed-out words, can be cut out and organized—and reorganized—as the reader sees fit, in true Nabokov style. It sheds light on how Nabokov structured his work and how he selected the best words to describe characters.

At the beginning of the 21st century, a "Manifesto for Agile Software Development" was developed by a team of dedicated, human-oriented software professionals. It states: "At regular intervals, the team reflects on how to become more effective, then tunes and adjusts its behavior accordingly."[3] The manifesto was authored by some of the most influential software engineers of our time: Robert C. Martin, Jeff Sutherland, Alistair Cockburn, Martin Fowler, Andy Hunt, Kent Beck, Ken Schwaber, and others.

Two years later, Ken Schwaber and Jeff Sutherland compressed their ideas about an "advanced product development method" into a single word: *Scrum*. Regular reflections were also baked into the core of Scrum: "After the Sprint Review and prior to the next Sprint Planning meeting, the Scrum Master holds a Sprint Retrospective meeting with the Team."[4] The Sprint Retrospective was born.

How do you conduct a Sprint Retrospective? According to the Scrum Guide,[5] it should be both an enjoyable and effective way to look back at the work done and inspect what could be improved with regard to people, relationships, processes, and tools—depending on the team's Definition of "Done." Over the years, several inventive techniques have surfaced to set the stage, gather data, generate insights, decide what to do, and close the reflection. The *Check-In, Mad Sad Glad, Five Whys, Circle of Questions, Temperature Reading*, and many other methods provide helpful guidelines to conduct an enjoyable and efficient retro.

---

[1] Robert Golla. Conversations with Vladimir Nabokov. University Press of Mississippi, 2017.
[2] Rearranging also frequently happened in a box in the back of the car en route to his beloved butterfly-hunting locations.
[3] See http://agilemanifesto.org/.
[4] Ken Schwaber. Agile project management with Scrum. Microsoft Press, 2004.
[5] See https://scrumguides.org/.

8.1   On filling a creative toolbox

What is the greatest common divisor between Marcus Aurelius' bird's-eye-view approach to ruling an empire during troubled times; Vladimir Nabokov's flexible index card system, which allowed him to easily change the entire structure of a novel; and various agile retrospective techniques? All three examples showcase the use of creative techniques to overcome roadblocks and generate novel insights.

Without a firm background in Stoicism, Marcus Aurelius might not be considered today the last of the Five Good Roman Emperors. He could have ruled as ruthlessly as Nero and Julius Caesar, but he chose not to: he had been given the tools to deny malice and hypocrisy. "Take care not to be Caesarified, or dyed in purple, it happens. Keep yourself simple, good, pure, serious, unpretentious, a friend of justice, god-fearing, kind, full of affection, strong for your proper work. Strive hard to remain the same man that philosophy wished to make you," he wrote in his *Meditations* when he was older.

Without index cards, Vladimir Nabokov might never have recovered from writer's block. Just like Niklas Luhmann's *Zettelkasten* system, Nabokov's cards boosted both creativity and productivity. Just like Luhmann, Nabokov was another great polymath, or *multipotentialite,* as a novelist, poet, translator, professor of literature, and lepidopterist.

Without the creative tools to facilitate an agile retrospective, the fortnightly meeting ends up like any other meeting: a boring and useless waste of time. Knowing one or more of the aforementioned methods will keep things enjoyable and effective, something all professional gatherings should aim for.

In that sense, the premise of this chapter is similar to that of chapter 2: a baseline of technical knowledge—not of programming but of these tools—is required to overcome creative roadblocks. By connecting this chapter back with the second, we have come full circle!

You might be wondering why the topic deserves its own chapter instead of being integrated into the previous ones. After all, aren't personal knowledge management workflows, diffuse thinking, and self-imposed constraints creative techniques? Of course, they are. However, in our focus group studies, the concept emerged as an intertwined but separate theme. Programmers seem to love talking about their creative toolbox. And that's exactly what we're going to do here.

Coding has remarkable similarities to both art and writing—with art, because we're creating something out of nothing, within a given set of constraints. Depending on the amount of freedom, this can be different from pushing papers or assembly-line labor, where external practices dictate the work. The artist, just like the coder, doesn't have to comply with the universal laws of physics: a quick glance at M. C. Escher's seemingly infinite constructions will tell you that.

Note that I wrote "coding has similarities to art" not "coding (or the result of it) *is* art." That's still up for debate. Again, what is art? Self-expression? Imagination? Creation? Freedom? What do you think?

Coding has similarities to writing because coding involves writing—in a structured manner to make sure the compiler understands what we're trying to say while also making sure our coder colleagues and end users understand what we're trying to say. The compiler doesn't care about the name of the function `buyNewBook`; it cares about the `() {` that comes after it. But we care: readability is much more important than parsability, or even performance.

Every imaginable discipline, including programming, comes with its own set of techniques. Many of these are interdisciplinary. It pays to take a look beyond the boundaries of software. However, the pool is simply too large. In the following sections, we'll limit our investigation of creative tools to a subset of the artist's, the writer's, and, of course, the programmer's. This is by no means a complete list, but it will, I hope, be sufficient to get the conversation started.

> ### Problem-solving techniques vs. creative techniques
> When is a problem-solving technique considered a creative technique? Is something as simple as asking "Why?" five times really that creative? A quick glance at chapter 1 can help answer this. Creativity techniques are techniques and methods that encourage creative actions. Remember that something is creative if deemed as such by you *and* your peers.
>
> That is why I hesitate to reduce this chapter—and the entire book—to a cookbook of practical techniques. Some will strike a chord. Some will sound too far-fetched. And some will induce a "Been there, done that" mumble. Instead, let this selection of creative techniques inspire you to come up with adaptations of your own.

We will focus on problem solving, although many creativity techniques can also be used in therapy or artistic expression.

8.2   A selection: The artist's toolbox

When I encounter the words *creative techniques* without context, I envision vigorous mixing of pigments with secret ingredients, Jackson Pollock's drip technique of splashing more paint on the floor next to the canvas than onto the canvas itself, and purposely bleeding watercolors into one another with the wet-on-wet technique.

As intriguing as these art-based techniques are, none of them are particularly helpful for the Creative Programmer. Or are they? We shouldn't dismiss the artist's toolbox entirely. With a bit of effort, some more high-level practices, techniques, and habits can prove to be valuable tools for the programmer. Let's take a closer look.

8.2.1   Art-Based Learning

In an attempt to re-create a progressive variant of continuous learning, without pursuing the often all-too-present economic goal, cultural history researcher Jeroen Lutters introduced the concept of Art-Based Learning.[6] This technique allows the viewer to

---

[6] Jeroen H. R. Lutters. In de schaduw van het kunstwerk: Art-Based Learning in de praktijk. PhD thesis, Faculty of Humanities, Amsterdam School for Cultural Analysis, 2012.

engage in a dialogue with works of art. The purpose of Art-Based Learning is to help answer life's pressing questions. The object at hand can guide us through an inner adventure, eventually, we hope, arriving at the answer to our question. Associative free thinking is central to this approach. Lutters compares the method with artistic self-expression: "[Art-Based Learning] is not unlike artistic mimesis—inimitable new personal creation as a result of inner research."

Does that sound a bit vague to you? That's because it is a very scholarly way to emphasize the personal intimacy of the method. How does Art-Based Learning work? It can be summarized as a four-step process, as visible in figure 8.2.

First, you ask (yourself) a relevant question. In his dissertation, Lutters provides some examples: "Why am I afraid to die?" or "How can I better enjoy living in the moment?" After you've settled on a question, a work of art must be chosen—or perhaps it chooses you. This can be a simple book, poster, or painting you're attracted to at that moment, an intriguing machine, or even attending a concert. According to Lutters, choosing an object mostly happens subconsciously during daydreaming: "We are not free to only use objects in this manner; sometimes, they choose us." Choosing therefore requires not only the ability to appropriate something but also, and above all, the ability to allow it to be appropriated.

Next, you let the artwork do the talking. The viewer becomes the listener. This can be done only by "close reading": observing attentively and being open to the possibility of inspiration. It's almost a form of meditation. Do not actively search for an answer; instead, admit, register, and become transformed.

In the third step, the viewer becomes detached from the current world and sees all other possibilities thanks to the expression of the artwork. It's about seeing and internally discussing the possibilities. At this point, the artwork stops being a simple work of art. I hope you're still with me; we're almost there!

The fourth and last step is a reflective one where understanding and meaning are transformed into a personal story. Art-Based Learning should result in a new story, new knowledge, and a tentative answer to the initial question.

Clearly, Art-Based Learning is intended to help cope with the bigger philosophical questions in life, not with the pragmatic ones we're trying to answer, such as "Why doesn't my breakpoint get hit?" or "How can I make this asynchronous?" How can we as programmers integrate Art-Based Learning in our creative problem-solving activities?

Figure 8.2   The four steps of Art-Based Learning: (1) ask your question and choose an artwork, (2) let the art talk, (3) see possibilities, and (4) transform them into an answer.

The technique has remarkable similarities with Henri Poincaré's subconscious theory of creativity: ponder a question, let the subconscious mind do its thing (with the help of a piece of art), and emerge victorious. Perhaps use one of the many inspirational television shows, fables, and tales that the Oliver twins devoured during the development of their games or the inspirational objects that Freud liked to surround himself with.

Art has a therapeutic effect. Our appreciation of it might inspire and thus help clear out personal roadblocks. Some programmers my colleagues and I interviewed for our creativity studies showed appreciation for modern highway bridges, like the one pictured in figure 8.3, as creative engineering marvels:

> *Person 1: I think when I admire creativity somewhere, it's primarily how something fits together. The simplicity and, you know, the complexity made simple in an existing solution to a problem. Apart from software and IT, for instance, a traffic interchange done right. Like, that's really well made!*

> *Person 2: Now that you mention it, that new highway bridge at that time, I thought it was solved nicely; there are no more traffic jams.*

> *Person 1: Indeed!*

> *Person 2: And that was a drastic change they did there.*

Figure 8.3   The highway interchange in Lummen, Belgium, redesigned between 2008 and 2012. Twelve new bridges, some weighing 8,000 tons, were built and moved around. This elegant engineering solution inspired our interviewees and can be beautiful, just like a work of art. Photo courtesy of Davy Govaert.

In their controversial book *Art as Therapy*, renowned philosopher Alain de Botton and art historian John Armstrong propose a new way of looking at art, suggesting that it can be useful, relevant, and therapeutic. "Great works offer clues in managing tensions and confusion in everyday life," de Botton argues.[7] That sounds an awful lot like Art-Based Learning! While Vermeer's *Melkmeisje* (Milkmaid) or the new highway interchange will probably not hold the answer to that caching problem you're struggling with, a thorough look can help us better understand both art and ourselves, thereby providing the clues needed to successfully invalidate the cache.

8.2.2 Steal like an artist

"Steal Like an Artist"—the title of Austin Kleon's provocative manifesto for creativity in the digital age—manages to grab our attention. In it, Kleon summarizes 10 things he wished he'd heard when he was starting out as an artist:[8]

- Steal like an artist.
- Don't wait until you know who you are to get started.
- Write the book you want to read [check!].
- Use your hands.
- Side projects and hobbies are important.
- The secret: do good work and share it with people.
- Geography is no longer our master.
- Be nice. (The world is a small town.)
- Be boring. (It's the only way to get work done.)
- Creativity is subtraction.

This list formed the basis of a talk at a community college in New York, which quickly went viral online. Can you find the similarities to the seven creative problem-solving domains in this book? "Subtraction" is constraint work. "Being boring" is being persistent, in the flow, and showing grit. One of the illustrations in the book states, "You will need: curiosity, kindness, stamina, a willingness to look stupid." Sharing work is a central theme of chapter 4.

Even the first entry, stealing "like an artist," occurs in the introduction of chapter 2, where we saw that the Kotlin programming language was purposely built on top of the shoulders of existing giants and where Seneca often peeked at and learned from the writings of Epicurus, his philosophical competitor. In a sense, this book came to life in the same way.

According to Kleon, there are good theft and bad theft. Good theft involves honoring, studying, stealing from many, crediting, transforming, and remixing. Bad theft involves degrading, skimming, stealing from one, plagiarizing, imitating, and ripping off.

Sadly, in the software development world, bad theft is commonplace. For example, Microsoft's recent GitHub Copilot project, "Your AI pair programmer," at first sounds like a really clever idea—and it probably is. However, the machine learning–powered

---

[7] Alain de Botton and John Armstrong. Art as therapy. Phaidon Press, 2013.
[8] Austin Kleon. Steal like an artist: 10 things nobody told you about being creative. Workman, 2012.

copilot that suggests code and entire functions in real time is trained by billions of lines of code directly lifted from hosted GitHub projects, without ever taking licensing considerations into account. No accreditation of any sort was put forward. Copilot, as a closed for-profit product, is made possible by unethically leaning on thousands of coding hours from open source developers and blatantly ignoring their licenses, of which most, in fact, require proper attribution. Eventually, the Software Freedom Conservancy put out the message "Give Up GitHub!"[9] Many open source software maintainers are migrating to other solutions, such as Codeberg, Source Hut, or a self-hosted Gitea instance. Yet another big tech company that ends up taking advantage of "free" data.

This happens all too often. I've worked at multiple companies where project dependencies are happily `yarn add`-ed without ever taking a closer look at the `LICENSING.md` file. At one employer, an observant developer was simply laughed at for remarking that we're using GPL software and selling the product as closed source. Bad theft, Austin Kleon says. "Who cares?" the company replies.

"Stealing" and remixing the best parts are often requirements to push a domain forward. These practices are clearly visible not only in art but also in the automotive, software development, and hardware-engineering industries. Sometimes, remixing results in bland and forgettable imitations of the original. Sometimes, remixing previously unthinkable combinations somehow works, even though the parts sound like impossible matches.

What do you get when you cross-breed the pinball genre with the run-and-gun shoot-'em-up genre? *Nitro Ball*, a 1992 arcade oddity from Data East that, against all odds, sold quite well. What about mixing the 2D exploration metroidvania genre with flying pinballs? The result is *Yoku's Island Express* (figure 8.4), a 2018 "platforming pinball adventure" by Villa Gorilla, where you play as a dung beetle?

> **EXERCISE**   When was the last time you "stole like an artist"? Did you commit a bad theft or a good theft? Did you study, or did you skim, like my students love to do? (I admit, I've been there!) Perhaps now is the time to quickly scan your project's dependencies and correctly accredit them. Many programming ecosystems have plug-ins to access this information, such as in Node.js (license-checker), Go (go-licenses), Gradle (gradle-license-plugin), and Elixir (licensir). Remember that not all licenses are compatible with each other.

---

[9] See https://sfconservancy.org/GiveUpGitHub/.

Figure 8.4   **Villa Gorilla somehow managed to fuse the best mechanics of the metroidvania and pinball genres into the cheerful adventure that is** *Yoku's Island Express*.

8.2.3   *The power of time off*

Every seven years, graphic designer Stefan Stagmeister leaves his studio behind to take a year-long sabbatical. During his prolonged time off, Stagmeister absorbs everything he encounters like a sponge. Remarkable cultures, humbling forests, sprawling cities: all impressions form the basis of his future creative work. Some places he has visited "spontaneously evoked wonderful inspirations."[10]

I must admit, I'm quite jealous. Taking a whole year off to chase nothing but inspiration requires both financial stability and a lot of guts. In his TED talk on the power of time off, Stagmeister makes the distinction between a *job* (a nine-to-five one done for the money), a *career* (climbing up the ladder), and a *calling* (intrinsically fulfilling). He argues that we often lose sight of what we really want and that, by regularly taking time off to rethink our working strategy and getting inspired, we're more likely to see what we do as a calling instead of a job.

One year off every seven years equals 12.5% time devoted to chasing whatever you want. Is it really that much? Compared to Google's former 20% time or 3M's 15% rule, it's actually less! Of course, those times "off" are never really off, and they are always taken with an eye on business profits. Since 2011, as Google exponentially grew

---

[10] See Stagmeister's TED talk, "The Power of Time Off," at https://www.ted.com/talks/stefan_stagmeister_the_power_of_time_off.

in size, it began cutting back this "free time" presumably to focus more on the operational side of the business and to adopt a "more wood behind fewer arrows" strategy.

Taking a sabbatical doesn't mean not working—it means working on whatever you'd like. It almost always is a trigger for inspiration for your main job. Many authors, like psychologist Daniel Gilbert, write books while on sabbatical. Gilbert is lucky enough to be a tenured professor, which obviously makes the sabbatical much more doable. Stagmeister still designed and sold artwork during that period. I know of psychologists who close their practice for four months to think, write, organize retreats, and get inspired. Slowing down to let the inspiration unfold is one of the key advantages of a long-term leave. It can even be enough to fuel creations for years to come, as Stagmeister witnessed: "Everything we designed in the seven years following the first sabbatical had originated in that year."

Taking a sabbatical also doesn't mean not planning anything. Stagmeister explains that his first sabbatical year was a disaster. Instead of generating ideas, he just fiddled about and reacted to anything that was sent his way. A better approach would be to convert a list of interesting things into an actionable plan that can serve as a starting point.

But perhaps the most important benefit of Stagmeister's sabbatical was falling in love with his job again. The job he resented became a true calling. Our feelings have more influence on our creativity than we'd like to admit. If you can't stand the thought of getting up in the morning because of your work, the chances of achieving that much-needed creative breakthrough are next to zero. It might even be a clear sign of a looming burnout.

Psychology research has claimed for decades that emotions and moods deeply influence our cognitive abilities, including creativity and analytical problem solving. This claim wasn't verified in software engineering research until recently, when Daniel Graziotin and his research team discovered that, indeed, happy software developers solve problems better and more creatively.[11]

The study's participants were limited to 42 computer science students, who could arguably not serve as true software developers. In a follow-up study, Graziotin's team interviewed 317 experienced programmers about the consequences of (un)happiness for productivity and software quality.[12] Happy programmers reported positive outcomes on both external processes and their own well-being:

> *The most significant consequences, in terms of frequency, of happiness for the developer's own being are: high cognitive performance, high motivation, perceived positive atmosphere, higher self-accomplishment, high work engagement and perseverance, higher creativity and higher self-confidence.*

The other way around is also true: reduced creativity is reported as a consequence of unhappiness.

---

[11] Daniel Graziotin, Xiaofeng Wang, and Pekka Abrahamsson. Happy software developers solve problems better: Psychological measurements in empirical software engineering. PeerJ, 2014.

[12] Daniel Graziotin, Fabian Fagerholm, Xiaofeng Wang, and Pekka Abrahamsson. What happens when software developers are (un)happy. Journal of Systems and Software, 2018.

What can we as programmers learn from this—should we collectively rush to our boss to ask for a sabbatical? I will leave that up to you. The essence of taking time off is to lighten the mood and get inspired (without corporate pressure), to feel that child-like curiosity again—perhaps even being happy, as we explored in chapter 6. Other drastic and less drastic ways to experience this include a prolonged vacation, becoming self-employed, switching teams, part-time work, working in different sectors and becoming a *multipotentialite*, setting up a blog or writing a book, and so forth.

It doesn't have to be a "sabbatical," which perhaps sounds a bit invasive (or sometimes downright impossible). Even taking limited time off—for example, an extended weekend to just noodle around and completely detach from work—has proven to recharge creative effectiveness at work.[13] Organizational psychologists discovered that emotional and physical detachment from work positively affects employees' health and even creativity. Taking time off—however short—to discover new things and meet new people is certainly beneficial to both our creativity and our health.

Yet at the same time, the previous study also reports that complete cognitive detachment from work can have negative effects on learning and creativity, since you leave the job resources behind that might help support creative thinking (your immediate colleagues, available work resources, etc.).

The authors conclude that employees need to take time off from work to balance health and creative problem-solving abilities. We will further explore the relationship between well-being and creativity in chapter 9.

8.3   A selection: The writer's toolbox

Taking a peek at the tools of the trade of writers, next to artists, could also prove to be instructive. After all, a writer's toolbox is full of effective techniques for jumping past roadblocks, pushing past the much-dreaded blank page, and making novel connections between ideas. Slight modifications allow these tools to be competent techniques in the hands of the Creative Programmer.

A quick internet search for "creative writing techniques" nets more than two billion results, ranging from metaphors, rhetorical questions, alliterations, personification, free-form writing, dictating and transcribing, act structuring to plot development, and even serious data mining techniques to extract specific language usages from different user groups.

These endless lists of writing techniques are less compelling than the writing advice formulated by great authors. The sections that follow offer a selection of the latter that might help improve the creative writing of our code. You'll recognize many tools of the trade from previous chapters.

---

[13] Jan de Jonge, Ellen Spoor, Sabine Sonnentag, Christian Dormann, and Marieke van den Tooren. "Take a break?!" Off-job recovery, job demands, and job resources as predictors of health, active learning, and creativity. European Journal of Work and Organizational Psychology, 2012.

8.3.1 *Vladimir Nabokov's toolbox*

Nabokov himself was always ready to dish out advice in various interviews and lectures. In the book *Conversations With Vladimir Nabokov*, edited by Robert Golla, these interviews come together to form an overview of the life and work of the Russian-American literary master.[14] The following paragraphs provide a selection of the advice I found to be fitting in the context of programming.

Study other artists. Said Nabokov: "A creative writer must study carefully the works of his rivals, including the Almighty. He must possess the inborn capacity not only of recombining but of re-creating the given world. In order to do this adequately, avoiding duplication of labor, the artist should know the given world." Steal like an artist *and* like a writer!

Be inspired by the world around you. "The art of writing is a very futile business if it does not imply first of all the art of seeing the world as the potentiality of fiction." Of course, there's a big difference between fiction writing and implementing business requirements in software, but that doesn't mean we can't be inspired by the things we see in the world outside of IT. For example, the postal system that delivers our mail can be seen as an asynchronous message broker like the popular software RabbitMQ or the distributed event streaming platform Apache Kafka.

Every writer is a great deceiver (and enchanter). Nabokov compared the writing of fiction with nature's deceptive simplicity. This comparison translates itself well to programming: write deceptively simple code that, in Nabokov's words, is a prodigiously sophisticated illusion, yet clearly able to convey intent. Style and structure are more important than implementing great ideas—a concept that has gained a clear following lately with Go programmers.

Caress the details! Nabokov's index cards allowed him to work, rework, and rework again, as clearly visible by the many pencil smudges in figure 8.5. "Every card is rewritten many times," he said—not a single word is left unedited. When programming, once the unit tests cover the initial requirements, we should code, recode, and recode again. Every line of code—including the tests—can be rewritten many times, until the tests signal the required functionality is implemented and the code is easily readable by others to facilitate maintainability and possible later reworks. Red, Green, Refactor. Again. "Kill your darlings," as writers like to say.

Style needs to be developed. "Style is not a tool, it is not a method, it is not a choice of words alone. Being much more than all this, style constitutes an intrinsic component or characteristic of the author's personality. Thus, when we speak of style we mean an individual artist's peculiar nature and the way it expresses itself in his artistic output." He continues: "It is not unusual that in the course of his literary career a writer's style becomes ever more precise and impressive." Programming is more of a collaborative activity than writing, but precisely because of that, I think Nabokov is onto something here. Our (collective) coding style is just as important as the choice of algorithms or frameworks.

---

[14] Robert Golla, Conversations with Vladimir Nabokov. University Press of Mississippi, 2017.

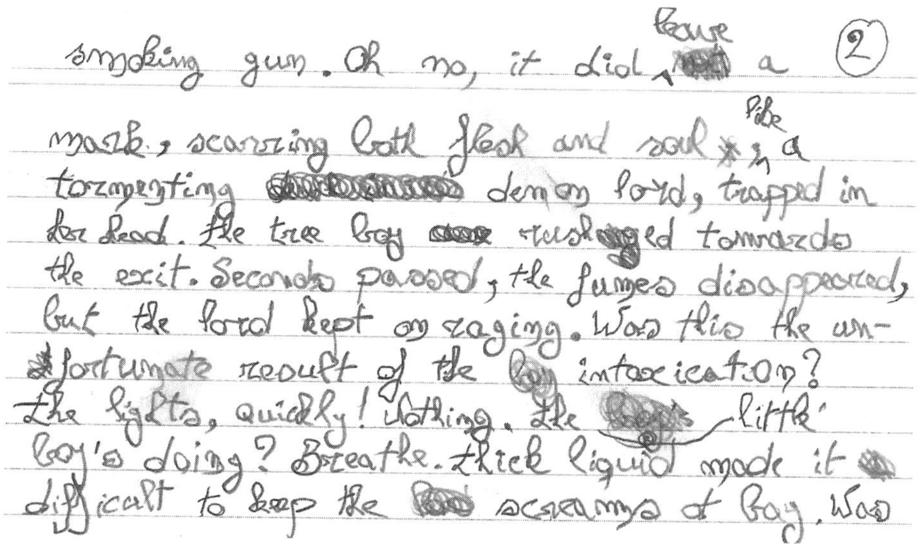

Figure 8.5 An index card with a piece of a plot modeled after Nabokov's sometimes quite messy novel-writing method. Depending on the order of these cards, the story will change. His final book, published posthumously, *The Original of Laura (Dying Is Fun)*, is subtitled *A Novel in Fragments*. In it, the reader is encouraged to alter the story by cutting out the present scans of Nabokov's index cards!

Don't necessarily start at the beginning. The flexible index card system allowed Nabokov to write a few sentences here and there, perhaps not starting with chapter 1 and dutifully continuing to chapter 2. We can heed that advice when implementing a complex piece of code. By breaking down the big piece into separate "index cards" with the help of unit tests, we can tackle the problem without having to start at the beginning.

8.3.2 Geoff Dyer's toolbox

English author Geoff Dyer writes both novels and nonfiction and has won many awards for his work. His writing advice, shared in multiple articles in *The Guardian*, is noticeably more pragmatic compared with the more erudite Nabokov.

Don't write in public places. "It should be done in private, like any other lavatorial activity." This is a nod toward Cal Newport's *Deep Work*: write (or code!) with closed doors; rework with open doors. Coding requires concentration. The idealized picture of working in a coffee shop doesn't facilitate concentration. If we are to believe Dyer, it actively impedes it.

Constantly refine and expand your autocorrect settings. Finally, a writer who openly advocates the use of productivity tools to help make space for more creative thoughts. Build up muscle memory for those IDE shortcut keys. Fine-tune the autosuggestions. Your code editor is your best friend.

Keep a diary. Other writers, like Brazilian Paulo Coelho, deny its advantages: "Forget taking notes. What is important remains, what is not goes away." When it comes to contemporary programming, that is a very dangerous point of view because the many details we are told to pay attention to also tend to slip away. Stick with Dyer's advice or reread chapter 2.

If something is proving too difficult, give up and do something else. "Writing is all about perseverance," Dyer explains. "You've got to stick with it." As we saw in chapter 7, sub-consciously processing the roadblock is an added benefit of temporarily doing something else.

Make a habit. Write every day. Remember, it's about perseverance. "Gradually, this will become instinct." Some authors' writing schedules are really impressive. Stephen King, for instance, writes 10,000 words every single day. No wonder he's one of the most prolific American fiction writers of our age. Other writers are content with a few heavily reworked sentences. It's not about quantity, but daily habits do make the road to creative success easier.

8.3.3   *Anne Lamott's toolbox*

Anne Lamott's *Bird by Bird*[15] is a classic work when it comes to uncovering the pain, grace, love, and fear of the writer. Compared with Nabokov's and Dyer's advice, Lamott's is more personal and emotionally laden but far from less important. The next few paragraphs provide a selection of her advice that stood out to me as especially provocative.

Write your own unique story. "You own everything that happened to you. Tell your stories," Lamott writes. Don't be afraid to unleash your Pythonic skills as a former Python programmer currently plodding in the Java universe. This isn't about syntax—for instance, `camelCasing` versus `snake_casing`—but about inventive ways to apply personal past experiences to present coding problems. Only you can pull it off.

Just sit down. Echoing Dyer's advice on making a habit, Lamott writes, "You try to sit down at approximately the same time every day. This is how you train your unconscious to kick in for you creatively." It can take a while for inspiration to come. Don't stress—be patient: "You look at the ceiling, and over at the clock, yawn, and stare at the paper again. Then, with your fingers poised on the keyboard, you squint at an image that is forming in your mind—a scene, a locale, a character, whatever—and you try to quiet your mind so you can hear what that landscape or character has to say above the other voices in your mind." During our creativity surveys, some programmers mentioned they "just sit down and start to write." They won't even bother with syntax and usually type out global ideas in pseudocode, just to "get it out there." Then, they'll call in help from others and gradually reshape it into a workable solution.

Don't fake it. Your end users will immediately notice it: "You must assume that we, your readers, are bright and attentive, even if we have lost the tiniest bit of ground in the last few years. So we are going to catch you if you try to fake it." Lamott mentions that *your readers* are bright and attentive. For programming, this isn't limited to end users! Your current and future colleagues, who will probably read your code many more times than you did, should also not be fooled with needless fluff. Creative programmers take the end user into account, whether the software is a video game, an

---

[15] Anne Lamott. Bird by bird: Some instructions on writing and life. Anchor Books, 1995.

administrative web application, or a mobile parking app. If possible, meet with them, get to know them and their world, and carefully analyze their business needs. Be critical of half-baked customer profiles and business logic. Only then write code tailored to their needs.

Ask people around you for help. Lamott gives the example of a passionate gardener who could help you include an accurate description of a garden in your writing. Build on the expertise of others to "make the words come alive." If you have to implement a music-streaming web server, it might pay off to talk to musicians to learn about pitches and typical waveforms to better understand how to encode data efficiently.

Write step by step or "bird by bird." Sometimes, it's okay to not know where you're heading. Stubbornly focusing on the destination means closing your eyes to everything that passes along the way. Lamott quotes novelist and professor E. L. Doctorow: "Writing a novel is like driving a car at night. You can see only as far as your headlights, but you can make the whole trip that way." Just seeing a little bit ahead of you is enough.

Stop trying to perfect things. According to Lamott, "Perfectionism is the voice of the oppressor, the enemy of the people. It will keep you cramped and insane your whole life, and it is the main obstacle between you and a shitty first draft." She continues:

> *I think perfectionism is based on the obsessive belief that if you run carefully enough, hitting each stepping-stone just right, you won't have to die. The truth is that you will die anyway and that a lot of people who aren't even looking at their feet are going to do a whole lot better than you, and have a lot more fun while they're doing it.*

EXERCISE   Imagine a new colleague asks you for code-writing advice. What do you say? Do you point the colleague to the team's coding style guideline? Do you sit down and tell a personal success story? Do you hand over your copy of Robert C. Martin's *Clean Code*? Or do you postpone the answer and instead propose to pair up this week?

Sometimes, our dogmatic self will keep on reworking and refactoring a piece of code, well beyond the point of futility. Be mindful of your pragmatic self: don't let it cut corners too rashly. But also be mindful of your dogmatic self: don't let perfectionism take over. Remember the mantra of critical thinking in chapter 5: *creativity is the means, not the goal.*

8.4   A selection: The programmer's toolbox

Creativity research has produced more than 100 different creative, problem-solving techniques: for analyzing the environment, recognizing and identifying problems, making assumptions, generating alternatives, and so forth. The question then becomes whether any of those techniques are applicable to the field of programming.

Software developers know more creative techniques than they like to admit. Every two weeks, I've seen these consistently applied in retrospectives, based on the excellent *Agile Retrospectives* by Esther Derby and Diana Larsen[16] or websites like https://funretrospectives.com. Yet I wonder, why don't we reach for these techniques when

---

[16] Esther Derby and Diana Larsen. Agile retrospectives: Making good teams great. Pragmatic Bookshelf, 2006.

outside of the meeting room? What's wrong with variations of invigorating retrospectives—for example, *Triple Nickels*—during development? During the Triple Nickel activity, small groups first brainstorm and write down ideas on paper individually. After five minutes, each person passes their paper to the person on their right, who gets another five minutes to build on that idea, until the paper returns to the original writer. This is a great way to quickly discover the limitations of your idea and to strengthen it, without running the risk of immediately dismissing less conventional ideas. These small but fun exercises can be organized ad hoc when hitting a wall during coding sessions. Obstacles should be overcome during a sprint, not in between them.

In the following sections, we'll let experts highlight an assortment of creative techniques that are underappreciated or commonly misunderstood. Let's remove the rust from those programmer's tools and make them shine. I promise no vinegar soaking is required.

8.4.1   *Anna Bobkowska's toolbox*

In 2019, software engineering researcher Anna E. Bobkowska explored the potential of creative techniques in software engineering using a specific training–application–feedback cycle.[17] Participants left the experiment with an increased appreciation of creativity techniques, claiming that a mix of these techniques is likely to be useful in practice. Bobkowska zoomed in on the following seven techniques:

- Asking *naive questions* to discover hidden assumptions and implicit knowledge ("Imagine we'd only need one input form for this webpage!").
- Wondering "What if . . ." or searching for hidden sequences of consequences ("What if I pressed the submit button twenty times?").
- Completing the sentence "I could be more creative if . . . " to understand personal obstacles ("I could be more creative if thought walks weren't frowned upon.").
- Using the *Lunette* technique: look at the problem at different levels of abstraction (switching between generalization and specialization; zooming in on code and zooming back out by applying a bird's-eye perspective).
- *Using reverse brainstorming*: first express criticism and then motivate to improve ("What don't you like about the database structure?").
- Using what Bobkowska calls the *Chinese dictionary, as derived from the presentation of old animal taxonomies*, a technique to create atypical classifications (create unusual taxonomies of concerns related to the project).
- Using the "Let's invite them" technique: use creativity patterns of (imaginary) experts in creativity ("Suppose we invite Linus Torvalds; what would he have to say on this?").

Some of these techniques will probably be very familiar to you. In the interviews my colleagues and I conducted on exploring creativity techniques for programmers,

---

[17] Anna E Bobkowska. Exploration of creativity techniques in software engineering in training-application-feedback cycle. In Workshop on Enterprise and Organizational Modeling and Simulation, Springer, 2019.

letting the imagination run wild was frequently mentioned as a great technique for uncovering unknown constraints and assumptions:

> *Person 1: . . . or also a little bit of out-of-the-box thinking; one thing that we applied in a retro recently was a technique that asks in what different ways can we break the system, to find all different ways things can go wrong, from another angle so to speak.*

> *Person 2: Yeah, I do that a lot implicitly when modeling. Like, if this is a solution, then what happens when this, and what happens—does it break, and if it breaks, is that okay? If not, on to the next solution that does handle this.*

Peeling the onion by repeatedly asking "Why?" was also a common theme—either in dialogue or as a monologue. Thinking out loud, what scientists call *self-directed speech*, is proven to help the brain perform better during visual processing.[18] By explaining a problem to someone—or something—else, whether it's debugging with the help of a rubber duck,[19] a convenient piece of art on the wall (as in Art-Based Learning), your cat, or a colleague, the solution often magically presents itself. Explaining, or even teaching, forces us to slow down and approach the problem from different directions, which is usually followed by a deeper understanding.

While most techniques are helpful tools to identify and clear implementation-related roadblocks, some, like reverse brainstorming and creating atypical classifications, can be used earlier, during ideation. Bobkowska groups techniques into four themes: *interpersonal skills* (create team spirit, remove personal obstacles), *creativity skills* (associative thinking and ideation), *motivational* skills (which help to discover negative aspects), and *overcoming obstacles.*

Brainstorming: The bad parts

What is more stereotypical than a brainstorming session recommended by creativity consultants? It is the most frequently mentioned method, in both our studies and the ones I encountered while digging through the literature.

Still, a few things have to be cleared up here. A multitude of studies has demonstrated that brainstorming, as we know it, does not work. First, people produce twice as many ideas alone as they do in a meeting room in front of a whiteboard. Second, connecting the dots—the one "big" idea we're all waiting for—is also better practiced in solitude. Third, as Eric Weiner noted, many brainstorming sessions come with a hidden agenda that puts pressure on the kettle, suppressing truly great ideas. Fourth, haphazardly blurting out ideas influences the thinking process of others. We all know that irritating colleague, shaking his head while interrupting us by saying, "That's never gonna work." Fifth, as mentioned in chapter 3, the genius cluster can work only if the minds are sufficiently heterogeneous.

---

[18] Gary Lupyan and Daniel Swingley. Self-directed speech affects visual search performance. Quarterly Journal of Experimental Psychology, 2012.

[19] In software engineering, rubber duck debugging is a method of debugging code by articulating a problem in spoken or written natural language. It was first introduced in *The Pragmatic Programmer*. For more information, see https://rubberduckdebugging.com/.

> **(continued)**
> Does that mean we have to give up on brainstorming? Respectful collective gatherings are still great ways to gather ideas—in the coffeehouse, not the corporate meeting room.

8.4.2   *The Pragmatic Programmer's toolbox*

The *Pragmatic Programmer* bible[20] recommends learning a new programming language each year. Each new language comes with its own guidelines, style, devoted followers, and a unique approach to problem solving. The more languages you have under your belt, the more likely it is that you'll be able to creatively combine and convert practices from one language into another, although, as explained in chapter 4, we need to stay mindful of cross-language clashes.

Bruce Tate didn't like the recommendation of Andy Hunt and Dave Thomas. Just *one* language each year? Why not seven in seven weeks? In *Seven Languages in Seven Weeks*, Tate provides practical tips on how to quickly learn any new programming language[21] based on the journey of learning seven languages in two months. Its success led to the inevitable follow-up four years later, *Seven More Languages in Seven Weeks*. Tate's books cover the technicalities of a language and give the reader a taste of how other programmers across broadly different communities solve complex problems.

Thinking in terms of multiple languages is an effective way to approach difficult problems in code. Imagine you're stuck on a problem and you have no idea how to move forward using the current technology. But what if you could write in JavaScript? Or Elixir? Or Kotlin? Would it be easily solved if you could rely on C's pointers? Or on Ruby's reflective extensibility? What if you could express it in a functional language? Would that make things easier or harder? How about pipelining `filter()` and `map()`? What about nullable types from other languages? Should the business logic be expressed in Prolog? Can you benefit from the advantages of a scripting language, such as Squirrel? How about a custom domain-specific language to express the logic?

If it can't be done in the current language, try out another one. And another one. Just one more. Is this your seventh yet? Perhaps back-porting the idea is good enough. Perhaps your virtual machine is able to interpret the language: Ruby and Python run on the JVM and CLR, Clojure is a Lisp dialect on the JVM, and pretty much anything runs JS code nowadays.

Many programmers are stuck in their daily routine and way of thinking. That tunnel vision actively prevents you from discovering other, sometimes better, possibilities. Interestingly, none of our focus group participants mentioned switching languages or thinking about patterns in other languages as a creative activity. Instead, someone in our interviews posed struggling with syntax as distinctively not creative:

---

[20] Andy Hunt and Dave Thomas. The Pragmatic Programmer: From journeyman to master. Addison-Wesley Professional, 1999.

[21] Bruce A. Tate. Seven languages in seven weeks: A pragmatic guide to learning programming languages. Pragmatic Bookshelf, 2010.

What's not creative, if you're like in this mode of syntax errors, that's the extreme, you've typed out everything and then you have to let it run (laughter) and you have to fix a misplaced comma three or four times, depending on your language, that's going to take longer. And the mechanical errors in your unit tests. And what I also wrote down is new technology, if you're reading documentation of something new, how it works, how does that protocol work . . .

The last remark hints at the baseline of technical knowledge needed to be creative as explained in the first chapter.

In addition to the recommendation to learn a new language each year, *The Pragmatic Programmer* introduced the concept of martial arts "katas" to the world of software development. A code kata exercise is usually a small snippet of code that is repeatedly rewritten to build muscle memory and practice the craft, just like a martial arts choreography.

The most popular code kata exercise I know of is probably the bowling game. After everyone reacquaints themselves with the scoring rules of bowling, coders try to implement it using a test-first approach. Where do you start? Create a `Game` class? Or a `Player`, or a `ScoreCalulator`? Should you use inheritance to reuse scoring logic for spares and strikes? Such a seemingly simple assignment can quickly get pretty messy in code. At that point, it's time to toss everything and retry.

The katas I've been involved in always comprised small isolated exercises that had nothing to do with the codebase we were working on. Online code kata training platforms, such as Codewars, focus mostly on improving knowledge of syntax and algorithms. Instead of fixating on the bowling rules, the concept of a code kata can also be an effective tool to quickly ideate possible solutions in your production codebase.

> **EXERCISE**   Pair up and try to implement a feature or a small subset of it. Now let your pair revert the changes—that hurts, doesn't it? When working alone, revert it yourself and pretend it was code written by a colleague. Can you do better than that person? But not everything is lost, as possibilities were explored and options were considered. New routines of thinking were examined. The next iteration is sure to be superior.

8.4.3   *Emily Morehouse's toolbox*

In 2015, Emily Morehouse attended her first PyCon conference, in Montreal, Canada. There, Guido van Rossum—the creator of the Python language—announced the search for female Python Core Developers, as none were enlisted at that time. It took another year for Emily to jump at the opportunity, only she had no idea where to start or what a Core Developer actually does. Luckily, Guido was there to mentor her.[22]

As figure 8.6 illustrates, the CPython source code is enormous: it contains more than 550,000 lines of C code and 629,000 lines of Python code. Where does one start contributing to such a huge and long-running project? Fixing small bugs reported on

---

[22] Watch Emily Morehouse's keynote talk for PyCon Colombia 2020 on how she became a Core Developer, at https://youtu.be/TSphDJdco8M.

GitHub would be pointless: the easy ones are, of course, already tackled. Instead, with the guidance of a mentor, Emily started studying the source code. This allowed her to understand how other Core Developers work, which patterns are repeatedly applied, how decisions are made, and perhaps even where improvements are in order.

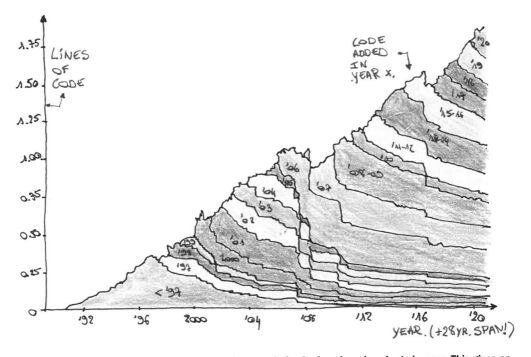

Figure 8.6   A historical plot of CPython's codebase evolution broken down in cohorts by year. This gives an impression of how the code evolved and grew over more than 28 years. Based on data collected by Pablo Galindo Salgado and generated by Eric Bernhardsson's *git-of-theseus* tool (available at GitHub).

By studying the source code of others, we can extract valuable lessons to use in our own work, just like Austin Kleon's "Steal Like an Artist" manifesto. Ask any novelist for advice, and the first thing they will say is "Read more." To become a good writer, first read.

It baffles me how little we as programmers deliberately read and learn from others' code, in particular outside of our comfortable daily project codebase. Our past reading groups covered books about programming, but never free and open source software (FOSS) code. To become a good programmer, first read. And perhaps write as well, as famous hacker and open source software advocate Eric S. Raymond suggests in his article "How to Become a Hacker"[23]—text, not code, that is (see chapter 1 for a workflow example on writing).

Social coding platforms such as GitHub and GitLab help tremendously in reading and understanding FOSS code. Many of these big projects are actively looking for con-

---

[23] See http://www.catb.org/esr/faqs/hacker-howto.html.

tributors. Although it can be daunting to try to wade through the never-ending stream of problems and lines of code, contributing to FOSS is a great way to sharpen your own creative programming toolkit.

If you want to take contributing seriously, like Emily Morehouse's ambition to become a Python Core Developer, having a mentor to check in on how you're doing is not a luxury. Emily admitted that, without guidance, she would have bailed out. The mentor can re-create much-needed context that otherwise remains invisible. Some code parts become relics nobody dares to touch anymore. Why were certain weird C functions grouped in this file? Why didn't they use x or y instead? Without proper documentation, that collective knowledge rapidly becomes lost in time.

In addition to reading code and having a mentor, Morehouse also emphasized the importance of gaining the trust of the development community. This is a very time-consuming process. Building empathy is conveniently never mentioned in any CONTRIBUTING.md guide. After successfully blending in, it is your job to support new contributors and deal with anonymous annoying people over the internet.

It turns out that a Python Core Developer, like any other developer, does much more than simply write code.

Summary

- When approaching a complex problem, remember to switch tools now and then. Do not stay zoomed in—try to zoom out to look at the problem from another perspective.

- Take good care of the tools in your creative toolbox. Critically evaluate and resharpen them now and then. Perhaps it's time to throw out the blunt ones?

- Appreciating masterpieces outside of tech might help spark an idea and inspire you to mirror its concept in code. Let the masterpieces do the talking; when it comes to creativity, do not listen only to yourself.

- Avoid degrading, skimming, and ripping off ideas. Instead, honor, study, and remix ideas. Steal like an artist, not like a con man.

- Scratch your own itch. Exploring side roads are effective ways to improve your creative problem solving and potentially create new products.

- When writing code, remember that there is a backspace attached to your keyboard. Sometimes, subtractions create more clarity than additions.

- Build downtime into your career and take time off now and then to recharge your creative-thinking batteries. Exploring new techniques and meeting new people beyond your day job are guaranteed to inspire and enhance your work.

- Remember that your current mood and emotions also positively and negatively influence your cognitive abilities—and, thus, your capacity for creative problem solving. Not every day needs to be a creative day.

- When it comes to code, style and structure are just as important as contents and functional correctness. Exaggerating creative programming might result in reduced maintainability.

- If the beginning proves to be difficult, start at the middle, or perhaps even at the end. If syntax proves to be difficult, just write, and ignore syntax errors. Getting down the basics of the idea first will make implementing it in your target programming language easier.

- As a programmer, one of the most important tools in your creative toolbox is probably your code editor. Get to know it well. Spend time fiddling with shortcuts and various settings. This will pay off greatly once you've mastered the basics.

- When faced with a roadblock, it's okay to temporarily just give up and do something else. Perhaps an hour or a day later, the solution will present itself.

- Put your personal history with certain programming languages to good use. If you know Ruby's message-passing syntax well, you'll have little trouble with Elixir's methods. As an extension of this, flex your linguistic muscles and take on the challenge of learning two new languages by next month!

- Try out some of your favorite agile retrospective brainstorming tools outside of the classic meeting room.

- Discuss coding problems with your parents, your children, your friends who aren't programmers, and your clients. Their nontechnical view might point to a simple solution that you, as the expert, overlooked.

- When organizing code katas, see whether you can isolate pieces of code from your current project source repository. Perhaps those pieces are better candidates to train you and your fellow colleagues compared with traditionally more isolated examples.

- If you don't have one yet, start looking for a mentor who'll help you forge your own creative tools.

Final
thoughts on creativity

This chapter covers
- Creativity as an attainable skill, not a preset one
- Different perceptions of creativity based on experience
- When not to be creative
- Further reading suggestions

We started out this creative adventure with the premise of awakening your inner *homo faber*. By investing in technical knowledge, communication, constraints, critical thinking, curiosity, a creative state of mind, and creative techniques, I guarantee that you will gradually progress toward becoming a Creative Programmer. Yet one of the hardest quests is yet to come: putting theory into practice. That is something you'll have to undertake by yourself. Roadblocks will appear to test your curiosity and persistence. I hope I've inspired you to press on and continue down the path.

And with that, I'd like to thank you for staying with me on this mission of exploration. It has been a wild ride, but as they say, "The best is yet to come." My job as a writer offering insights into creative problem solving in software engineering is now done, while your job as a graduate Creative Programmer is only beginning.

Good luck on the journey ahead! Remember that if the going gets tough, this book will be there to act as a guide. Flip through the chapters now and then to remind yourself that creativity isn't rocket science: everyone can be creative.

9.1 Remember, everyone can be creative

Charles Darwin suffered from severe anxiety and had to lie in bed for hours almost every day, yet he still made a huge contribution to the world. Many Nobel Prize winners interviewed by cognitive psychologist Mihaly Csikszentmihalyi were humble when asked about their creative process. Some even admitted that anyone could have done it; they just happened to be at the right place at the right time.

These stories are very encouraging: anyone can become a creative genius—it's not (only) attributed to genes, IQ, or aptitude. Again, like Albert Einstein said, "It's not that I'm so smart; it's just that I stay with problems longer." Most geniuses weren't especially intelligent or sociable. They were just like you and me: committed, hardworking, curious.

Psychologist Carol Dweck proved that a fixed mindset can be turned into a growth mindset. The same is true for creativity, as we explored in chapter 6:

> *If you show students—or, in our case, programmers—that creativity is a skill that can be learned and thus is not fixed, their creativity blossoms.*

If there is one thing I want you to take away from this book, it is a malleable view of creativity as a skill that can be learned and mastered, just like programming in Elixir or Scala, just like fluency in Unix command-line usage, and just like knowledge of enterprise software design patterns. Everyone can be creative. Creativity isn't something you are born with or need to have special talent for. Creativity isn't magic exclusively reserved for the Rembrandts, Kandinskys, van Goghs, Madonnas, Michael Jacksons, Linus Torvaldses, or Steve Jobses of the world.

Instead, creativity is a relatively modern sociocultural verdict. The potential to be creative isn't limited to just one major contributor, such as your lateral thinking ability. It indeed isn't complicated rocket science, but it is complex: creativity concepts are highly interconnected and based on relationships—in other words, it is *systemic*.

If creativity is, just like programming, an attainable skill, then it, too, can be trained and grown, like a muscle. There is plenty of scientific evidence, which I have touched on throughout this book, that supports this statement. That's exactly like a reinforcement learning loop: by being a more creative programmer, you're learning to become more creative!

Creativity "best practices" can be dangerous

I'm always a bit reluctant to hand out advice to others to do this or that to increase their creativity: that is not how it works. Consider the mindfulness example from chapter 7. Simply exercising mindfulness will have little effect, yet it is being massively prescribed as a cure for work-related problems by managers who think only in the short term and are too focused on the data.

It is very dangerous to reduce creativity—or mindfulness, for that matter—to a set of best practices, even though each chapter ends with a bullet-point summary. A book has to be structured in a certain kind of way. I know that programmers are pragmatic folk who can be impatient and love to skim over walls of text to extract the essence, so please do not make that mistake here. Remember: systems-thinking, not parts-thinking!

9.2 On the evolving perspective of creativity

As decades fly by and we grow older, it becomes more challenging to be open to new perspectives, while at the same time, our increased wisdom makes it easier to think critically. In his book, *Successful Aging: A Neuroscientist Explores the Power and Potential of Our Lives,* researcher Daniel J. Levitin explains that our personality can (and will) change multiple times throughout our lifetime. If you've ever taken the popular Big Five personality test, which maps your personality across five domains (openness to experience, conscientiousness, extraversion, agreeableness, and neuroticism), don't be surprised if the results radically differ as you grow older and retake the test. You are not cursed to spend the rest of your days being too disagreeable or too extroverted: these traits are nothing more than snapshots in time.

The concept of age-related personalities can have big ramifications when it comes to creativity. Less openness to experience means it becomes more of a challenge to stay curious to keep up with the latest and greatest, which, as I hope you know by now, is a major part of creativity (chapter 6). At the same time, Daniel Levitin also mentions that young people are less inclined to work together—another important aspect of creativity (chapter 3).

In another study of the interplay between job resources, age, and what psychologists call *idea creativity,* or the ideation part of creativity, researchers have found a positive relationship between age and idea creativity, provided the right corporate support for creativity is given.[1] In other words, as we grow older, more experience from previous projects greatly boosts our capability for ideation, resulting in more creative breakthroughs.

9.2.1 From technical individualism to a creative team player

The research of my colleagues and myself indeed confirms that graduate students and junior software developers interpret creativity differently from more seasoned programmers: they tend to focus on the technical challenge and the creative freedom of bootstrapping a greenfield project and emphasize the creative freedom one experiences when working alone.

Of course, most graduate students and junior devs simply lack experience. They've never properly worked in collaboration with others on a bigger coding project, except

---

[1] Carmen Binnewies, Sandra Ohly, and Cornelia Niessen. Age and creativity at work: The interplay between job resources, age and idea creativity. Journal of Managerial Psychology, 2008.

for the neatly bounded assignments that also happen to be easy to assess. Adam Barr, a former technology consultant at Microsoft, partially blames university computer science curricula. In his recent talk, "Lessons From the Fifty-Year Quest to Turn Programmers Into Software Engineers,"[2] he explains that individual and small exercises in higher education focus too much on the single programmer, while industry requires an engineer who knows how to handle living code (and work together). See figure 9.1.

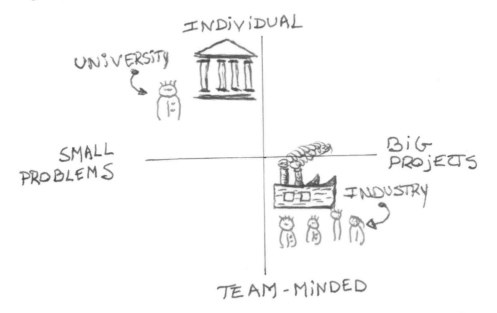

Figure 9.1   The academia–industry gap as illustrated by Adam Barr. University focuses on small programming problems, mostly at the individual level, while industry expects collaboration on big projects.

I can't disagree with Adam. My colleagues and I have noticed the same thing when studying the creative behavior of students. For example, when we ask graduate students in CS when they're creative, the first thing they answer is usually very technical:

> *When I have this particular problem where there is not really a right solution yet. For sorting algorithms, there's a lot already known, and it's easily found [on the internet], what the right thing is, but for other stuff where there isn't information available, you have to come up with something yourself.*

Answers to the question "When are you creative while coding?" were very consistent. At the same time, when we asked programmers with at least seven years of experience exactly the same question, their answer is usually along the lines of the following:

> *When it's time to be creative, when I can or have to think along [with others] about the end-to-end solution and we discuss alternative roads instead of staying on the beaten track.*

---

[2] See ACM Tech Talks at https://learning.acm.org/techtalks.

In those answers, collaboration (thinking along with others) and critical thinking (exploring and evaluating alternative paths) are usually placed front and center while the pure technical challenge is put in the backseat—but still considered important and relevant.

We found these differences to be very striking. Our survey results seem to confirm the suggestion made by neuroscientists that major personality traits—which can be correlated with our domains of creativity—differ from age group to age group.

These findings can help when working in teams with diverse age groups. Perhaps we shouldn't expect the same level of creativity from a graduate student compared with a seasoned developer: after all, they can't yet draw from the same vast pool of previously stored knowledge to tie together information into a novel idea. Still, that doesn't mean that we as educators can't put more emphasis on the parts of creative problem solving that a student is less likely to explore.

Creativity can help battle cognitive decline

Several people we interviewed hinted at the idea that general psychic and physical well-being is a prerequisite for creative success. They were right: consecutive nights of bad sleep will interfere with our focused and diffuse thinking modes, potentially blocking our ability to generate and recognize insights. It gets worse: as we age, parts of our brain (e.g., the prefrontal cortex) literally shrink, and we more easily experience trouble with cognitively demanding tasks such as programming.

Fortunately, if you've kept yourself busy during your lifetime with creative problem solving and brainstorming, you've constantly trained and pushed your brain in many interesting ways. Neuroscientists like Daniel Levitin have proven that "keeping the brain busy in interesting ways" triggers the neuroplasticity of our brain, thereby keeping it young, and helps keep cognitive disorders like dementia at bay. Keep on challenging yourself!

9.2.2 Revisiting the CPPST

Since you've reached the conclusion of the book, now is probably a good time to revisit the Creative Programming Problem Solving Test (CPPST) introduced in chapter 1. Perhaps the newly yielded insights on the topic at hand will net a higher average score for each domain. Remember not to reduce the test to a numbers comparison game with others or between different projects.

There's something I intentionally left out about the CPPST when I first presented it at the beginning of our adventure. The nearly 300 students who took the test comprised roughly an equal amount of first-year and last-year computer science students. When inspecting the statistical analyses of both groups separately, we noticed slightly different correlations.

For example, overall, last-year students scored lower on communication-related questions. Surprisingly, they agreed with the statement "I regularly ask for feedback from fellow students and peers" much less often than first-year students did. Perhaps graduates feel too confident and think they don't need feedback. Perhaps the individualism Adam Barr talked about was, by the time they were about to graduate, fully baked into their brains. What is more likely, however, is that feedback is perceived not as something that can enhance your own creative ideas but as something obligatory related to grading. First-year students are more used to asking for feedback (both from peers and instructors) because they simply know less.

The analysis also revealed that the seven domains of creativity we explored can be regrouped into three overarching constructs: *ability*, *mindset*, and *interaction*. Note that this categorization is relevant only to students, since most of the questions that turned out to be relevant again focused on (technical) ability. In other words, students' incorrect perception of creative problem solving skewed the results in favor of the "individual programmer" problem. Is this yet more evidence of age-related creative differences?

EXERCISE Think back and reflect on your professional programming career. When it comes to the seven main themes of creativity introduced in this book, did your preference or proficiency change as your career evolved? Are you sure it wasn't the project but a subtle change in your own personality that caused this?

9.3   *When not to be creative*

In *The Creative Habit: Learn It and Use It For Life,* dancer and choreographer Twyla Tharp shares practical tips to stay on top of your creative game and grow a lifelong creative habit. While that sounds exactly like what we're trying to do for programming, Tharp seems to identify creativity with almost divine dedication. Sentences such as "Your work is your life" and "Don't expect anything less than perfection" make me want to run away from creativity instead of embrace it![3]

I do admire people like Tharp and Jiro Ono, a famous 97-year-old Japanese chef who dedicates his life to one humble thing: sushi. In a search for the perfect sushi, Jiro Ono still gets up at 5:00 a.m. and still goes to the fish market himself to select only the best of the best pieces. Research confirms that giving up work (the thing we call *retirement*) increases the chances of social isolation and cognitive—and thus creative—decline, so it is certainly admirable to see these people continuing their dedication to a craft.

However, the way creativity is portrayed in *The Creative Habit* makes it virtually impossible to achieve without putting in the required 10,000 hours or more. I'm not a big fan of this view, although I recognize that deliberate practice is certainly an efficient way to evolve from journeyman to master. Technical knowledge brews creativity—it's even a requirement to be creative (chapter 2)—and, of course, practice makes perfect, but demanding nothing less than perfection cuts us off from 90% of that which we'd like to be more of: creative.

---

[3] Twyla Tharp. The creative habit: Learn it and use it for life. Reprint edition. Simon & Schuster, 2006.

The problem with putting creative perfection on a pedestal is quite worrisome. First, perfectionism easily leads to burnout and depression, two societal problems that already receive too little attention and that are mostly approached from an economic perspective.

Second, the harsh and pretentious interpretation of "Big-C" creativity—such as huge scientific breakthroughs or the invention of a new AI algorithm, which most of us will probably never achieve—as the only worthwhile type of creativity tends to dismiss smaller victories that are easily reachable for everyone.

Third, the holiness of a craft leads to ignoring the reason why you're doing what you're doing. Programmers who see coding as a craft tend to overachieve on the clean code principles and underachieve on delivering a product that the customer wants.

As mentioned in chapter 5, creativity is the means, not the end. A creative mind knows when *not* to be creative. Creativity can be very demanding, or, put another way, you and your peers might demand too much from your own creativity. Be wary of your mental oscillation: staying in overdrive for too long can impart lasting damage. Sometimes, it's a requirement (and a big relief) not to be a Creative Programmer and just execute a few less demanding tasks while also recharging your batteries.

9.4   Further reading

What if your thirst for creative knowledge isn't yet quenched? No worries; there's plenty of interesting material left to delve into. This section provides a selection of recommended readings grouped by each of the seven creativity themes. Some of these books have already been touched on throughout the previous chapters but are more than worth reading on their own. I've intentionally left out academic material, which can be a bit hard to get into (and get your hands on, thanks to ridiculous paywalls):

- Technical knowledge
  - *Pragmatic Thinking & Learning*, by Andy Hunt—A pragmatic approach to learning and behavioral theory, sprinkled with a few cognitive and neuroscience toppings. Simply a required read that fits seamlessly with *The Creative Programmer.*
  - *How to Take Smart Notes: One Simple Technique to Boost Writing, Learning and Thinking—for Students, Academics and Nonfiction Book Writers,* by Sönke Ahrens—The reference booklet to getting to know Niklas Luhmann's *Zettelkasten* note-taking methodology as introduced in chapter 2.
- Communication
  - *The Geography of Genius*, by Eric Weiner—Travel around the world and discover the social dimension of creativity with the help of history's greatest creative thinkers and Weiner's witty remarks that connect the findings back to our modern age.
  - *Where Good Ideas Come From: The Natural History of Innovation,* by Steven Johnson—Learn how cities originated and evolved as ideas and creativity flowed between them, just like the liquid networks discussed in chapter 3.

- Constraints
  - *Creativity: Flow and the Psychology of Discovery and Invention,* by Mihaly Csikszentmihalyi—A seminal work full of interviews with creative geniuses of our age, reassuring us that, with the right amount of dedication and curiosity, everyone can be creative. This book also neatly summarizes a lot of academic research on creativity.
  - *Creativity From Constraints: The Psychology of Breakthrough,* by Patricia D. Stokes—Draw along with Patricia to trace the steps of early cubists to find out how artists use self-imposed constraints to create superior artworks.
- Critical thinking
  - *Thinking, Fast and Slow,* by Daniel Kahneman—A groundbreaking tour of the mind that explains the two systems that drive the way we think and live: a fast, intuitive, and emotional system and a slow, deliberate, and logical system. Daniel also explores countless critical thinking fallacies.
  - *The Programmer's Brain: What Every Programmer Needs to Know About Cognition,* by Felienne Hermans—Aimed at programmers, this book explores how our brain works and how to hack it to improve our thinking when it comes to coding. If *Thinking, Fast and Slow* explains the academic theory, then *The Programmer's Brain* highlights the engineering practice.
- Curiosity
  - *Mindset: Changing the Way You Think to Fulfill Your Potential,* by Carol S. Dweck—This is one of the best-selling psychology research books ever, and with good reason. If you are looking for more information about the psychology of the growth mindset from chapter 6, this is the book for you.
  - *How to Be Everything: A Guide for Those Who (Still) Don't Know What They Want to Be When They Grow Up,* by Emilie Wapnick—Required reading if you like the idea of generalism but don't know how to apply it to your coding job.
- Creative state of mind
  - *Deep Work: Rules for Focused Success in a Distracted World,* by Cal Newport—A critical view of our modern interruption-invaded world and a possible solution to it: close the door—but not always—mute the notifications—but not always—and get more deep work done.
  - *Flow: The Psychology of Optimal Experience,* by Mihalyi Csikszentmihalyi—Another classic work by Csikszentmihalyi that contains tales of flow in sport, music, art, writing, education, and more. While most examples are outside of the world of engineering, they can be effortlessly translated into our coding environment.
- Creative techniques
  - *Steal Like an Artist: 10 Things Nobody Told You About Being Creative,* by Austin Kleon—A witty, practical, visual, short, and, above all, humorous approach to giving creative advice that fits remarkably well for programmers.

- *Seven Languages in Seven Weeks: A Pragmatic Guide to Learning Programming Languages,* by Bruce A. Tate—If you're familiar with the book *The Pragmatic Programmer: From Journeyman to Master, Seven Languages in Seven Weeks* will shift your programming language knowledge into higher gears and highlight techniques to master future and ever-shifting trends.

index